D1106255

MY
JERUSALEM

Secular Adventures in the Holy City

MY
JERUSALEM

Secular Adventures in the Holy City

BRONWYN DRAINIE

Doubleday Canada Limited

Copyright © 1994 Bronwyn Drainie

All rights reserved. No part of this publication may be reproduced, stored in
a retrieval system, or transmitted, in any form or by any means, electronic,
mechanical, photocopying, recording or otherwise, without prior written
permission by the publisher.

Canadian Cataloguing in Publication Data
Drainie, Bronwyn, 1945–
    My Jerusalem

ISBN 0-385-25474-1

1. Drainie, Bronwyn, 1945–   . 2. Jerusalem - Social life and customs. 3. Women -
Jerusalem - Social conditions. 4. Authors, Canadian (English) - Jerusalem -
Biography.* I. Title.

DS109.86.D73A3 1994 956.94'42054'092 C94-930980-X

Cover illustration by Thom Sevalrud
Cover design by Tania Craan
Text design and maps by David Montle
Printed and bound in the USA

Published in Canada by
Doubleday Canada Limited
105 Bond Street
Toronto, Ontario
M5B 1Y3

"JERUSALEM" from THE SELECTED POETRY OF YEHUDA AMICHAI
by YEHUDA AMICHAI. Edited and translated by Chana Bloch and Stephen
Mitchell. English translation copyright © 1986 by Chana Bloch and Stephen
Mitchell. Reprinted by permission of HarperCollins Publishers, Inc.

This book is dedicated to two mothers:
to my own, Claire,
and to the memory of Tamar

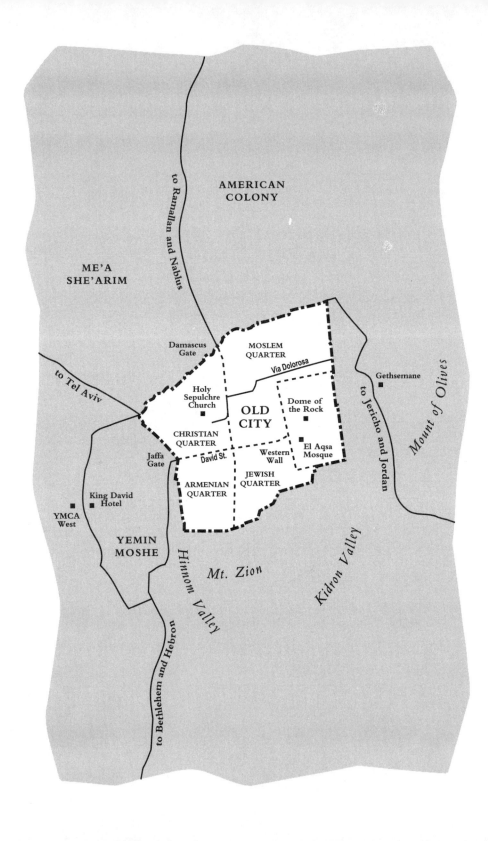

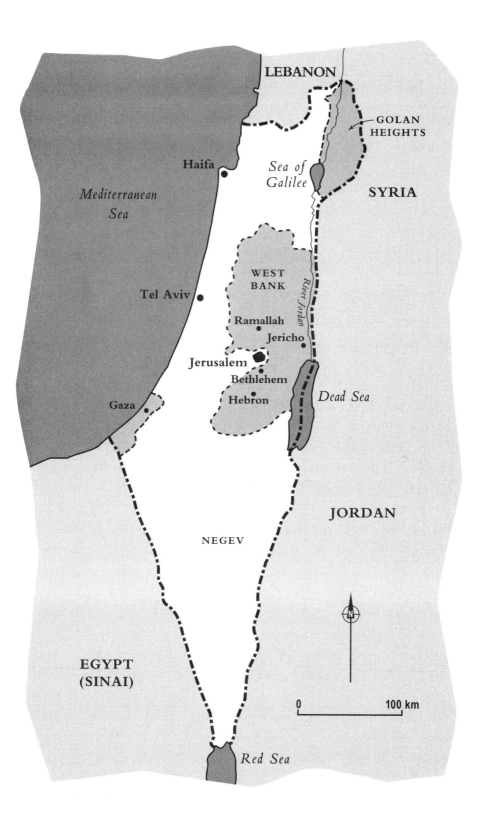

Acknowledgements

Most of the people who helped with the content of this book appear in the text, and I thank them all. Some others are absent, and I name them here to indicate my appreciation for the time they spent with me and the insights they gave me: Janet Aviad, Menachem Brinker, Hania Aswad, Nabil Anani, Dany Peter, Lea Shamgar-Hendelman, Max Apple, Talia Fishman, Serge and Elena Makarov, Eric Cohen, Danny Rabinovitch, Avshalom Farjun, Moshe Lissak, Etia Dan, Suha Hindiya, Hidaya Husseini, Carol Morton, Sahir Dajani, Tom Segev, Noam Baram, Yaser Barakat and Hagop Antreassian.

Thanks are due as well to those who helped bring this project to fruition: my agent, Dean Cooke; John Pearce, Susan Folkins, Christine Harrison and Maggie Reeves of Doubleday Canada; and artist Thom Sevalrud for his beautiful cover illustration. A special thank-you to Judylaine Fine for her criticism and support.

Finally I must express my gratitude to Patrick Martin, without whose initiative and enthusiasm I would not have spent the two years in Jerusalem that enabled me to tell this story; to my parents, Claire and Nat, who provided a quiet, comfortable place to write; and of course to my wonderful sons, Gabriel and Sam, who put up with a distracted mother during all the difficult months of creation and never complained about having to order in pizza when I couldn't pull myself away from the computer screen.

INTRODUCTION

"**G**ET HER!" I can hear my readers saying, especially the ones who disagree with any of my observations in this book. "She spends two years in the place and then has the presumption to write about *her* Jerusalem, as if she had lived there all her life."

And, of course, on one level they're right. Jerusalem places such a heavy weight of history and tragedy and human folly on the shoulders of its inhabitants that only those who have breathed its restless air from birth are truly qualified to reflect on its troubled existence to the rest of the world.

On the other hand, no foreign writer has ever been able to set foot in Jerusalem and shut up about it, and a lot of them have pronounced on the place after spending a great deal less time there than two years. René de Chateaubriand, for example, the great French essayist of the early nineteenth century, stayed four days in the city, in 1806, before writing his *Itinéraire de Paris à Jerusalem*. His impressions were lugubrious, to say the least: "The only noise in this city of deicide is the occasional clatter of the hooves of the desert cavalry; it is a janissary carrying the head of a bedouin or riding off to pillage the *fellahin*." Charming. In fact, if there is one common theme to all the travel writing that has been produced about Jerusalem in the past thousand years, it is the dashing of expectations. Because it is the centre of all three of the great monotheistic religions, Judaism, Christianity and Islam, no other city in the world bears Jerusalem's burden of hope — "city of peace," "Jerusalem of Gold," "Al-Quds" (the holy one) — and no other has failed so consistently to live up to its advance billing.

Herman Melville came in 1857 and found the place "a sickening cheat." Gustave Flaubert went further: "It's all whorish to the last degree: hypocrisy, cupidity, falsification, impudence... I resent not having been moved: I wanted nothing better than to be so." Even Theodor Herzl, the father of Zionism, decried the "musty deposits of two thousand years of inhumanity, intolerance and uncleanliness [that] lie in the foul-smelling alleys" of Jerusalem.

That's the city. The people come off no better. The Moslem traveller Muqaddasi, writing about A.D. 985, observed: "Learned men are few, and the Christians numerous, and the latter are unmannerly in the public places." The French writer Constantin Volnay, in 1784, declared the Jerusalemites to be "the most wicked people in Syria, not even excepting Damascus." And Margaret Thomas, an English water-colourist who spent two years wandering and sketching in the Middle East in the late nineteenth century, noted that "the keeping of three successive Sundays — Mohammedan, Jewish and Christian — leads to much loss of time, for the lazily-disposed observe all three."

As for the surrounding countryside, Mark Twain probably captured it best in *The Innocents Abroad:* "Every outline is harsh, every feature is distinct, there is no perspective— distance works no enchantment here. It is the most hopeless, dreary, heartbroken piece of territory out of Arizona."

After I had been living for six months in Jerusalem, filling my head full of the dyspeptic writers quoted above plus many more modern ones who have reported on the trials and tribulations of the Middle East right up to the present day, I was ready to pack my bags and go. I thought I knew how to handle culture shock, but Jerusalem knocked me flat on my back. In those early weeks, every excursion out of my house and into the cauldron of ethnic and political tension in the city felt like rape; I would crawl home with my head spinning, licking my wounds and longing for the boring civility of Toronto.

Finally, though, one dreary February afternoon when the winter rain was falling for about the fiftieth day in a row, I hit the right book, the one that made me want to stay. It was Israeli writer Amos Elon's brilliant meditation on his city, *Jerusalem, City of Mirrors.* Sometimes, rarely, an author and his subject are so perfectly wedded that what is produced is not so much a book as a miracle: in this case, a miracle of complexity made clear, of history made meaningful, of horror made human. The book's effect on me was instant and comforting: any city that could produce a writer capable of such art and honesty was worth checking out a little longer.

But as my knowledge of the place deepened and broadened, I realized that the city Elon had captured in his book was not the same city I experienced every day. Jerusalem is truly a prism with thousands of facets, and one's approach to it — including one's ethnicity, age, education and religious beliefs — entirely determines its effect on one's mind and heart. Looked at that way, it was completely appropriate for me to speak of "my" Jerusalem (just as veterans speak of "my" war): a personal construct that exists at the interface of "my" expectations with the place's undeniable, beautiful, terrible actuality.

No matter how many books I read, by Israelis or Palestinians, by Jews from the diaspora or outsiders with no stake in the conflict, by novelists or poets or journalists or historians or cultural anthropologists, none of them ever quite captured the reality of *my* life in Jerusalem, and so there seemed, amazingly, to be room for yet another book on the shelf of Jerusalem travel memoirs.

I make no pretence to objectivity or to political balance in these pages. You will not find interviews here with the usual spokespeople, politicians or lobbyists for any of the groups who see Jerusalem as theirs by God-given right. Rather, you will meet the people I met as I went about my mundane affairs in the heavenly city. Some of them knew I was writing a book when they met me; many did not. For that reason, except for those who already have a public reputation, I have called them by their first names alone, to give them all the same degree of semi-anonymity.

I have written this book, as all writers do, first and foremost for myself. But as well, I have written it for those thoughtful, intelligent readers who believe they ought to care about what transpires in the Middle East but have neither the background nor the energy to follow the labyrinthine strands of claim and counter-claim, boast and recrimination, treachery and absurdity that have characterized the Arab–Israeli conflict for the past hundred years or more. This book does not unravel those complicated strands, though I hope it will make them seem part of a very human tapestry, in which joy and laughter, and even fun, are improbably interwoven with intolerance and fear.

I cannot count the ways in which that region of the world surprised me, moved me, expanded my mind and challenged all my received notions about ethnic conflict and the too-easy apportioning of blame. But let me give you three examples.

At the Jerusalem Tennis Centre, where I would take my boys for twice-weekly lessons, a foursome of young Israeli men turned up to play every Tuesday. They were in peak form and were always given the most prominent court, right below the clubhouse, so we could all admire their prowess. All four were paraplegics, casualties of who knows which chapter of the deadly conflict between themselves and the Arabs. The sight of healthy young athletes in wheelchairs, at first so heart-wrenching, eventually became commonplace and unremarkable in Israel. It never made me more sympathetic to their government's tough tactics against the Arabs in the occupied lands, but it fleshed out the human face of a hard-nosed country that has known nothing but war since the first day of its existence.

My second example: One day I was strolling with a young Palestinian journalist through the British military cemetery in the Gaza Strip, a tiny haven of neatness and civility in the middle of one of the world's most chaotic hell-holes. As we walked between the meticulously tended gravestones, I asked my companion how he felt about the British, who, after all, had promised this land to the Jews out of one side of their mouths and to the Arabs out of the other. "Of course the British have been our greatest disaster," he said matter-of-factly. We walked a few more steps and then he stopped. "No, that is not correct. Our greatest disaster has been our Arab neighbours, the Egyptians, the Syrians. They have never helped us. The British come second." The Israelis weren't even on his list.

Finally, let me tell you about Janet, a Jewish American from Pittsburgh who lived in the Arab sector of Jerusalem and did human rights work on behalf of the Palestinians. She went into the most dangerous areas of the West Bank and Gaza, gathering information that could be used before the Israeli military courts to make a case for reuniting Palestinian families that had been torn asunder by the occupation. Her tiny salary was paid — irregularly — by an Arab women's group based in the Gaza Strip. When she couldn't pay her rent, her Arab landlady would turn up on her doorstep with food.

Janet lived a double lie. From the Palestinians among whom she worked, she hid her Jewish identity and was assumed to be a Christian. If she hadn't, she would have been unable to function in Arab society and her life could have been in danger. To her Jewish family back home in America, she was simply working "in Israel," with no details given about which ethnic group she was working for and with. (She is the only person in this narrative whose name I have changed.) Janet had left Judaism behind many years before and become a Buddhist. That religion appeared to give her strength and solace as she struggled with the contradictions, the poverty and the loneliness of her life.

By the time I met Janet, she had been living this difficult existence for six years, and truthfully, she was half mad. She was my age, in her mid-forties, but her hair had gone completely white. She suffered seriously from asthma. She hitch-hiked alone on dangerous West Bank roads that Israeli military jeeps hesitated to travel. Whenever I tried to pull her out of her damp little flat off the Nablus Road, to give her some respite from the tension of her life by taking her to the mall or the movies, it was futile. She could not talk or think of anything else but the accumulated rage she felt against the Israelis for what their military occupation had done to the lives of Palestinian families. Mercifully, she eventually received a fellowship to return to the United States and turn her experiences into a research monograph on human rights techniques. The last time I saw her she told me that as soon as she had the report written, she would be off to Thailand to see what she could do to stop the sex traffic in children from remote villages.

Janet continues to haunt me. How often, in my comfortable North American existence, have I felt a revulsion for my ease and affluence, a discomfort over the inadequacy of writing cheques to charities, a desire to act, to escape the triviality of my concerns and really do something to improve the lot of those vastly less fortunate? Well, that was what Janet had done and it had almost destroyed her. And I am not sure, in the end, whether her sacrifice had been of great benefit to those she was seeking to help. After six years of unceasing effort, she had been instrumental in reunifying only a small number of families, and I have little doubt that most Palestinians whom she encountered viewed her, at best, as a harmless eccentric with her heart in the right place. What, in the larger global sense, would do the greater good: Janet's presence in the middle of such a conflict or my cheque written from the safe haven of Canada? It was a question that hung over my two years in the Middle East, and I still don't know the answer. Perhaps there is none.

It was stories and scenes and people like these that made me want to write this book, and now it is done. Just one final word before we set out together. My time there, from mid-1991 to mid-1993, was just a microsecond of Jerusalem's history; you are reading this during another microsecond. Events have occurred in between, signatures have appeared on documents and hands have been reluctantly shaken, the police of one nation have started to replace the soldiers of another, the coercive machinery of an occupying force is beginning to be dismantled. Yet these are all events that Jerusalem has witnessed before, not once but dozens of times in its extraordinary existence, and it is hard to believe that the end is in sight. Let's agree to call this a brief chapter in one of the longest, strangest and most compelling tales in the history of the world.

CHAPTER I

THE DAY WE LEARNED we were posted to Jerusalem, we let our children drink alcohol for the first time. We sat, dazed and thrilled, on the front steps of our Toronto house in the slanting sun of a May afternoon, unable to believe our good fortune. The boys — Gabriel and Sam and Sam's friend Anthony — swooped and crowed around us, knowing that something momentous was happening although they really had no idea what. Then Patrick remembered the half-bottle of Veuve Clicquot that had been sitting in the refrigerator for six months waiting for the perfect occasion. He filled flutes for us and tiny liqueur glasses for the boys, and we drank: *l'chaim*.

We were toasting the end of a long road as well as a beginning. Ever since Patrick had joined the staff of the *Globe and Mail* seven years before, he had been quietly but insistently lobbying for the Toronto-based newspaper to open a bureau in the Middle East. It was one of the few major papers in the world that did not have a correspondent there, and its reasoning was curious: the *Globe* considered the Middle East to be, in news-gathering terms, a temporary story. Its editors were sure that no sooner would they go to the expense and trouble of setting up a bureau there than the Story would evaporate. Peace would break out, Jews and Arabs would learn to love each other, we'd all learn to live without Arab oil, radical Islam would stop its push for domination and we'd never hear a peep out of the region again.

But the Middle East has been front-page news certainly since the creation of the state of Israel in 1948 and, the historically minded might argue, for approximately 3,500 years before that. Each of us in the West may have a different idea of where and when civilization began — in the rolling valleys of Mesopotamia between the Tigris and Euphrates, on the Nile delta of Egypt, on the rocky outcrop of Mount Moriah in the Judean hills, at the foot of a cross in Roman Jerusalem — but they are all in the Middle East. During some periods, such as the first three hundred years of the Ottoman Empire (1517–1817), the area has dozed off and been relegated to the back pages, but it always bounces back as headline material. And with the millennium just around the corner, isn't this the part of the world to look to for the fulfilment of W. B. Yeats's prophecy in "The Second Coming," the "rough beast, its hour come round at last," that "slouches towards Bethlehem to be born"? The *Globe and Mail* did a good thing setting up a Middle East bureau. Better two thousand years late than never.

The Jews say "Next year in Jerusalem" at the end of their Passover Seder, and Patrick and I echoed that prayer for seven years. As we waited for the newspaper's top brass to make up their minds, we carried on with our work and family life. I worked in broadcasting, wrote a book, and then began a column, also for the *Globe and*

Mail, on cultural issues. Patrick toiled at the newspaper as both editor and writer, and continued to feed his Middle East passion with courses and conferences and the occasional journalistic foray to the region. We ran our home, shopped for groceries, raised our boys, went skiing. Jerusalem floated before our eyes, like the heavenly city of myth and mysticism, approaching then receding with successive editorial and budgetary regimes at the newspaper.

Towards the end we had given up hope: several months had gone by without a whisper of the Middle East bureau. Patrick had made his case many times over; he knew that raising the subject further would constitute nagging and would engender nothing but irritation among his superiors, so he shut up. Then, with the breathtaking swiftness of the Rabin–Arafat peace accord, the bureau was announced, the candidates were screened, and the job was Patrick's. We never knew exactly what turned the *Globe and Mail* around on this, but the decision was made right at the end of the Gulf War. It seemed to me that the editors realized that the dynamics of the Middle East situation were becoming more complex, not less, and that the West was being drawn into the region on many fronts. A top-flight newspaper needed someone on the ground to help its readers make sense of it all. Whatever the reason, my husband was delighted. As soon as we had gulped our champagne that May afternoon, he was booking a flight to go house-hunting in Jerusalem. Patrick was in hack heaven.

I was happy too, although apprehensive about having, for the first time in my life, to leave work I loved to follow a man. But I was determined not to let feminist misgivings spoil a great adventure. Whatever life in the Middle East held in store for us, I promised myself I would never blame Patrick for dragging me after him. It would prove to be a hard promise to keep.

The *Globe* had to decide not only whether to open a bureau but where. Cairo, Amman and Nicosia were all contenders, as well as

Jerusalem, but they ruled themselves out for various reasons. Cairo, it could be argued, had the largest concentration of humanity in the region, the despair of census takers, estimated to contain about fourteen million souls. Unfortunately, the infrastructure of a city that massive and that poverty-stricken is none too healthy, and the telecommunications requirements of an international newspaper bureau might find Cairo wanting. Amman, the capital of Jordan, is often dubbed the Switzerland of the Middle East because of its clean streets, smooth functioning and dull atmosphere; it would work well technically, but Jordan itself would generate little news. Moreover, at the time this decision was being made you couldn't pick up a telephone in Amman and call Jerusalem forty kilometres away, a major logistical drawback if the bureau was going to cover the entire Middle East. Nicosia, the capital of the island of Cyprus, was a hot location for journalists all through the long years of the Lebanon civil war, a window on the Beirut action but a safe haven for journalists at night. But with the miraculous end to hostilities in that war-ravaged country, Nicosia had gone cold, a sleepy island town with few stories to tell, except for the occasional blip in Greek–Turkish relations.

The usual rule of thumb in siting a news bureau is that the location itself should generate at least fifty percent of the stories. Any less than that and your correspondent is spending too much time and money on the road. The problem with being based in any Arab capital in the Middle East is that it's impossible to keep abreast of the Arab–Israeli conflict from there, so you'd be spending half your time in Jerusalem anyway. From Jerusalem it is difficult, but not impossible, to keep tabs on developments in the Arab world. Even now, with Israeli and PLO signatures on a declaration of peaceful intentions and Palestinian self-rule gradually creeping through the occupied territories, the relationship between Arab and Jew will continue to fascinate the world. This tiny speck on the world map has become a microcosm of so many pressing themes of the late twentieth century: an

East vs. West cultural clash of epic proportions, racism, demographic politics, ecological battlefronts. Most of all, though, the future of Jerusalem — that glowing, throbbing heart of the great desert religions, Judaism, Christianity and Islam — is still nowhere near resolution and could yet bring the fragile structure of peace down around the heads of Jews and Palestinians alike. So it's the right place to be, for all kinds of reasons.

Over the next few weeks, people's reactions to our news were varied and intriguing. Our families predictably fussed over the distance and the danger. A Jewish friend assured me I would discover my roots. (I am a non-practising half-Jew, on my mother's side.) My neighbour down the street, a TV commercial producer, had just returned from a film shoot in Israel. "Three days was more than enough for me," she said vehemently. "Too many guns."

But it was my piano tuner who first made me realize that there were different Jerusalems and that perhaps I wasn't going to the one I had imagined at all. Gunther was German and an evangelical Christian. I had called him in to tune our old upright before I shipped it across town to my brother's for the next few years. As I was writing out Gunther's cheque at the dining-room table, I told him our destination and then watched his face undergo a complete and disconcerting transformation. His rosy complexion turned several shades plummier, sweat stood out on his brow, his eyes looked as though they had been lit up from behind by wax tapers. His hands twisted his tweed cap tightly and his voice shook: "Jerusalem, Jerusalem, oh how fortunate you are! It has been our dream, my wife's and mine, all our lives to save enough money to be able to see Jerusalem." Yes, I agreed, it must surely be a very beautiful city. "Not *a* beautiful city," he insisted, "*the* beautiful city. It is the City of God and our Redeemer. We *must* see it before we die. You are so fortunate, so blessed." He shook my hand fervently at the door, as if my touch could impart some holiness to him even though I was still in a pre-Jerusalem state. That day I began to get an inkling of the city's extraordinary dual existence.

We were not only moving to Jerusalem, the holiest city in the world — a billing that always seems to send the place orbiting out of space and time — but to Jerusalem, the hotly disputed and very earthly capital of two warring peoples, the Israelis and the Palestinians. This was a chunk of political real estate in which each stone, spire and cellar could tell a tale of blood and treachery, triumph and transmutation. So could each of its citizens, living and dead, if given half a chance. It was also a city in which, despite its prayers and other-worldly pretensions, people presumably still had to buy laundry soap, get their cars fixed and go to the dentist. I knew I was heading for the laundry-soap level, while my journalist husband was going for the blood and treachery. The millennial aspirations of the city we intended to leave strictly alone, because they made us feel creepy and uncomfortable. It would take the next two years for me to learn that the prayers, the blood and the laundry soap were of a piece, ingredients in an urban alchemical stew that some find indigestible but for others is a serious addiction. I became addicted to Jerusalem.

On August 24, 1991, we set off for Israel, and of course we did it all wrong. Patrick was the expert in these matters, having flown to and from Israel many times, while the children and I had never been there. On his house-hunting expedition two months earlier, Patrick had flown direct for fourteen hours on the Israeli national airline, El Al, and he came back convinced that this was not the way to introduce his family to their new home. The aggressive forty-five-minute grilling from the Israeli security staff at Toronto Airport was a bad enough start, followed by the extra-tight seating, the kosher airline food, the appalling washrooms, the bone-wearying length of the journey and the less than friendly cabin service that are all part of the

El Al experience. Israeli diplomats and prominent North American Jewish fund-raisers and lobbyists seldom fly El Al, although they tend to keep their alternative travel arrangements quiet for nationalistic reasons. But there are other curiosities on an El Al flight, like the groups of black-suited Orthodox Jewish men who gather at mysterious times at the back of the airplane to bob and chant. When prayer times happen to coincide with arrival times, it can be quite diverting watching the cabin crew struggling to get the worshippers back to their seats. And for Patrick, who was already known to the Jewish community of Canada for his analysis of Middle East politics, there was the unpleasant surprise of finding himself seated beside a Toronto rabbi who had denounced his appointment to Jerusalem just the previous week in his synagogue. One can avoid a lot of these problems by not flying El Al.

We chose to fly Lufthansa, with a stopover in Frankfurt. It was a random choice that left an indelible impression in our minds. Apart from the Israelis, there is no one in the world more concerned about Israeli security than the Germans. The shadow of the Holocaust still looms over German–Israeli relations, and the rise of neo-Nazism in the newly united Germany has brought that shadow into troublingly sharp focus. Then there was the harrowing 1972 nightmare when eleven Israeli athletes were murdered by Palestinian terrorists at the Munich Olympics. Since that time Germany has done everything in its considerable power to avoid another Middle East terrorist incident in German jurisdiction. Over the next two years we would go in and out of Israel many times, to different destinations and on different airlines, including El Al. No other airport or border experience came close to approaching the grimness or sense of foreboding of our security clearance at Frankfurt.

We were travelling heavily loaded. Although we had shipped our household furnishings and appliances by sea two months earlier, all our clothes and personal effects were in the twelve pieces of luggage we were carrying with us. While the boys and I tried to catch a few hours of fitful sleep in the airport hotel, Patrick attempted to check in the baggage and select seats from Frankfurt to Tel Aviv. He was sent back and forth from one end of the vast Frankfurt airport to the other, achieving absolutely nothing. The German officials refused to lift a finger until the whole family was assembled to go through security with all our luggage. They shrugged ruefully. "What can we do? There are special procedures. It's the Middle East."

So we collected our impedimenta on four luggage carts and set off for Gate C-69, which turned out to be the most distant and isolated gate in the airport. At first we walked past glassed-in departure lounges that held hundreds of passengers travelling to more benign destinations, families with diaper bags and teddy bears, businessmen with laptop computers perched on their knees, sulky teenagers making last-minute phone calls to abandoned lovers. Then the glass walls ended and were replaced by a corridor of grey concrete blocks that gradually narrowed and curved to the right. We walked half a kilometre, a floating anonymous distance punctuated every hundred metres by a German soldier patrolling with a submachine-gun.

Eventually we reached the x-ray machines, where Patrick was instantly whisked away to a closed room for a special examination of his camera, tape recorder and laptop. He told me later that this process involved carefully wiping all surfaces of the equipment with a paper towel, then doing a computerized detection of the dust in a search for explosives residues. It took a long time.

Back at the x-ray machines, my sons and I were unloading the twelve pieces of luggage. The very first bag through the scanner contained Gabriel's baseball bat, which the security officials pounced on with great consternation. "It's just a sports bat," I explained, "and besides, this bag isn't going in the cabin with us."

"Follow me — quickly," shouted one of the officials, brandishing the offending bat and marching at a clip around the curve of the corridor. I couldn't follow him, I was still dragging heavy bags onto the x-ray table and off onto the luggage carts again. "Gabe, you follow him," I said, and my ten-year-old trotted off obediently into the bowels of the airport and disappeared.

In a few minutes, Patrick returned from the computer examination, and he and Sam and I set off in the direction Gabriel had gone, along more grey corridors and down two flights in an elevator. The doors opened into a cavernous white examination room full of officials who meticulously searched every sock, Tampax container and cassette tape in our luggage. Beyond the phalanx of security personnel at their tables, we could see Gabriel on the far side, clutching his baseball bat. After the bag search, each of us entered a curtained cubicle for a body search. My matron was thickset and jolly and did her job breezily enough but still managed to rummage pretty thoroughly around my breasts and crotch. I closed my eyes and thought of Canada.

Past the security barrier we were reunited with Gabriel and could finally check in at something like a normal airline counter. Boarding cards in hand, we shuffled into a departure lounge and found it, to our surprise, already quite full of passengers. During our entire odyssey from the mothership of Frankfurt airport terminal to this distant satellite, we had seen no other passengers at all and we assumed we were excessively early for the flight. We reached the departure lounge an hour before flight time and yet most of the passengers had clearly come through before us and were comfortably settled in.

I looked around the lounge. Everyone seemed relaxed and normal, but the procedure we had all just been through was not normal in the least. Most of the passengers were returning Israelis, for whom these security super-checks must be commonplace. A young mother in a headscarf grabbed her son by the elbow to slow him down, two men in rumpled suits laughed loudly at the coffee bar, a sleek foursome of Israeli cyclists sprawled on a pair of plastic couches, mute behind their mirrored sunglasses. The low, guttural buzz of Hebrew filled the room. People read an eclectic mix of newspapers, *The New York Times* and *The Herald Tribune, Le Monde, The Guardian, Die Frankfurter Zeitung.*

Our flight was announced. But we did not walk down a carpeted corridor to a waiting plane. Instead we were loaded onto several articulated buses, under the tense gaze of half a dozen more armed soldiers, and driven far out on the tarmac, as distant as possible from the building. "You'll get used to this," said Patrick as we bounced along. "The planes bound for Israel always park far away. If there's a bomb, at least it'll only blow up the plane, not the terminal." This was small comfort as we climbed the metal staircase to the jet.

It had been an hour of extraordinary emotional stress and exhaustion. Nothing I had read or heard about the Middle East situation had quite prepared me for the sense of isolation and danger I felt in Frankfurt airport. We were leaving the normal world behind, a world where people were assumed to be peaceful, friendly and trustworthy until proven otherwise, and entering one where everyone could be a potential enemy, where one slip in security could spell disaster.

As the passengers settled in with pillows and headphones, I asked myself for the first, but certainly not the last, time how Israelis could live this way, with this knowledge, this mindset, twenty-four hours a day every day of their lives. The answer, I eventually came to realize, was by sublimation. They bury the fear and suspicion deep inside themselves and get on with daily concerns, as if they were truly living in a normal place. Within their own borders they relax, more or less confident in the ability of their army to protect them. But when they come and go from Israel, they must feel the clash of two different realities, as I did on that first approach. My friend Racheli confirmed this a few months later when she told me, "I breathe easy inside Israel and I breathe easy outside Israel, but moving from one to the other takes my breath away."

I think I was in mild shock as I sat back and watched the safety video of obedient passengers sliding down the inflatable ramps into the sea. Perhaps it wasn't too late for us to bail out. I pictured a soft landing on the island of Crete an hour before we got to the Middle East. I glanced sideways at Sam, my eight-year-old, and wondered how I could have so blithely agreed to bring him to this armed fortress of a country where children got blown up on buses and wild-eyed religious fanatics stalked the streets with knives, killing in the name of Allah.

Come to think of it, what did I actually know about Jerusalem or Israel? Very little, although probably a touch more than the average North American, for two reasons. First, I was married to the just-appointed Middle East correspondent of a major newspaper. Patrick had been thinking and writing about the Middle East for ten years. That meant that, in the name of family diplomacy, I had had to read at least *his* articles on the subject, just as he had had to read mine on the chronic distribution problems of the Canadian film industry. I knew who Yasser Arafat was, and Yitzhak Shamir (prime minister of Israel), although I tended to mix him up with Yitzhak Rabin (once and future prime minister of Israel). I could recognize a photograph of Jerusalem because of its golden dome, although I didn't know exactly what the dome was. I knew two words of Hebrew, *shalom* and *l'chaim,* and none of Arabic. Most Moslems were Sunnis, but the ones who lived in Iran were Shiites. I had only the vaguest idea of the difference between the two, something to do with the prophet Mohammed's son-in-law. King Hussein of Jordan was married to a former American airline hostess. Anwar Sadat had been assassinated by radical Egyptians who despised the Camp David peace accords he had signed with Israel. In Saudi Arabia you couldn't drink and they cut off your head if you committed adultery. Lebanon was a murderous morass where they kidnapped journalists. Topol was Israeli, Omar Sharif was Egyptian. Falafel was the regional cuisine, claimed by both Jews and Arabs.

This stellar breadth of knowledge about the Middle East was slightly deepened, in my case, by my aforementioned half-Jewish ancestry. My mother had grown up Jewish in Swift Current, Saskatchewan, which is to say she had hardly grown up Jewish at all. Her marriage to an Anglican put an end to any future feeling of tribal or religious solidarity among her children. We grew up nothing, like so many North Americans, but we lived on the fringes of the more focussed Jewish lives led by other branches of our family. We spun draidls in my cousins' basement, and searched for Hanukkah gelt (usually silver dollars), which expansive uncles hid among the sofa cushions. We celebrated secular versions of Passover and Easter and Christmas, and teased our cousins about having to go to Hebrew school, although we felt jealous when we went to their bar mitzvahs. One day my beautiful Jewish aunts were cooking bacon in the kitchen when their father made an unexpected appearance. The bacon slid into the garbage in an instant, but the smell lingered deliciously and guiltily in the air. His anger and outrage were unlike anything I had ever witnessed in my own house; there was a profound sense of customs broken, traditions betrayed, hopes dashed.

In my early twenties, on a brief and confused quest for spiritual enlightenment, I attended High Holy Days services at various synagogues a couple of years running, thrilled to the music of Kol Nidre, fasted on Yom Kippur (good for the figure) and joined a Jewish reading group. As we puzzled our way through Saul Bellow and Isaac Bashevis Singer, I found a stiff resistance inside myself to discussing these authors *as Jews*. I had just completed a B.A. and M.A. in English literature at the University of Toronto. If I had learned anything through that process it was that although every writer is specific and individual, the great ones are great by virtue of their ability to transcend specificity and reach for the universal in all of us. T. S. Eliot's "Great Tradition," don't you know. Well, that was all pre-Derrida, pre-deconstruction and pre-ethnic consciousness. Times have changed, and I can now understand, if not exactly sympathize with, what my Jewish friends in that reading club were groping towards. At the time I was very intolerant.

We moved around from house to house in that group, and one week we met in the house of a young newlywed couple who had decided, against their family backgrounds, to keep a kosher home. Shelley gave us a tour of her kitchen, with its separate sinks and banks of drawers, all neatly Mac-Tacked, "spoons — meat," "spoons — milk," "forks and knives — milk," and her four sets of dishes, meat and milk for regular days, meat and milk for Passover. I thought the pair of them were certifiable. I realize now that they were in the vanguard of what's known as the *baalei tshuva* movement, the Newly Religious or born-again Jews, a largely North American phenomenon of young people from secular or mildly religious Jewish backgrounds discovering their religious and cultural roots. Large numbers of them now live in Jerusalem, adding a curious yuppie quality to life in that Middle Eastern city.

Growing up on the outskirts of Judaism meant that I was slightly aware of Israel and its influence on Jewish life. If you weren't sure what to do with your future, you should go to a kibbutz and pick oranges for a year. Somehow this would miraculously straighten you out. (How do these pieces of smugly received wisdom ever get started?) Women had absolute equality in Israel; everyone had seen the pictures of them carrying guns and driving tanks. And look at Golda Meir. The Six Day War of 1967 was a cause for general celebration, as gallant little Israel gave what-for to the big bad Arabs and captured the Sinai and Gaza Strip from Egypt, the West Bank and half of Jerusalem from Jordan, and the Golan Heights from Syria.

Thoughtful Jews cast a darker shadow over the heroics, though. My friend Geri, who worked at a local television station with me in Ottawa, invited some of us singles for dinner one frigid winter night in 1969. Over coffee and cake the talk turned to Israel. "You can't imagine what it felt like in those last months leading up to the Six Day War," she reminisced. "Nasser had blocked the Straits of Tiran. Everyone thought it was an act of war. In the Jewish community here, we were absolutely convinced that Israel would be wiped out. And if Israel was wiped out, what would happen to us? We didn't see how Jewish life could survive without Israel."

"Yeah, it's a good thing we won," growled her husband, Bert, lighting his cigar. "But what do we do now with the million Arabs we won? The West Bank and Gaza are no prize, you know, just a colossal headache for the Jews."

Until we began to make preparations to move to Jerusalem, I had met only one Israeli in my life, and it was love at first sight. It happened that same year in Ottawa, 1969, when the gallant-little-Israel myth was at its height. To be a *sabra,* a native-born Israeli Jew, particularly one who had fought in the Six Day War, was one of the sexiest and most romantic things a man could be that year. And suddenly there was one virtually on my doorstep. He was to be my introduction both to the romance of the Israelis and to their universally noted contrariness.

His name was Menachem, but he called himself Mouky. He was six foot four and his wiry khaki-covered legs went on forever. He held his back and shoulders in a gangly slouch that belied his peak fitness and feral reactions. His face was simply beautiful to look at, perhaps the most perfect male face I've ever seen. Ocean-blue eyes with silky black brows, a fine straight nose and firm but delicate mouth, a strong, uncomplicated chin, clear olive skin glowing with good health. Binding these classic features together, a look of pouting, wary intelligence that made him untouchable and irresistible at the same time.

Mouky was on his way around the world, his reward from an adoring family for his heroic achievements as a paratrooper in the Six Day War. He had been in on the capture of East Jerusalem from the

Jordanians, I remember that much, although the specific sites of battles he described slid by me at the time. He was crashing with a mutual friend in Ottawa for a couple of days, and I made it my business to spend every waking moment over there. Nothing happened between us; I was content just to feast my eyes and fantasize, and Mouky seemed too self-absorbed to notice. It didn't matter; I was blissfully happy. We smoked grass and ate pizza and listened to endless hours of Janis Joplin.

In my bedazzled state I wanted to do something for Mouky, give him something that would make him remember me out of all the women he casually encountered on his global drift. One of my brothers, I knew, was setting out on a cross-country trek in a couple of days and would probably welcome someone to share the driving. Mouky accepted the suggestion that he should be given free transportation across North America with the noblesse oblige of a gracious hero humouring his adoring public. I drove him five hours from Ottawa to Toronto to link up with my brother, and the next morning we exchanged addresses and parted with a tender fraternal kiss. It had been, from my point of view, a perfect brief encounter with a perfect human being.

Three weeks later, when my brother returned to Toronto, I got a phone call. "Your friend Mouky," Mike began with barely suppressed fury, "he's a madman. He practically got us both killed half a dozen times." Then followed a tale I could hardly credit. After Mike's initial stint of driving, Mouky took the wheel and proceeded to drive down the middle or left-hand side of the road across the heartland of America at a hundred miles an hour. He completely ignored my brother's protestations, pleadings, threats and prayers, dipping back into his lane in the face of oncoming traffic but immediately recapturing the middle of the road. He was impervious to the shouts and honks from other outraged drivers, his eyes grimly locked on the horizon and his foot clamped to the floor. Incredibly, they had no accidents and they never got pulled over for speeding. Michael spent the next three days desperately trying to stay awake so he wouldn't have to surrender the wheel to Mouky any more than he could possibly avoid.

But the worst moment was not on the highway. The third evening, just as dusk was coming on, they reached the lip of the Grand Canyon. Mike proposed that they sleep in the car and get up at dawn to make the descent. Mouky was having none of it; they would sleep at the bottom under the stars. He set off at a loping run, with Michael desperately trying to keep up behind him, down the narrow stony trail to the canyon floor. He ran like a demon possessed, and when darkness fell completely he ran even faster. One false step and they would be over the edge into oblivion, but Mouky ran with absolute recklessness and not a jot of visible fear or caution. In an hour they were safely at the bottom, but my brother had added several years to his life. "It was *inhuman* for him not to be afraid under those conditions," he told me, "and that was what scared me most of all."

I hadn't thought of Mouky in years, and now as we flew over the Mediterranean the idea that we were going to what might turn out to be an entire country of Moukys was more than a touch unsettling. I must have sighed deeply or started muttering dire warnings to myself because Sam's little hand crept into mine.

"Are you worried about Israel, Mom?"

"Not really," I lied. "I think it was just the sight of all those soldiers with guns back at the airport that shook me a bit."

"Here, Mom, I've got a song to cheer you up." Sam is the Al Jolson-cum-Orson Welles of the family, and he launched into a lusty rendition of "You Gotta Have Heart" from *Damn Yankees,* his favourite musical that summer.

I was touched, but I was also a mother on an airplane. I shushed him so that he wouldn't bother the lovely young woman sitting on his other side. She was dripping with inexpensive but flamboyant silver jewellery and she had spent the whole trip concentrating on a complicated-looking music score.

She smiled. "He's not bothering me." The accent sounded like Philadelphia. "In fact, that song really takes me back. Do you know I played Lola in my high-school production of *Damn Yankees?*"

Sam and I both nodded. We could easily picture this exotic creature in fish-net stockings doing wildly provocative things in a men's locker room, just like Gwen Verdon.

"And what takes you to Israel?" I asked, now that the ice was broken.

"I'm going to Jerusalem to study for a year."

"Oh, yes? And what's your field?"

"I'm studying to be a cantor." She indicated the score on her lap. The cantor is partner to the rabbi in conducting the religious rites of a Jewish community. While the rabbi concerns himself with the intellectual content of services, the cantor is the custodian of ritual, of the chanting or singing that is such a distinctive and mournful-sounding aspect of Jewish worship. Every cantor I had ever come across was male and looked quite different from Jennifer.

"Do the Israelis know you're coming?" I asked a little incredulously, since one of the few things I knew about Judaism in Israel was that it was entirely Orthodox, which meant, among other things, entirely run by men.

She laughed. "Let's just say I don't broadcast what I'm doing too widely. I've gotten into some horrible wrangles with Orthodox Jews in Israel." Jennifer then explained that it was the congregation of Reform Judaism in North America that was beginning to license female rabbis and cantors. In order to complete their studies, though, they had to spend a year at Hebrew Union College in Jerusalem, Reform Judaism's tiny toehold in the spiritual centrepoint of Israel. The Conservative wing of Judaism, halfway between Orthodox and Reform, also has a minuscule presence in Jerusalem. These "progressive" offshoots of Judaism are barely tolerated by the Orthodox establishment in Israel, and laughed at by most Israelis, even secular ones. "Some of my Israeli friends send me Christmas cards as a joke," admitted Jennifer sheepishly, "just to underscore how un-Jewish they think I am."

Suddenly I felt refreshed and eager to land. My thoughts of Mouky and my encounter with Jennifer made me remember why I had been so excited about coming to Israel in the first place: it was quite simply, by all accounts, one of the most interesting places in the world. Guns, terrorism, the claustrophobic isolation, the conquering of fear: these were all elements to be dealt with and got used to, to be sure, but they couldn't begin to detract from the prospect of seeing wondrous things and fascinating people in dramatic circumstances.

As we emerged from the airplane at Ben Gurion Airport, we slammed into a wall of heat so intense it felt solid. It was the last week of August, and that year would prove the truth of the Israeli saying, "The end of summer is the worst of summer." As we rushed for the air-conditioned terminal, I expected to see more guards or soldiers on duty, but there were none in sight. Of course not; now we were *inside* the fortress, and the bored blonde who stamped our passports seemed to be the only official around.

Her eyes flickered with mild suspicion as she looked at our Canadian passports. They were clearly marked, "For use in Israel only." Journalists and diplomats from most countries are quietly issued with two passports when they are moving to the Middle East, a fact that underscores the extraordinary circumstances of Israel's existence. Because most of the Arab countries have been boycotting Israel since it came into being in 1948, they refuse to accept passports that contain Israeli stamps. So each of us had one passport for use everywhere else in the world, and a second one we used only for entering or leaving Israel. They were essentially two halves of the same passport, but I never got over the nervousness of approaching a border convinced that I was going to proffer the wrong document. Handing our "general" passports to Israelis was not a problem; they were aware of the messiness of their situation vis-à-vis the Arabs and pragmatically made no fuss about it. But if we had mistakenly handed over our Israel-only passports on our way into Lebanon or Jordan, we would have had a major diplomatic incident on our hands.

It had not occurred to me that the first emotion I would feel when setting foot on Israeli soil would be pity. As the blonde stamped my passport and handed it back to me without a word or glance, I realized we were both playing an elaborate game that had been constructed over the years to allow this aberration called Israel to exist. I felt embarrassed for the Israelis, embarrassed that they should be so hated and shunned, not only by their Arab neighbours but by large swatches of the world community as well. I also knew instinctively that if I were ever to share this sentiment with an Israeli citizen, I would feel the back of his hand in a second. The last thing Israelis want is pity from outsiders. I tucked the emotion back inside my travelling bag with the pariah passports.

We had arrived. As we emerged from the terminal building we hit a bewildering microcosm of Israeli life in the milling crowd of meeters and greeters. We had our first glimpses of ringlets and Homburgs, of Arab head-dresses, of khaki-clad soldiers, male and female. Families shouted and sobbed and shrieked around us, while an Israeli Air Force jet streaked deafeningly overhead. We had chosen this tense, overwrought place to be home. How long would it take, I wondered, before its raw sights and sounds and emotions began to seem commonplace, before this confusing tapestry of humanity started to break down into manageable, knowable individuals?

For the first time, obvious though it seems now, the thought struck me that apart from these three people, my husband and two sons, fighting their way through the crowd with me at this moment, I didn't know a soul in this country. At the age of forty-six, I would have to start making a completely new set of friends. Somehow that realization seemed more difficult to bear than any of the other culture shocks I knew we were in for. This was going to be quite a challenge.

Out on the shimmering asphalt we loaded our luggage into the Eldan rental car that was waiting for us, drove down the palm-fringed avenue that connected Ben Gurion Airport to the country's main east–west highway, and turned left for Jerusalem.

CHAPTER 2

I F YOU LOOK AT THE WEST BANK on a map (something you can't do in Israel because Israeli maps tend not to show it) it resembles a foetus, with its backbone along the Jordan River and its top and bottom halves folded in on themselves at its navel, which is Jerusalem. Or if you reverse the image and look at the long dagger shape of Israel, then the spur of land that connects the rest of the country to Jerusalem has a distinctly phallic thrust to it, digging deeply eastward into alien territory.

As we approached Jerusalem from the west, from the airport, with the Mediterranean and Europe at our backs, we felt that curious mapmaking in our bones. First we crossed the great coastal plain, that graceful strip of lush farms and kibbutzim that are the glory of the new Israel. The Judean Hills hung suspended before us in the blinding haze of late August, and as soon as we entered their narrow defile above the monastery of Latroun we were surrounded by the dangerous echoes of history. In those desperate days of the War of Independence in 1947, when the fighting went on from village to village as the Israelis tried to carve as much of a country as they could out of the land they had been theoretically awarded by the United Nations, the call went out: We must have a lifeline to Jerusalem. No matter how deep in Arab territory it lies, no matter how many lives it costs, we must. And so they did. As we drove those steep curves for the first time, beautified now with sparse green forests of pine punctuated by the graceful exclamation points of cypresses, we caught glimpses of old artillery and rotting tanks, rusted orange and crazily askew on the hills, left there for the past forty-four years as a ghostly reminder.

There's a special artificial smile humans plaster on our faces as we approach a new place where we know we are going to live. It's the same smile we use to meet the in-laws for the first time. Critical judgements will creep in soon enough, but for the time being we are desperate to like this place, to imprint a positive first impression on our brains. Jerusalem is not a wonderful city to approach in that frame of mind, certainly not from the west. The dizzying climb through the Judean Hills ends with a final pair of hairpin turns and a dusty shrubbery bed that spells out the name of the city in Hebrew script: Yerushalayim. From that point on, the narrow mountain highway widens into a confusing maze of major arteries, clogged with traffic spewing leaded exhaust in all directions. Scaffolding and unfinished buildings loom on every side, dense tract housing carpets the nearby hills, seedy gas stations moulder by the side of the road. Directly ahead, the Hilton Hotel perches against the hot blue sky, dazzlingly tall in a city that likes to keep itself low to the ground.

We plunged into a green valley and climbed another hill, now driving through the older and more settled residential neighbourhood of Rehavia. Feathery pines shaded the sidestreets from the blazing sun, instantly marking the area as a place of privilege. At the crest of this hill sat another modern hotel of breathtaking ugliness, the Sheraton. Patrick pointed out a dingy supermarket at the base of the hotel with the remains of that day's produce liberally heaped around the sidewalk and parking lot. This was the Supersol, where I was destined to spend many eventful and expensive hours.

We descended again, gently this time, past a serene green space on our left, Independence Park, with its ruinous Moslem cemetery, and increasingly old and interesting buildings on our right — the Alliance Française, the mission of the Sisters of the Rosary, the U.S. Consulate with its beefy marines on duty, and a vast, elaborately carved building, now Israeli government offices, which had begun life as a hotel for Moslem pilgrims visiting the Holy City. A right turn took us up another hill onto King David Street, with its two enormous landmarks directly facing each other. On our left, the King David Hotel, part of which had been blown up by Jewish terrorist squads back in 1946 when the hotel was being used as military headquarters by the British. On our right, the YMCA building, surely the most beautiful YMCA in the world (Jerusalemites call it Yimca) with its broad gardens and steps up to a popular terrace restaurant, a gracefully arched portal and a rounded tower soaring fifty metres above the city skyline.

All of this was impressive, but we were still craning our necks for a sight of the Jerusalem we were familiar with from picture books and tourist videos: the golden Dome of the Rock, the Wailing Wall, the Via Dolorosa, where were they? As soon as we had pulled into the nearby LaRomme Hotel, the best of the five-star hotels in the city because it had the good taste to remain low, Patrick took us out on our balcony and gave us our first lesson in Jerusalem geography.

Everything we had been driving through so far was West Jerusalem, or the new city. Its earliest buildings dated to about 1860, and feverish development was constantly pushing the boundaries ever westward. But most of the interesting things to see were inside the walled Old City, the crenellated towers of which we could see directly across the next valley to the east. To reach the great Jerusalem sights, we would have to cross that valley and plunge into the Old City on foot. And the only way to get the familiar panoramic view of classic Jerusalem with its golden dome was to approach the city from the east, from the Mount of Olives, from the Arab side. This was a revelation. Somehow, it seemed, the Arabs "owned" the treasures of Jerusalem, no matter who patrolled the streets with machine-guns or whose flag flew atop the public monuments. It would in fact be several days before we would venture over there and it would feel as if we were travelling to another world.

Down the middle of the valley between us and the Old City wall, known as the Valley of Hinnom, ran the now non-existent Green Line, which had marked the mined and barbed-wired boundary between Israeli and Jordanian forces from 1948 until the Six Day War of 1967. In that war the Israelis "liberated" the Old City and its holy places from centuries of Ottoman and Arab rule, along with the rest of East Jerusalem, a series of sprawling Arab neighbourhoods. By the time we arrived in 1991, the Israelis were still working on the massive urban renewal scheme that they hoped would eradicate the Green Line forever from people's minds. The Valley of Hinnom had been transformed from a dank and dangerous no-man's-land between the warring sides to a paradise of parkland, historic monuments, an open-air amphitheatre, cultural venues such as the Jerusalem Cinémathèque and exclusive, exquisite housing, in the neighbourhood of Yemin Moshe.

And this was where we were going to live. It seemed hardly credible that we should end up, not just in Jerusalem, but in one of the loveliest and most dramatic parts of the city. When Patrick had done his whirlwind house-hunting tour three months earlier, he had been discouraged by what he saw. Everything he liked was steeply priced in American dollars, and in Israel, he soon learned, an unfurnished place meant four walls and a roof — no kitchen or laundry appliances and no built-in cupboards at all. Towards the end of the week, the agent suggested he look at a "cottage" in Yemin Moshe, and suddenly there was our house. It belonged to a member of the Israeli foreign service who had just been posted to New York. Amazingly, it contained everything we needed: a properly equipped kitchen, a washer and dryer, walls and walls of beautiful built-in cupboards, excellent gas-powered central heating for the chilly Jerusalem winters and a pair of air-conditioners for the bedrooms upstairs. Even more amazingly, it was considerably less expensive than other places Patrick had seen, $2,000 Canadian a month. But the most impressive thing about the house was its beauty and its location.

That first afternoon, as soon as we had settled in at our hotel, we set off on foot to see our new home. In spite of our impatience, we could not move in until our furniture arrived. It was waiting for us at the Mediterranean port of Haifa, but our physical presence in the country was required before the container could clear customs. We also needed to buy ourselves a bed. Still, a visit to our new neighbourhood was our first priority.

From the LaRomme Hotel we walked through manicured flower gardens eastward to the edge of the valley, where a squat white windmill dominated the horizon. It was the landmark of Yemin Moshe, a name that means the right hand of Moses. This referred to the biblical Moses, late of Mount Sinai, but locals also associated the name with Sir Moses Montefiore, whose stature in Jerusalem is almost as high as his biblical namesake's. Sir Moses was an English Jewish philanthropist who, in the mid-nineteenth century, took a look at Jerusalem and decided something had to be done. What he saw was a remote walled city filled with Jews and Arabs and bursting at the seams with human misery. Typhus was rampant, as were starvation, cholera, consumption and abject poverty. Most of its population was devoutly religious, adherents to all three of Jerusalem's great religions, clinging to the city's holy places and living, in the main, on charity from abroad. Although many of the tiny city's problems stemmed from outrageous overcrowding, no one was willing to leave the safety of its walls and begin expanding onto the desert hills beyond. Those hills were under the control of marauding bands of Bedouin who, the Jews were sure, would murder them in their beds the first night they ventured outside the six locked gates of the city. Sir Moses believed that the Jews could never re-establish themselves in their ancient kingdom of Israel unless they were willing to expand outwards and physically embrace the land.

He chose the western slope of the Valley of Hinnom to make his early Zionist statement. In 1859 he ordered a windmill constructed on the crest of the hill, and along its ridge, a pair of curious long buildings he named Mishkenot Shana'anim (Dwellings of Serenity), which look rather like an English Victorian railway station, with their delicate tracery of wrought iron, so out of place in this landscape of rock and sand. The buildings contained simple, one-roomed dwellings for workers and their families, and the entire precinct was surrounded by a crenellated wall with guarded gates, which mirrored in miniature the more splendid Old City walls across the valley.

The story goes that it was ten years before any families got up the nerve to move in permanently. But gradually Sir Moses' idea took hold, and a whole neighbourhood of little rowhouses was built along the valley. Because it was on a steep hillside, Yemin Moshe developed with walkways and staircases and no roads for vehicles. It has a classic late Ottoman Empire look, compact cream-coloured stone dwellings with dark wooden balconies and shuttered alcoves, terracotta roofs, mysterious stairwells and soaring palm trees here and there to emphasize the long, low, village-like structure of the place.

We'd been living there a year and a half before my neighbour Jessica pointed out to me, on a map of Yemin Moshe, that the streets had been laid out in the shape of a hand, a mystical element that made me love the neighbourhood even more. The open-palmed hand, or *hamsa* in Arabic, is a totem dear to both Arabs and Jews in the Middle East, a symbol of good luck that adorns doorways, Torahs, brass coffee-tables and car dashboards alike. In a place where animosities are so sharply defined, I warmed immediately to an icon that meant the same thing to both sides. I began collecting *hamsas* and ended up with an entire wall of them from all parts of the Middle East. The knowledge that I was living in the middle of a *hamsa* (actually out at the tip of its baby finger) was pleasing.

But Yemin Moshe had not always been the idyllic place we found it. After the creation of the State of Israel in 1948, when Jerusalem was sliced in two by the scythe of war, the neighbourhood became a dangerous place to call home. Since it directly faced the Old City across the Green Line, it was well within range for Jordanian snipers behind the walls, who took pot-shots at everything that moved in their rifle sights. Anyone with the means to move elsewhere got out of Yemin Moshe, the houses of which were now battle-scarred and in many cases roofless, and squatters crept in, poverty-stricken Jews from Iran, Turkey and Kurdistan. The crowding and misery must have echoed the conditions in the Old City a hundred years earlier that had pushed the Jews over to this side of the valley in the first place.

Then came the uneasy peace established by the Six Day War, and the natural Jewish desire to make a triumphal statement about their victory. Now they were in control of the walls of the Old City, and no enemy, they vowed, would ever again use that vantage point to shoot at innocent Jews across the valley. To symbolize Israeli hegemony, Yemin Moshe became the focus of a controversial urban scheme. The squatters were moved out, some by force, to accommodation far off in the dreary new suburbs of West Jerusalem, and the ruined houses of the little hillside village were put up for auction. Anyone bidding had to agree not only to pay the price of the house but to restore it exactly to its condition during the neighbourhood's heyday in the 1890s. But because the city planners also wanted to turn the whole no-man's-land area into a cultural precinct, they made especially easy conditions for painters and sculptors to purchase houses in Yemin Moshe, and the whole area took on the air of a jewel-like artists' colony. The original long buildings of Sir Moses were transformed into a music academy and an exclusive municipal guest-house for visiting artists, writers and academics. Over the years a pantheon of Western artists have taken up residence there: Marc Chagall, Saul Bellow, Jim Dine, Yehudi Menuhin, Mordecai Richler.

By the time we arrived, however, a further metamorphosis had occurred in the neighbourhood. For a combination of aesthetic and nationalistic reasons, Yemin Moshe properties were some of the most desirable in town, and the usual laws of the marketplace prevailed. Many of the artists who had worked there quietly in their studios for two decades were suddenly being offered enormous sums to vacate the premises, mostly by prosperous North American and northern European Jews who wanted to own homes in Jerusalem, even if they seldom used them. So, many of the neighbourhood's streets wore a shuttered and abandoned look for much of the year.

Fortunately, though, Patrick was leading us down, down, down to the lowest tier on the hillside, where only one row of houses faced across the valley. Directly in front of them, amazing in a desert city, was a large lawn of well-watered grass, planted with rosebeds and olive trees. The temperature was a comfortable ten degrees cooler than in the upper ranges of the neighbourhood where the sun bounced blindingly back and forth between the stone houses ranged on both sides of the streets. The people who owned houses down in this lower-level oasis really lived in them, or if they didn't, they were always full of short-term tenants.

Our street was named Pele Yoetz, a Hebrew phrase meaning wonderful counsellor. A ridiculous name for a street, no doubt, but when I heard the English translation it rang a bell. The phrase comes from one of the loveliest passages in the Bible, from Isaiah, where the prophet describes the One who is coming: "For unto us a child is born, unto us a son is given: and the government shall be upon his shoulders: and his name shall be called Wonderful Counsellor, The mighty God, The everlasting Father, the Prince of Peace." These same majestic words were inscribed over the portal of the YMCA up on King David Street. It is a passage of impossible hope and longing, and it brings tears to my eyes whenever I hear it. How could one live in a place that promised so much without feeling spiritually uplifted and broodingly mortal at the same time?

We stopped at number 41. A quick glance up and down Pele Yoetz confirmed my first impression: Patrick had done a first-rate job. This was the best house on the best street in Yemin Moshe. True, our neighbours on either side could make strong cases for their houses getting top rating, but ours was clearly better than theirs. Unlike most of the other houses on the street, which had rather cramped and very public front patios four steps up from the sidewalk, ours had a semicircular retaining wall of golden Jerusalem stone, which curved out gently into the walkway. Geraniums and portulaca cascaded over this wall, sweeping right to the ground, and the garden above held a graceful old olive tree that washed the whole patio in lacy silver-green shade. A grape trellis in full fruit canopied the front door. The house on our left had been built thrusting forward to the property line, forgoing a front terrace, so that our patio was defined on that side by a handsome wall of ivy-covered stone. The whole configuration felt cosy and cool and private, and yet gave us a close-up view of the comings and goings in the neighbourhood and, beyond that, through more olive trees, of the sweep of the Old City walls. As for the house on our right, which was the last house on the street, I gazed admiringly and envyingly at its exuberant flower garden but noted that it was bathed in white-hot sunlight. Sitting on our terrace,

I quickly realized, would give me the best of both worlds: shade from our own olive tree and the visual enjoyment of our neighbours' flowers. So far there appeared to be no neighbours in sight.

Inside, the house was cool, low and white-washed, and it stretched a long way back. The space was broken at the halfway point by a glass-enclosed atrium full of semi-tropical plants and trees. Behind that was a small space that would make a good workplace for me and, at the very back of the house, a square room that was destined to become the *Globe and Mail's* Middle East bureau. Upstairs there were small bedrooms for the boys and a lavish private area for us at the front of the house, looking out through a deeply sloping gable onto the by now tantalizing sight of the Old City walls.

Months later, my Israeli neighbour Jessica and I were sitting out on the green carpet of grass in front of our houses. She was the daughter of a prominent Jerusalem rabbi, and old enough to remember the neighbourhood in those terrible years from 1948 to 1967. "Look at your house," she said. "It fits you and your family just about right, doesn't it?" I nodded. I never liked to mention to Israelis that the house we had left behind in Canada was twice the size of this place, because to Jerusalemites our little house was palatial. "Well, just imagine it when the Jews from Turkey were living here," she continued. "Each floor of the house was divided in two, so there were four apartments in your house, with the atrium a common courtyard, filled with garbage. Each apartment was for one family, but the families were big — six, eight, ten children. No bathrooms, no plumbing at all — there was a well down there." She waved her hand a block to the south. "The misery was incredible."

That first afternoon, as the four of us wandered around those empty rooms, imagining how our furniture and our lives would fill them up, there was suddenly a crowd of people at the white-painted iron grille at the front door. No one knew we were coming that particular day, but obviously the neighbourhood telegraph worked efficiently because a reception committee had materialized out of nowhere. It consisted of two adults and a large contingent of young boys, which seemed promising.

David and Tina were the adults. They were American Jews, a pair of school psychologists, who had been living in Jerusalem for fourteen years, and they were close friends of our landlords. "We've been over every day, watering the plants, wondering when you would turn up," said David, making it not too subtly clear that he had a key and was going to be our neighbourhood watchdog. David wore a neat beard and a *kipa,* the little crocheted beanie that is the sign of the practising Orthodox Jew; his wife simply wore an expression of terminal fatigue. As we got to know David better, her expression made perfect sense.

Two of the children, Joshua and Rachel, belonged to David and Tina. Joshua wore a *kipa* like his father. Our boys eyed them cautiously, finding them strange in spite of their familiar American accents. The other three boys were Israelis who lived on the street. There was Amos, a pallid, scholarly teenager with thick glasses and a tremulous smile. And there were Jonathan and Chaim, an unlikely looking pair of twelve-year-old twins, one large and heavy-set, the other small and quick, both with the swarthy colouring of the Sephardic, or North African, Jews. There was another boy, much smaller and younger than all the rest, David from Montreal, also *kipa*-clad, with a wistful smile and fussy manner that instantly suggested he was the late child of elderly parents. Six pairs of juvenile eyes stared unblinkingly at Gabriel and Sam in their New York Mets and Bart Simpson T-shirts.

"So where will the boys be going to school?" asked David, as we shuffled uneasily on the terrazzo floor of the empty living-room. We mentioned the Anglican School, the only English-language school in Jerusalem. A shade of annoyance passed over David's face, and immediately I felt on the defensive.

"We gather it's a very multicultural place," I babbled, "with students from forty-five countries around the world. A lot of them are from UN families, I think." There has been a large permanent contingent of United Nations forces based in Jerusalem observing the Arab–Israeli disengagement since 1948.

"I hear there are quite a few Arab students there," said David. Ah, so that was the problem.

"Yes, and some Jewish students too," said Patrick, who had actually been to the school, as opposed to me, who had only read the brochure.

"Jewish students?" David scoffed. "Why on earth would Jews send their children to the Anglican School?"

"Because they want them educated in English, I suppose." The edge in Patrick's voice was surprisingly obvious. I felt the way he sounded.

David persisted. "It just makes no sense. Jews immigrate to a Jewish country and then send their kids to a Christian school. Why do they bother coming at all?"

Tina diplomatically changed the subject, and a moment later the welcome party left, with all the adults making pro forma noises about the boys getting together to play soccer on the front lawn. David drew us out of earshot of the children to admonish us never to allow the boys to go into the valley below to play. We were surprised; the valley floor looked particularly inviting for ball games, afternoon strolls and picnics.

"The Arabs are well known for molesting young boys," he whispered.

"Are you saying there have been incidents of that sort right in this valley?" Patrick asked, the edge returning to his voice.

"No, but that's because Jewish families never let their kids down there." It seemed that in spite of all the urban renewal in the Valley of Hinnom, Jews still didn't feel completely safe or comfortable there.

As our visitors left, Patrick and I looked at each other, amazed at the rush of angry adrenalin we were both feeling. We had just been hijacked by our first Jerusalem Jews, and it was an extraordinary experience. The boys came clamouring, asking if they could go and explore the valley. "Sure you can," we said defiantly. "Just keep your eyes open and your wits about you." When they returned half an hour later, they reported one human sighting.

"There was a father down there with his two kids, playing soccer."

"Was the man a Jew or an Arab?" Patrick tried to ask casually.

"I dunno," said Gabriel, exasperated with the question. "He was just a dad, Dad."

It didn't take long for us to find out more about people like David and to understand why he made us feel so uncomfortable.

That evening, we were invited for dinner at the home of Israelis we had never met. Nachman and Etti had been living in Toronto the previous year on an academic exchange program, and their two sons had been in our boys' classes at the local public school. Through the children, we agreed to meet as soon as we got to Jerusalem; they were our only personal contacts in the whole country.

On the telephone Etti told us with wifely pride that Nachman had just been named chair of his department at Hebrew University. This set off certain expectations in our heads about where they might live — perhaps in a place like that leafy neighbourhood of Rehavia we had passed through on our way in from the airport? As we followed the detailed but still confusing official map of Jerusalem, however, it became clear that Israeli academics did not live quite as well as their North American counterparts. Down through yet another green valley and swooping up to the next hilltop, we entered Givat Mordecai, a neighbourhood of densely packed six-storey apartment blocks, all made of the ubiquitous yellow-grey Jerusalem stone, with men in black suits scurrying homeward in the thickening golden dusk. The entrance to Etti and Nachman's block was like all the others, scuffed and dingy and jammed with children. It felt a great deal more like the Third World than I had expected a middle-class Israeli neighbourhood to feel, although the children, I'll admit, looked well fed and full of vibrant energy.

Inside our hosts' cramped but cosy flat, we were instantly at home. Having Toronto in common broke the ice immediately, and since they had just returned from a year abroad they were experiencing a little of the same dislocation we were feeling. Etti, a pretty blonde in her thirties, worked for the Jewish National Fund, one of the country's huge money-raising organisms whose purpose is to plant forests and create national parks and green spaces all over Israel. She had taken the whole year off while they were in Toronto, and clearly it had been paradise. "I slept in and didn't get dressed until eleven." She giggled disarmingly. "I watched all the soap operas. It was wonderful."

Nachman was a brilliant scholar with owlish glasses, a towering forehead and a charming, wicked smile. He was a complete iconoclast. Nothing gave him more pleasure than to dissect Israeli society and drag its myriad skeletons into the light of day. His field was the sociology of deviance, and he had already produced major works on Israeli prostitution and drug addiction and was just completing a book about Jewish political assassinations in Israel. He loved visiting discomfort on the many Jews who saw it as part of their job in life to do incessant public relations on behalf of Israel. "The first time I went to Toronto," he told us with barely suppressed glee, "I started getting phone calls from women organizing lecture series at the local synagogues — you know, visiting Israeli academic, we'd be so honoured, would you come and speak to our group? I told them I'd be delighted to come and talk about Jewish prostitutes and drug traffickers. I never heard from them again."

That first night, as we sat with our two pairs of boys over a delicious home-cooked meal of salads and beef brisket and chicken, we told the story of our troubling encounter with David and Tina. Nachman perked right up and began expounding. I never met a man so happy in the throes of controversy as Nachman. He proved to be a wonderful friend and a delightfully outspoken guide through the minefield of Israeli life.

"The first thing you have to understand is that there are two types of terrible religious Jews in Jerusalem. One group is the penguins and the other is the cowboys. The cowboys are the worst."

"No, no," interjected Etti, "the *haredim* are much worse. They refuse to go in the army. All the Israelis hate them."

We begged them to back up to the beginning. The penguins ("I hesitate to use that word," explained Nachman, "because it's such an insult to real penguins") were the black-suited and ringletted ultra-Orthodox Jews, known in Hebrew as the *haredim,* or God-fearing ones. The entire lives of *haredi* men revolve around religious observance and Torah study, the lives of their wives around kosher cooking, baby-making and obscure family-centred rituals. The most strictly observant of them do not accept the existence of the modern state of Israel at all. The State of Israel, they believe, will be God's creation and it will happen only when the Messiah comes. Those somewhat less observant accept the earthly state but refuse to serve in its army. Their holiness, they believe, is part of the nation's defences; their daily prayers and study in the yeshivas are as much a bulwark against Israel's enemies as thousands of conscripts with Uzis.

Naturally other Israelis, like Etti, tend to disagree with this view. "I went to the army, Nachman went to the army, Zach and Guy will have to go to the army, everyone should have to go." This wasn't always such a big deal for Israelis. When the state was formed in 1948, there were only about four hundred draft-age *haredim* in the whole country, and to give them an exemption meant nothing. Isaac

Herzog, who was chief rabbi of the country at that time, referring to the destruction of Jewish traditions in the Holocaust, said the *haredim* "are the tiny remnant of the great Torah institutions... The very soul of the Jewish people is dependent on their existence." But over the past forty-five years, life has been good for the *haredim* in their protected enclaves of Mea Shearim in Jerusalem and Bnei Brak in Tel Aviv, and they have enjoyed an enormous baby boom. David Landau, who recently wrote a book about the *haredi* community, estimates that there are now 25,000 able-bodied draft deferees and the number will grow by leaps and bounds in the years to come. To ordinary Israelis, for whom army service is itself a form of religion, this is completely unacceptable. I never saw Israelis register anything like the same distaste for the Arabs as they did for the *haredim* who will not serve.

"Then," continued Nachman, "there are the cowboys, and they are very dangerous. I think your new friend David falls into this camp." The cowboys are the modern Orthodox Jews who combine strong religious beliefs with intense nationalistic fervour. They call themselves religious Zionists, to distinguish them from the original Zionists who settled Israel, who tended to be aggressively secular and usually socialist. The men often dress in white shirts and black pants, with *kipas* and no ties, and with the curious *tsitsit,* or ritual fringes, hanging from their waistbands. Many of the new breed of Zionists carry loaded weapons, they have settled in large numbers in the West Bank and, as far as I could ever see, it is they, not the *haredim,* who are the true Jewish fundamentalists. In fact the *haredim* seem to be opposed to a literal reading of the Bible; everything of value to them is to be found in the Talmud, the accretion of centuries of rabbinical rulings and interpretations of the original five books of Moses. The cowboys, on the other hand, sweep all that learning aside and go back to the literal words of Genesis and Exodus, in which the Lord promised Moses all of the land of Canaan from the Mediterranean to the Jordan River, in other words all of modern-day Israel and the West Bank, or as the cowboys call it, Judea and Samaria. There are places in Genesis where the Lord promised Moses a whole lot more than that: a vast swath of land from the Nile River in Egypt all the way to the Euphrates River in present-day Iraq. I suppose the world should be thankful that only a tiny handful of Zionist fanatics take the Bible that literally.

Nachman had a further lesson for us that first night. "Jerusalem," he lectured, "is not Israel. Don't ever forget it, and don't draw conclusions about Israelis from your lives here in this city." We would soon learn how right he was. For example, about eighty percent of Israeli Jews are completely secular and couldn't care less about centuries of rabbinical teachings. Those Israelis live in sprawling down-at-the-heel communities on the coastal plain, from the working-class port cities of Ashdod and Haifa to the fleshpots of Tel Aviv. But of the twenty percent who are religious, the vast majority live in and around Jerusalem, which makes it an overwhelmingly pious city. It was a shock to discover early in our stay that the *haredim,* who seemed to represent such a doomed museum-like culture, actually made up fifty-two percent of the children entering the Jerusalem school system in 1992.

Nachman and Etti, vociferous members of the secular majority of Israelis, nevertheless wanted to live in peace and a genuine sense of community with their religious neighbours. "That's why we chose to buy a flat here in Givat Mordecai," Nachman explained. "It's the only one of the new neighbourhoods that was specifically designed to house secular and religious families together." But the psychological separation between the two groups is complete in spite of the physical proximity. "The kids don't intermingle, we don't intermingle, and on the sabbath they are completely intolerant about us using our cars. It really doesn't work." It was clear there were a lot more walls in Jerusalem than the beautiful ones that enclosed the Old City.

As we left Nachman and Etti's that night, it occurred to me how strange it was that we had talked all evening about Jews and Jewish Israelis and not at all about Arabs or Palestinians. Come to think of it, except for a couple of white head-dresses at the airport, I hadn't seen anyone I could identify as an Arab our whole first day in the city. This seemed odd in a place where Arabs made up close to a third of the population. We were soon to discover that although the Israelis thought they had unified the city of Jerusalem in the Six Day War, the Palestinians had effectively rent it asunder again with the start of the intifada in 1987, and there was very little crossover between the two halves of the city.

Before returning to the hotel, we detoured to Sir Moses' windmill to take another look at Yemin Moshe, the Valley of Hinnom and the Old City walls, now bathed in silver light from the most monstrous moon I had ever seen. Patrick used to send us postcards of Jerusalem-by-night that showed a moon so outrageously bloated I was sure the pictures were romantic fakes. The real thing was in fact twice as corny. Trucks loaded with watermelons from West Bank Palestinian farms snaked through the valley on the Hebron Road, grinding into second gear to climb up the far side, directly below Mount Zion and the Old City walls, towards the next day's Arab markets in East Jerusalem.

It had been an eventful day. In just a few hours we had acquired a home, a neighbourhood, some difficult new neighbours and some promising new friends. And we had started to learn the Monopoly game of Jerusalem passions and politics. Observing the game was to become our favourite pastime, with every day bringing dazzling new moves and strategies by ancient, familiar opponents.

A mountain breeze stirred the oleander bushes near where we stood. The scathing dry heat of daytime had disappeared, granting easy sleep through fresh summer nights. Tel Avivians don't envy Jerusalemites much — in fact, they hate the holier-than-thou sanctimony that billows out of their capital city — but in summer they droop in the muggy humidity of their seaside apartments, toss and turn in sweat-soaked sheets and dream of the cool desert winds that caress Jerusalem.

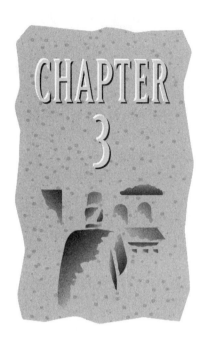

CHAPTER 3

AT THREE-THIRTY in the morning, the first night we slept in our new home, I was jolted awake by the call of the muezzin. During our initial few days in Jerusalem, as we scurried about dealing with our domestic affairs — opening bank accounts, getting telephones hooked up, having towering battles with Israeli customs agents over our computers — we would catch the occasional phrase of the Islamic call to prayer, wafting across the valley from invisible minarets on the Arab side of the city and tempting us to drop all our mundane concerns and go exploring. But it always sounded distant and muted, as if emerging from the wrong end of a time tunnel.

Now, in the deadest hour of the night, as we lay asleep on our brand-new kibbutz-manufactured mattress on the floor of our bedroom, the muezzin call literally blasted me to my feet. The sound seemed to be coming from everywhere, including the inside of my sleep-befuddled head. "Awake, awake. Prayer is better than sleep," is what the middle-of-the-night call exhorts the faithful in Arabic. Suddenly I was a little concerned that our stunning location on the dividing line between East and West Jerusalem was going to have its drawbacks. One always gets used to unfamiliar noises after a few days, but this noise was so all-encompassing, so vast, that I could hardly believe it was issuing from a human throat. It was probably a tape, of course; most mosques use them now all over the Islamic world. But the volume was cranked so ear-splittingly high that I could not help feeling it was designed as a political calling-card for the benefit of the Jewish neighbours. Perhaps it was a one-time-only prank: I never again felt it fill up my brain cavity to such a point of panic and pain.

Patrick had remained in deep slumber throughout the serenade. I could hardly believe it, especially as he was usually the light sleeper, not I. An hour and a half later, after I had dropped off again like a stone, we were both aroused by an infernal clanging that sounded like the volunteer fire department out on a drinking spree. As we peered out our window into the pink, opalescent dawn, it was clear that the cacophony was coming from the belltower of the Dormition Church on Mount Zion, just to the right of the Old City walls across the valley. This sound was almost as powerful as the muezzin, but considerably less euphonious. I am a great fan of church bells, as I am of bagpipes and other northern calls of tribal solidarity, but whoever was pulling the ropes over on Mount Zion was completely ham-fisted and tin-eared. And the bells, unlike the muezzin, did not disappear after one unforgettable performance: they were there every morning at five o'clock, announcing the beginning of another Christian day of worship and pilgrimage in the Holy City.

In the religious decibel war, the Jews are the clear losers in Jerusalem. In fact, they're not even in the competition. Judaism is a very quiet, contained religion that lays much greater stress on each person's private dialogue with God than on spreading the glad word. I'm not sure religious Jews would even say there was a glad word to be spread. Their religion has always been as much a burden as a joy to them, and they have no particular desire to see others join their faith. Still, there are moments when the Jews of Jerusalem do make joyful noises unto the Lord. The blowing of the shofar at the Western Wall each New Year is the most triumphant public sound the religion makes, a special compensation for the fact that it was forbidden in that holy place from 1931 until the Jews took control in 1967. And every Friday after sundown, when Jews gather in their unassuming synagogues all over the city, the chanting of the cantor insinuates itself through the open window grilles into the dark stone streets, telling its ancient tale of exile and longing and utter obedience.

A few days later was the eve of the Jewish New Year, Rosh Hashanah, and that afternoon, we had been assured, the shippers would finally deliver our furniture. We knew that unpacking and settling in would keep us housebound for the next while. Before that happened, it was time to visit the holy places. Unseen behind the Old City walls, they pulled us like a magnet in spite of our absolute dearth of religious belief. We had already attempted this exploration twice and found ourselves turning up at the wrong hours on the wrong days, but today all the signs seemed auspicious. Modestly dressed, even in 35-degree heat, we set off on the footpath across the valley, winding between huge aromatic bushes of rosemary and lavender, and climbed towards the Jaffa Gate.

For the first few months I lived there, I found it almost impossible to tell how old anything was in Jerusalem. Clearly it was an ancient city, four thousand years old, maybe five, but there had been so much building and rebuilding, sacking and looting, layering and recycling from the Bronze Age to our own era that anyone less than an expert was left floundering in an archaeological morass. And the morass was made even more confusing because from the beginning virtually all building in Jerusalem has been done with the identical building material: Jerusalem stone, a buttery-coloured limestone of extraordinary subtlety and beauty that has been quarried since prehistory throughout the Judean hills. There are squalid and rundown parts of Jerusalem, to be sure — it is per capita the poorest city in Israel — but because of the universal use of Jerusalem stone, every neighbourhood has a dignity and solidity that slums in the developing world, made of mud, tarpaper or corrugated tin, cannot hope to attain.

We had reached the base of the Old City walls. It was clear to me that the only way I was going to learn anything about Jerusalem was by asking stupid questions.

"Are these walls from ancient times?" I asked Patrick. They were in such perfect condition that they looked like Disneyland.

"Nope. Ottoman period. Built by Suleiman the Magnificent in 1534. They're only 450 years old." This seemed disappointingly new, under the circumstances. In a multilayered city like Jerusalem, which has seen dozens of civilizations and ethnic groups take up residence one after the other for thousands of years, the natural tendency is to place the highest value on the oldest things that have been uncovered and dismiss the more recent as parvenu add-ons. We gradually learned to stop looking at the city so simplistically.

As soon as we entered the Jaffa Gate, we made a delightfully gruesome discovery about the walls. Just inside the opening, there was a tiny alcove between two buildings on our left that held a couple of scrawny trees and two very weathered tombstones. Scrambling in our guidebooks, we learned that these belonged to the two gifted but luckless architects who had designed and built the walls for Suleiman. The emperor, in fact, never left his seat of authority in Constantinople, never travelled to Jerusalem to view his architects' magnificent handiwork. But he knew he was getting good press for their achievement throughout the Ottoman Empire and he wanted to keep it that way. He ordered the architects put to death so they could never create anything that would surpass the Jerusalem walls. (When we met Canadian architect A. J. Diamond a couple of years later, just as he was putting the finishing touches on the splendid new Jerusalem City Hall complex he had designed, Patrick and I suggested he take a contemplative moment to visit the graves inside the Jaffa Gate, and then get out of town quickly before eighty-two-year-old mayor Teddy Kollek started entertaining similar intimations of immortality.)

This tale has all the ingredients of a great Jerusalem story, including the strong possibility that it isn't true. One of the best things about the city, we soon discovered, is that you make the place up as you go along, that all who come there carry their own Jerusalem in their heads, and that whatever they bring to the city in the way of cultural or aesthetic or spiritual baggage, they are bound to find reinforced by what they see and experience there. If they come as devout Christians, they go away with their faith enormously strengthened. If they are skeptics about all spiritual matters, they will find Jerusalem the mother of all con games. If they were doubters to begin with, they continue doubting. If they just want to observe the unfurling of human history in all its glory and perfidy, they will never be happier.

Directly past the architects' graves, we plunged downward into the Arab souk, a narrow stepped alleyway called David Street, which leads straight to the heart of the matter, the Temple Mount. This was something most Jews — Israelis or tourists — had not done since 1987, when the intifada began, and which everyone we met in West Jerusalem advised us not to do. The intifada, which started with the stoning death of a Jewish truck driver who had lost control of his truck and killed four refugees in the Gaza Strip, was a genuine Palestinian grass-roots protest movement that spread instantly throughout Gaza and the West Bank. Its philosophy: we must stop letting the Israelis "normalize" their complacent occupation of us that has gone on since 1967. We will psychologically reconstruct the Green Line between them and us. We will make life so uncomfortable for Israelis that they will not come here. Thus we will reclaim Jerusalem and all the occupied territories.

If you look only at that one limited goal, the intifada was a complete success. Israelis were terrified to enter East Jerusalem, the Old City or the West Bank. They had to be crazy to go to Gaza, and the few who took a wrong turn and ended up there by accident paid for their mistakes with their lives. In Jerusalem, Israeli frustration at this state of affairs was acute. From 1948 to 1967 they had been barred from reaching the holiest site of Judaism — the Western Wall — because of Jordanian control of the Old City. Then for the next twenty years, Jews could wander freely throughout Jerusalem, worshipping where they chose, excavating and rebuilding where they wanted, rekindling ancient memories. Now once again, even though they had the upper hand and a massive military presence throughout the Old City and East Jerusalem, the constant low-level harassment by the Arabs — made up of scowls, sputum and stones in about equal parts — kept the Jews away in droves. The Israeli authorities had developed the area around the Dung Gate, on the south flank of the city walls, as a massive car park with complicated security access, so that Jews could be bused to the closest point of contact with the Western Wall, visit it briefly, then scurry back to their buses without having to set foot in the frightening Arab enclave the rest of the Old City had become for them. Technically they were still in charge of their holiest shrine, but no one was fooled. This was a *de facto* admission of crushing defeat for those who had proclaimed Jerusalem in 1967 "the eternal, undivided capital of Israel."

In September of 1993, just after Yitzhak Rabin and Yasser Arafat shook hands on the White House lawn, things began to change again. In the expectation of some kind of limited peace, West Jerusalemites began tentatively venturing into the lanes of the Old

City that they had not visited during the six years of the intifada. Azor, an Israeli cameraman we knew because he worked for one of the foreign television services, went exploring with his wife and children, and they were greeted in a warm and friendly fashion by Arab shopkeepers they hadn't seen for a long time. "Nice to see you back," said the Arabs in Hebrew, but then, switching to the Arabic they did not think Azor could understand, they continued, "Enjoy your stroll while it lasts. Soon we'll have you out of here for good."

All of this was on our minds as we made our way for the first time towards the Temple Mount. And it gave an extraordinarily piquant flavour to the experience, not just that first time but every single time we entered the Old City. That slight edge of danger, combined with the sheer exoticism of the Arab market and the looming monumentality of the holy places, made it an adventure over and over. Right from the beginning we also realized that we were in no rush, that we had years, not days, to absorb Jerusalem's treasures. There were always throngs of bone-weary tourists clogging up the narrow streets of the Old City, most of them Christian pilgrims travelling in flocks, colour-coded by sunhat so their distracted guides could separate the Day-Glo orange sheep from Nebraska from the lime-green goats from Manila. It was clear from the blank looks on their thousands of faces that they were being force-fed far too much Jerusalem history in far too short a time. "Every stone just looks like every other stone," I heard one moan to another in front of a pile of First Temple ruins. "I can't believe we have to visit three more churches before lunchtime," replied her friend. We had the luxury of time, the ability to build up a slow, rich accretion of experience; to visit a site, then go home and look it up in two or three guidebooks or historical accounts, hear stories about it from neighbours who would point out some telling detail we had missed, and then return, at a different time of the day or the week, when the light and the activity around the site would be entirely different.

On that first visit, David Street seethed around us. The shops near the top were all designed as multicultural tourist traps, ready to catch anyone of any religious or tribal persuasion. There were *hamsas,* crucifixes and Stars of David; inlaid backgammon games, carved wooden camels and electric menorahs; tea sets from Hebron, chess sets from Taiwan, nativity sets from Bethlehem. There were cocky Israeli T-shirts, like the one with a squadron of jet fighters streaking across the sky and the slogan: Don't Worry, America, Israel Is Behind You. (The more political Arab T-shirts, decorated with the Palestinian flag, and with blood-soaked images of intifada victims, were sold from under the counter.) Wedged between the tourist shops were tiny cafés and bakeries, where gnarled Arab elders watched the passing scene over delicious cups of cardomom-flavoured coffee while their restless sons and nephews swung their worry-beads, smoked incessantly and ogled the female tourists. Young Arab boys pushing green wooden delivery carts heaped with anything from fresh bread to chicken feet kept up a continuous shout of warning, "Allo, allo, allo," as they ploughed through the middle of the throng, narrowly missing the gaggle of pilgrims on one side and the hefty Palestinian matrons in their floor-length black embroidered gowns on the other. From the other direction came Israeli soldiers, three abreast, filling the space with their single-minded arrogance. I couldn't press closely enough to the wall to keep out of their way, and got painfully clipped on the forearm by a gun barrel.

We descended quite steeply, and then took a sharp right turn at Western Wall Road, which jigged and jogged until it opened high above an immense open square, and there was one of the famous Jerusalem pictures spread before us: the Western, or Wailing, Wall, with a smattering of religious Jews — men on the left, women on the right — in intense communion with the stones. Floating above the Wall, the green trees of the Haram esh-Sharif, as the Arabs call it, or the Temple Mount, as it is known to the Jews. Israeli soldiers were everywhere, on the floor of the huge plaza, on rooftops around the square, at the corners of the Haram. Six eternal candles burned on top of a religious institution to our left, symbolizing the six million Jewish souls who perished in the Holocaust. On our right, on the ridge above the plaza, massive recent construction had restored the Jewish quarter, which the Jordanians had virtually levelled when they controlled the Old City.

As we descended the wide stone staircase to the plaza floor, we tried to visualize what this area had looked like before the Israeli victory of 1967. It had not been a plaza at all but a crowded Arab neighbourhood that encroached to within three metres of the Jews' beloved Wall. Ever since the Jews had been cast out of Jerusalem by the Romans in A.D. 70, and the Roman emperor had ordered the Jewish temple completely destroyed, this one wall, actually part of a retaining wall built by King Herod to hold up the immense structure of the Temple Mount, was as close as Jews could ever get to their Holy of Holies, the rock on which they believe Abraham offered to sacrifice his son Isaac to God. Over centuries, the Wall itself — much more than the rock above — had become the main object of Jewish veneration, an eternal symbol of the Jews' loss of Jerusalem and their sweet but sorrowful relationship with their stern, avenging God.

But in the deadly balance of Jerusalem life, whatever the Jews revere the Arabs abhor, and vice versa. Once Islam established itself as the dominant religion in the city after the defeat of the Crusaders in 1244, the Jews were tolerated but reviled. The narrow lane in front of the Western Wall became one of the most squalid parts of the Old City, according to such nineteenth-century travellers as Mark Twain and Herman Melville. The Arabs regularly herded their sheep and goats back and forth behind the hapless Jews who were trying to pray, threw garbage into the area, contaminated the precinct overnight with piles of human excrement. Even under the more civilized British mandate before the state of Israel was created, the Jews were not allowed to keep chairs or benches by the Wall for their older congregants because furniture might constitute a *de facto* ownership of the Wall, which the Arabs hotly disputed. Given all that, it's perhaps no wonder that the minute the Israelis took possession of the Old City in 1967, they got a bit overenthusiastic. While the Six Day War was still going on, orders were given from on high to bulldoze the Arab neighbourhood immediately adjacent to the Wall, because hundreds of thousands of Jews were streaming in from all over Israel to see and touch the sacred stones. A few more streets than necessary were bulldozed "by mistake," rendering some six hundred Palestinians homeless and creating the gargantuan sun-baked plaza we see today. It is so enormous that it almost dwarfs the Wall.

I would return many, many times to the Wall over the next two years, seeing it in all its moods and manifestations. What I noticed on that first visit was that there were very few men praying in the ample Wall frontage they had allotted themselves, and very many women praying in the much more crowded space assigned to them. The worshippers at the Wall were, of course, vastly outnumbered by the tourists taking pictures of them. When I approached the Wall on the female side, a number of *haredi* women in their long skirts looked disapprovingly at my slacks and complained to the soldier on duty, who shrugged and couldn't care less. I was annoyed. I was modestly dressed, in the sense that most of my flesh was covered. That the *haredim* have a prohibition against women wearing what they deem to be men's clothing seemed to me completely beside the point. After all, as I understood it, the Wall belonged to all Jews, not just the *haredim*, and as a half-Jew I felt entitled to approach its warm rough stones and eavesdrop on some of the longings and hopes that had been whispered into its secret fissures for two millennia.

Right beside the Wall was a steep-sloping ramp leading up to the Mughrabi Gate, one of the eleven gates that give access to the Haram or Temple Mount. Israeli soldiers searched handbags and camera cases as an assorted mixture of Moslems and tourists entered the holy precinct. We had already made two attempts to enter the Haram, only to be rebuffed by the officious guards of the Wakf, the Moslem authority that retains control of all the Islamic religious sites in Jerusalem. "Only Moslems can come now. Time for prayers," we had been told. On those occasions, when we appealed to the Israeli soldiers for a ruling, they shrugged elaborately. Their business was to make sure no one smuggled a bomb into the holy sites; who was allowed to come, through which gates, at what times, on what days and wearing what clothes was up to the Wakf. Since we were entering what is probably the most contested piece of real estate in the world, it is perhaps not surprising that the lines of authority seem confused, overlapping and overbearing.

What lay before our eyes past the security checkpoint was a panorama more immense and impressive than any photograph can convey. The Haram is a huge open-air platform of 144,000 square metres, covering one-sixth of the area of the Old City. To the right was the graceful white oblong of the Al Aqsa Mosque, with its brooding black dome, the holiest mosque in Palestine. To our left stood the Dome of the Rock, by far the most beautiful building in Jerusalem, an octagon glowing with blue, green and white tiles under its magnificent golden dome. There were about a hundred other small open shrines, fountains and sculptures dotting the vast surface of the Haram, mixed in with delectable plantings of trees, bushes and grass. Moslem women in long shapeless gowns and white *higabs,* or headscarves, herded collections of young children before them towards the mosque for devotions. Groups of Arab men in white burnouses lounged in languorous conversation in the shade of cypresses. In one corner, a tall young man kicked a soccer ball around with a dozen Arab boys in blue jeans. Tourists moved in straggling waves between the Dome and the mosque, pacing the warm white slabs of marble in their sock feet, carrying their Reeboks in their hands.

It felt like paradise, a relaxed unselfconscious Garden of Eden. It was the first Islamic religious site I had ever entered, and what struck me was its cosiness, in spite of its monumental scale. I did not visit many other Moslem places of worship in the Middle East, because most of them prohibited entry to unbelievers, but every one I did see had the same atmosphere as the Haram: casual, communal, non-hierarchical. Quite apart from its religious significance, which Palestinians seemed to wear rather lightly, the mosque struck me as being rather like a British pub, a civil construct where classes and ages (but not sexes) mingled for gossip and politics and good times. Arab living-rooms always felt unbearably formal; if you wanted to see Arabs just hanging out, the courtyard of the mosque was the place to do it.

We deposited our shoes in cubby-holes outside the Dome. On advice from friends, we had not brought cameras or purses with us because the Wakf would not allow these items inside the holy sites and it seemed less than prudent to leave them on open shelves with thousands of people milling about. The Wakf officials watched the foreign women like hawks, thrusting shapeless pale blue coveralls at any who in their estimation were showing too much leg or forearm. "Look, madam," shouted one of them to me, pointing at my throat and motioning that I must do up the top button of my blouse if I wanted to gain entry. While he was keeping his prurient eyes on me, three men slipped into the Dome behind his back without showing their tickets. The Wakf officials took the prize as the most unpleasant Arabs we ever met in Jerusalem.

Inside the Dome of the Rock, all was quiet splendour and spaciousness. The combination of thick Persian carpets underfoot, patterned marble and mosaics on the vast curved walls and the softly filtered green light floating in through the stained-glass windows high in the dome made the whole atmosphere rich, muted and otherworldly. In the centre of the building, behind a wooden screen so high that you had to get on tiptoe to look over it, lay the rock itself,

flat and obvious and seemingly out of place in the glorious setting
around it. A huge imaginative effort was required to strip the building and its trappings away, to make the Haram esh-Sharif, the Old
City and the rest of Jerusalem disappear, and try to picture this rock
as Mount Moriah, the rounded top of a not very high outcrop of the
parched Judean Hills, with scrubby bushes and goat droppings all
about, which tradition has always associated with Abraham's attempt
to fulfil God's command by sacrificing his son Isaac.

From that act, which God stopped in the nick of time, and from
this rock, flowed monotheism and the indestructible covenant
between humans and an unseen, all-powerful single deity. God's conditions to Abraham and his offspring were simple: give me complete
obedience and circumcise all your males as a sign of that obedience.
His promise: you will be my chosen people and I will bless you and
protect you. Moreover, in God's exact words from Genesis, "by your
offspring shall all the nations of the earth gain blessing for themselves,
because you have obeyed my voice." In other words, the well-being
of the entire world was to depend in some mysterious way on the
covenant between God and the Jews.

These are weighty matters, and to contemplate them as you
stand beside the rock of the sacrifice is to feel that you are indeed
standing at the very centre of the world. And if, like me, you do not
believe in any extrahuman force called God or Yahweh or Allah or
anything else, then the overwhelming question becomes: why this
place? What is it about this particular rock on this specific patch of
the earth's surface that touched those ancient wellsprings of human
need and set our civilization in motion more than five thousand
years ago?

The later manifestations of belief attached to this sacred place are
easy to track: in 1000 B.C. King David bought the property, known
at that time as a threshing-floor, from a member of the Jebusite ruling family that controlled Jerusalem before the Jews took power;

King Solomon, David's son, built a temple on the spot in 960 B.C., calling it the Holy of Holies, where only the high priest of the Jews could enter. The Babylonians destroyed that First Temple in 586 B.C. and sent the Jews into bondage. The Jews returned seventy years later and erected their Second Temple on the ruins. In 20 B.C., King Herod aggrandized the whole site and his reputation by building the Temple Mount platform all around the Second Temple, including what is now known as the Western Wall. In A.D. 70 the Roman emperor Titus kicked the Jews out of Jerusalem again and reduced the Temple to rubble. The next Roman emperor Hadrian erected a temple to Jupiter on the site, but that was destroyed when the Roman Empire turned Christian under the rule of Byzantium. When Islam swept into Jerusalem in 638, the ruling caliph, Omar Ibn Al-Khattab, cleared away the garbage from the rock and built a small mosque nearby.

The site is holy to Moslems for two reasons: first, they accept that they too are descended from Abraham, but through his bastard son Ishmael rather than his legitimate son and heir Isaac. This was intelligent public relations on the part of the prophet Mohammed, who founded Islam in 622. Instead of beginning afresh, he traced his new religion's origins back to the same source as that of Jews and Christians, so that Islam would be seen not as a usurper, but as a continuation and fulfilment of Judaism and Christianity. (Moses and Jesus are frontline prophets in the Islamic worldview.) Just to nail the connection down more securely, Islam developed its own story about the rock. This was the legend of Mohammed's famous night ride from Mecca to Jerusalem in a dream, on the back of his beautiful winged horse, El-Burek. From the rock he rose to Heaven to discuss the creation of Islam face-to-face with Allah. The dream story was the only way the Moslems could establish a connection to the rock because in real waking life Mohammed never set foot in Jerusalem. The building of the Dome over the rock in 691 cemented the Moslems' control over Jewish and Christian roots, and with the construction of the Al Aqsa Mosque beside it, Jerusalem was declared the third holiest site in Islam, after Mecca and Medina, where the Prophet Mohammed had lived and preached. Moslems do not call the city Jerusalem, however; to them it is known simply as Al-Quds, the Holy One.

That still wasn't the end of the story. When the Crusaders lumbered into Jerusalem in 1099, they took over the Haram esh-Sharif, converted the Dome to a Christian church and turned the mosque into a royal palace. The Knights Templar took their name from the Temple Mount, and built a vast underground area to house their horses, which they called Solomon's Stables. When Saladin reconquered the city for Islam a hundred years later, he tore down the cross from atop the Dome and burned it. Since then, except for fifteen years when the Crusaders reconquered and lost it again, the precinct has remained in Moslem hands, even after the 1967 Israeli conquest of the Old City and their annexation of all Jerusalem. The story goes that the officials of the Wakf fully expected to have to give up their precious Haram to the modern Jewish warriors as the natural spoils of war, but that Moshe Dayan, the general in charge of the conquest of Jerusalem, told them no, there was no need to hand over the keys to the Dome and Al Aqsa, that as far as Israelis were concerned these monuments could and should remain in Moslem hands.

When the vexed subject of Jerusalem would come up in conversation, a number of times I heard Israelis express the opinion that they should have grabbed the Temple Mount when they had the chance. It is one of the more intriguing "what ifs?" in modern world history. Undoubtedly the Arab and Islamic world would have announced jihad, holy war, against Israel after such a move. But given how poorly Israel's enemies have generally been able to cooperate in pursuing their common goals, the Islamic effort might have remained more rhetorical than practical. If Israel had grabbed the Temple

Mount and had prevailed, would Jerusalem today remain the most bitterly contentious aspect of any possible peace settlement between the Arabs and the Jews?

We decided to leave an exploration of the Al Aqsa Mosque and the Islamic Museum beside it to another day, and plunged back into the Old City to touch base with Christian Jerusalem. On our way over to the Church of the Holy Sepulchre, though, we left the Haram by way of the Street of the Cotton Merchants, a medieval vaulted street, pitch-black except for the thin, square beams of blinding sunlight that pierced the darkness from holes in the roof high overhead. It was frightening to plunge into so much blackness in the middle of the Moslem quarter, but as soon as our eyes became accustomed to the dark our fears evaporated. Throngs of Palestinian children, dressed in blue smocks and with bookbags slung across their backs, were cutting through the lane and the Haram as a lunchtime shortcut from school to home. There was a store selling the cheap pink and green plastic toys that seem to be ubiquitous in Third World marketplaces. The covered street contained tightly shuttered shopfronts, neatly labelled with Arabic numerals, used now as storage vaults.

The only other place open for trade was a tiny café. Really it was nothing but a serving table set up in the gloom with a two-burner gas stove for boiling water, from which a young Arab man and his little boy dispensed the most delicious mint tea we had ever tasted, very sugary, scalding hot, served in tall glasses with enormous sprigs of fresh mint. There was a built-in stone bench running the entire length of the street, and the owner had appropriated the section near his tea-stand by throwing down some rush matting and half a dozen rickety tables. A couple of his regular customers were sharing a hubble-bubble in the corner, the elaborate Arab waterpipe that feels so deceptively mild until you have sucked on it three or four times. We sat and drank and repopulated the street in our imaginations with medieval cotton merchants from Jaffa and Damascus and Tyre, trading feverishly under the watchful eyes of the Mameluke janissaries who controlled Jerusalem from the thirteenth to the sixteenth centuries. That café became our favourite in the Old City, particularly when we explored the Haram on bright, cold winter days and warmed our hands afterwards on hot glasses of tea, huddling close to the little charcoal braziers where our tea-maker's son tended singed cobs of corn and tiny skewers of lamb.

At the bottom of the Cotton Merchants' Street, a few quick turns brought us into the lower half of the Via Dolorosa. The wonderful Israeli writer Amos Elon talks about the "extraordinary economy of religious sites" in which the same crowded spaces are used and reused through the centuries by one faith after another; Jerusalem is the best, in fact the most laughably obvious, example in the world. Does it strain credulity just a touch that the momentous events in three of the world's most powerful religions should have all occurred within a city block of each other in a small walled mountain town? Here at the intersection of El-Wad Road and the Via Dolorosa, the ultra-Orthodox Jews heading for the Wall jostle with the Arabs on their way to the Haram, and both are swamped every few minutes by another wave of Christians toiling up the route of Jesus' Passion to the place where tradition says he was crucified, buried and resurrected, at the Church of the Holy Sepulchre.

I'm sure that you, like I, have seen *Ben Hur,* so we know what Calvary is supposed to look like. A high hill outside the city gates, the three crosses silhouetted against a lowering sky split every few moments by shafts of lightning. Roman soldiers play dice at the foot of the cross, Mary and her women friends weep and mourn, Joseph of Arimathea wrings his hands. We know the holy tomb as well from countless Renaissance paintings, an ancient rock cave surrounded by vaguely Italian-looking shrubbery, with the three Marys keeping their long lonely vigil.

Now put all that aside and picture the Holy Sepulchre. It is a holy mess, a confusing and ugly agglomeration of kitschy chapels, statues, stairwells, scaffolding, domes and hanging oil-lamps, the result of sixteen centuries of non-stop turf wars, sackings, lootings, reconstructions, miracles and horse thievery by all the princes and potentates who have staked their claim on Christendom's holiest site. It all began around A.D. 320, when Constantine the Great, the Byzantine emperor, dispatched his mother, Queen Helena, to the Holy Land to definitively identify the important sites of Christ's birth, life and death. What qualified Helena for this job no one has ever known, except that she was the mother of the man in charge. The good queen (whom we in our family took to calling "the human divining rod") wandered the Middle East locating the big sites, the manger in Bethlehem, Mary's well in Nazareth and of course the Holy Sepulchre sites in Jerusalem. She is even believed to have found the True Cross in a cave under the Holy Sepulchre site, still intact after three hundred years. An amazing, enterprising woman. Everywhere she pointed, official churches sprang into being, smothering the natural locations or tiny local shrines in massive Byzantine overbuilding. In the case of the Holy Sepulchre, the enormous Byzantine cathedral Helena created was soon destroyed by the Persians. What stands before the confused visitor today is a collection of small chapels pertaining to many varied sects, overbuilt by the Crusaders into a unified structure, then divided up again into at least five warring Christian communities, the Greek Orthodox, the Armenian, the Roman Catholics, the Syrian Jacobites and the Copts. The poor Ethiopians lost their bit of turf two centuries ago and now insist on their hegemony from a precarious position on the roof!

It was difficult not to snicker at the gaudy decoration and crass opportunism of the Holy Sepulchre. If it had set out deliberately to demonstrate everything that was worst about organized religion, it could not have done a better job. The place had no class at all. What it had, though, was something much more intangible and astounding: it had people's trust and belief. I stood enthralled as little Greek widows, clothed from top to toe in deepest black, slathered holy oil over the Stone of Unction in the main vestibule of the church, said to be the site where Jesus was anointed when his body was brought down from the cross. Sobbing, crossing themselves, beating their breasts, they pushed the oil over the surface of the stone with small white cloths, then kissed the oil-soaked cloths, put them carefully into plastic bags and dropped them in their stiff black purses to carry home as a precious reminder of their pilgrimage. Weary bus loads of the faithful from every corner of the globe lined up in an interminable queue to enter the sepulchre itself, a long nondescript rock inside a tiny chapel that could hold only two people at a time along with the vigilant ever-present Greek Orthodox priest. Because of the constant pressure of numbers, each pilgrim could spend only ten, fifteen seconds at most touching the tomb and praying before the priest made shooing motions to keep the line moving.

At the top of a high, dangerous staircase of slippery marble steps, another steady line of worshippers knelt and crawled under the altar to touch a bronze disc set into rock, reportedly the spot where Jesus' cross had stood. (On one of our numerous later visits to the Holy Sepulchre, a friend and I overheard an American mother explaining to her young son, "And this is where he died." Whereupon her husband, obviously suffering from holy-site overload, said, "No, no, this is where he was born.")

What seemed to make these pilgrims believe was belief itself, the centuries of belief that preceded theirs. They were not interested in archaeological evidence or proof that the sites they were venerating were the real McCoy. The fascinating academic argument about whether the site of the Holy Sepulchre had been inside or outside the city walls at Jesus' time (the dead were never buried within city walls) was tedious to these pilgrims and completely beside the point. They came to Jerusalem, having saved their hard-earned money for years to make the journey, because millions of others had come to Jerusalem before them, had worshipped these exact same stones as far back as the collective memory of their communities could take them. Seeing such faith in action was a humbling and extraordinary experience.

We were suffering from holy-site overload ourselves by this time, so we quick-marched back through the David Street souk and out of the Old City through the Jaffa Gate. From the gate's commanding position, we had a beautiful view of our own neighbourhood, with its charming red-tiled roofs, spread out on the other side of the valley below us. When we arrived back home, hot and very thirsty, we noticed that the door to our next-door neighbour's house was open, with Brahms wafting out into the blazing summer air. This was exciting, because until now all of Pele Yoetz Street seemed to be away on vacation and we had met none of our neighbours. We brought a jug of icy lemonade out onto our terrace and awaited further developments.

A loud male voice lifted above the strains of the piano concerto, and suddenly a short fellow with a bushy moustache and grizzled grey curls burst out the door shouting in Hebrew into a portable telephone. As soon as he saw us he waved expansively, made a curious movement in which he bunched all his fingertips together and lifted them towards us, and then disappeared into the house. (It was, we learned, a very Israeli gesture that meant "*Rak rega*," or "Hold on a minute," and depending on the movement of the hand it could be a polite request or as rude as a middle finger.) The gentleman's flow of Hebrew never stopped. A moment later he emerged again, still engrossed in his conversation, nodded to us a second time and started picking deadheads off his crimson geraniums. Three or four more times he appeared and disappeared before he eventually flung himself, still talking, into a chair at his white plastic patio table, which was identical to ours. If you just listened to his stream of words, the man sounded angry, as if he was chewing out an incompetent employee. But his sparkling eyes and frequent braying laugh belied his tone and made us keen to make his acquaintance, should that ever prove possible. Finally, after several false endings, the conversation was abruptly terminated, the man telescoped the aerial of his telephone, ducked between the sharply pointed palm fronds that separated his property from ours and approached us with expansively open arms, as if we were long-absent friends.

"So you have finally arrived!" he said, in fluent but heavily accented English. He gave the impression that he had spent days waiting for us, rather than the other way around. "We just got back from our summer holidays. A package tour to Bulgaria. Really hot. Terrible food. Too many Israelis. But it was cheap. *Ma laasot?*" This last phrase, one of the most common in Hebrew and always accompanied by an elaborate shrug, seems to pinpoint the basic Israeli philosophical position on everything: whatcha gonna do?

We were delighted to find our new neighbour so friendly and forthcoming, but we were still a little cautious. After all, we had been warned that he was a would-be murderer. On the surface this seemed unlikely, but you can never tell.

We had received this startling information from David, our landlord's watchdog, who had made it his business to come around two or three more times to make sure we were settling in correctly. He had had to give us little seminars on how to fire up the gas water-heaters and how to set the oven, which came with Hebrew-only instructions and no pictures. David was helpful; he just wasn't very pleasant. He always made us feel on trial because, as foreign journalists, we could be counted on, in his experience, to give Israel an undeserved hard time in our dispatches. Many Jerusalemites, particularly the transplanted North American ones, automatically shared this view of journalists.

At the end of one of his visits, when we had wandered onto the patio making awkward small talk, I commented on the lovely bed of white roses just across the pathway from our house.

David agreed they were pretty, then paused. "The trouble is, they're in the wrong place."

"What do you mean?"

"Well, the bed wasn't supposed to be here at all," David said, his exasperation building as he told his tale. "All the gardens in Yemin Moshe are planned and taken care of by the East Jerusalem Development Corporation, you know, the management which runs this neighbourhood like a condo. But your next-door neighbour here" — he indicated the locked door of number 43 — "wanted more flowers around his property, so he planted all these." His sweeping hand took in our whole enchanting corner of the street, which indeed had many more flowers and flowering bushes than the rest of the area. "But to make that rosebed he took away some of the grass. And sometimes, if the kids are playing soccer, the ball gets into his rosebushes. It's only natural. The rosebed shouldn't be there in the first place." David glared daggers at the offending plants. "Anyway, one day our kids were playing and the ball came over here, and your neighbour came flying out of his house and threatened to kill me if it ever happened again. Threatened to shoot me. So just watch out."

Everything else being equal, I'm the sort of person who would side with the soccer players rather than the gardener in that story. But everything else wasn't equal because I had taken quite a dislike to David. So I was curious to meet the man who had threatened to kill him.

"My name is Avraham," said our neighbour. "*Naim meod,* pleased to meet you." (In Israel people often say something in Hebrew and immediately afterwards in English. This solidifies their commitment to the national language but indicates they are cool as well. The most commonly used bilingual phrase is "*lehitraot*-bye.") "My wife is

Tamar. She is somewhere." He waved vaguely towards his house. "You will meet her," he said brusquely, in the tone of voice that always made Israelis sound impatient to newcomers. Whether they really were as peremptory as they sounded was one of the intriguing mysteries about these people. In their own eyes, their national personality was much more sentimental: the word *sabra,* Israelis never tired of telling us, meant the fruit of the cactus, prickly on the outside but soft and sweet on the inside.

We began to explain our presence to our neighbour, but he had already been briefed by our landlords. At least he knew what Patrick did. When I explained that I was also a journalist, specializing in cultural matters, Avraham's eyes lit up.

"This is wonderful, because I am a painter and sculptor. You see?" He indicated the three-metre-tall wrought-iron birdbath in front of his house. It was not particularly to my taste, too whimsical and gawky, but it blended in enough with the plentiful foliage that it didn't create an eyesore. And it was clearly a favourite haunt for the neighbourhood birds, especially on those endless hot summer days.

"Are you a professional artist?" I asked, wondering if he was one of the originals the government had encouraged to settle in Yemin Moshe.

"Well, I sell my work, if that's what you mean," said Avraham, adding reluctantly, "but I did have a real job until I just retired. I costed heating systems for apartment buildings, factories, things like that. And Tamar, my wife — where is she? she must be resting — she's a, what do you call it? She runs a high school. She's the boss."

"A high-school principal?"

"Yes, yes, principal," Avraham shouted with glee, thrilled to have bagged an elusive English word. Then he rushed back to the subject that clearly had his heart's devotion. "But now I can paint all the time. My studio is up there." He pointed to a window on the second floor. "I started very young, when I was growing up on the kibbutz.

You know Streichmann, the famous Israeli artist?" We shook our heads regretfully. "Ach, he is the best, the best. You must go to see his work at the Israel Museum. He lived on my kibbutz and I learned painting from him. You want to come and see my work?"

Usually I am reluctant to enter an artist's studio unless I have seen his or her work and admired it. But I guess it was some measure of how instantly we warmed to Avraham that we felt no qualms at all about entering his inner sanctum. I knew in advance we would like what we saw. The main floor of his house, exactly the same space as ours, felt smaller and more den-like because it was crammed with dark comfortable furniture and lace-topped tables and every inch of wallspace was covered with Avraham's work, from tiny framed sketches to large oils and water-colours. Also, they had preserved both a front and a back staircase to the second storey, the front one leading up through the living room to Avraham's studio.

They were all paintings of Jerusalem, the water-colours lyrical and soft-edged, the oils more playful and semi-abstract. "I am stuck, I admit it," said Avraham, shepherding us through a pile of water-colours on his work table, "always Jerusalem, Jerusalem. It is hard for artists who live here to paint anything else. The light, the stones, they are always changing, there are always new things to capture. Still, I am getting a bit tired of the subject."

With little discussion, Patrick and I knew which ones we wanted. First, a water-colour in moss greens and browns of people buying and selling in a place we had yet to visit, the Mahane Yehuda, or Jewish market. That was destined to go over our bed. Then a large square oil that was still on the easel, showing a lively cubist tumble of houses and domed buildings curving up the right side of the canvas, with the left side an almost abstract impression of huge looming walls washed in faint pinks and blues. The painting captured perfectly, uncannily, the feeling we had both had walking the streets of the Old City that morning, the feeling of a living city teeming with the energy of everyday life and yet somehow stifled, paralysed by the walls and stones of its long, cruel and too-important history. We had to have it.

"I don't think it's really finished yet," said Avraham, frowning at the left-hand side of the painting. "What do you think?"

What kind of question was that for an artist to ask potential clients? We said we loved it as it was, but it was up to him. "At least let me keep it a couple of days. I'll frame it for you — don't worry, nothing fancy," he said hurriedly, catching the alarm in our faces. "I always used to get my paintings framed in the Old City, until the intifada. My Arab friends over there told me, don't come, you could be in danger, just don't come. I haven't been there for five years," he said matter-of-factly, as if he was talking about Paris instead of the streets and laneways just a hundred metres from his front door. "Now I make my own frames."

As we descended the rickety stairs, a short blond woman with a polio limp and a gentle face came out from the kitchen area. "This is Tamar," said her husband, sounding offhand but looking at her as if she were the only woman in the world.

"*Naim meod*," said Tamar, and explained that her lovely name was the Hebrew word for date or datepalm.

"They are buying two paintings," said Avraham, preening.

A slight cloud passed over Tamar's face. "Which ones? No, don't tell me. I love them all so much, I have told Avraham for years not to sell any of them. I can't bear to see them go."

We assured her they would be right next door, as would we. Suddenly Pele Yoetz Street felt like home.

CHAPTER 4

I
F YOU'RE LIVING IN A WAR ZONE, it's best to move around in a
tank. That was the conclusion Patrick and I came to after witnessing our first week of Jerusalem driving. It wasn't only that
you might find yourself straying across the invisible Green Line
and into hostile territory on the way home from the supermarket, although that was always a possibility. The more clear and present danger in the Middle East is simply from the traffic. Israelis and
Arabs may differ culturally in many respects, but on the road they are
all maniacs. Let me fine-tune that: Israelis are aggressive maniacs;
Arabs are friendly maniacs. It makes little difference when they rear-
end you.

The pressing question, then, was what type of tank to purchase,
and here regional politics immediately reared its head. Unlike most

Israelis, we expected to spend a fair amount of time driving in the occupied West Bank, where our yellow Israeli licence plates would elicit a Pavlovian response from Palestinian stone-throwers. Foreign journalists, it turned out, were not entitled to the quasi protection of white plates; that was only for diplomats and UN personnel. West Bank residents themselves carried blue or green plates. The people who really got burned (literally) by this system were the Palestinians who lived inside the municipal boundaries of Jerusalem. They were issued yellow plates like the Israelis and not infrequently found their cars mistakenly vandalized by fellow Arabs. One night it happened to our friend Kamil, a Christian Arab who worked tirelessly for the Palestinian cause from his base at the East Jerusalem YMCA. He turned up late for dinner at our house, sheepishly announcing that his car had been torched. "Sometimes the revolution gets a little too enthusiastic," he admitted with what seemed, under the circumstances, an overly charitable chuckle.

If we had to drive around with a yellow beacon on our car, it was important that the vehicle itself be as neutral as possible. Citroëns and Peugeots were out; the Israeli army and important government functionaries drove those. BMWs and Audis just felt wrong in the land of the Jews (although a surprising number of Israelis do buy and drive German cars, especially old Mercedes-Benzes that were part of the war reparations Germany paid to many Holocaust survivors.) The Dodge Caravan we had left behind would have been perfect for our family, but that whole line of high, roomy vans was the vehicle of choice among the settlers, Nachman's cowboys, the tough religious pioneers who run the gauntlet of Arab displeasure every day to establish and maintain a Jewish presence in what they call Judea and Samaria and what the rest of the world calls the occupied territories. The settlers tend to customize their Plymouth or Toyota vans with chain-link fencing over the windows and a large guard dog in the back seat. We had no desire to be mistaken for them. Eventually we settled on a Volvo station wagon — a white, neutral heavyweight of a car that looked as though it would roll away from any encounter and live to tell about it.

As it turned out, our research was not quite thorough enough. We hadn't reckoned with the *haredim,* Nachman's penguins, who are bursting out of their crowded Jerusalem neighbourhood of Mea Shearim and spreading fast throughout the city. The *haredim* have enormous families, and the more affluent among them seem very partial to white Volvo station wagons. Still, in the wonderfully convoluted world of Middle East politics, it is healthier to be mistaken for a *haredi* than for a settler when you are driving through the West Bank. The Arabs are aware that the *haredim* are not Zionists, that they live in the land of Israel for purely religious reasons, and that they have no designs on the occupied lands.

The only Jews we would regularly see walking with no fear at all through the Moslem quarter of the Old City were the *haredim* on their way to pray at the Western Wall. They were blind to the Arabs around them, as indeed they were blind to the modern city of Jerusalem and the modern state of Israel, rushing with speed and single-minded purpose towards the vestiges of their two-thousand-year-old temple. The Arabs treated them with respect and distance.

To make our car purchase, we were directed to the Talpiot Industrial Zone, a Jerusalem neighbourhood as ugly as its name. The Volvo showroom was deserted, except for one salesperson, Ayala, a drop-dead *sabra* far more concerned with the state of her flawless nails than with selling cars. "It will take at least three months to get one from Sweden," she said in the husky baritone voice that so many Israeli women surprisingly possess. She was clearly hoping this information would discourage us from pursuing the matter. It didn't. Could she tell us how much the car would cost? "You have a B-1 visa, for working in Israel?" Yes. The fingernails clattered over the calculator keys. "That's 49,800 shekels" — about $25,000 Canadian or $20,000 U.S. We made the universally understood eye-rolling response to this figure. "But you are lucky," Ayala protested. "You know what Israelis would have to pay?" The fingernails flew once again. "For the same car, 98,000." We were beginning to understand that it takes a heap of taxes to run an armed fortress like Israel on constant red alert.

The next half hour was spent on paperwork, a fine Mediterranean and Middle Eastern custom, inherited from those masters of bureaucracy, the Ottomans. As Patrick ploughed his way through one meaningless form after another, I observed Ayala. Like many beautiful Israeli women — and if they are below the age of forty they are almost all beautiful — she had an enormous mane of permed, frizzed and hennaed hair, eyelids that drooped heavily from a combination of makeup and sultriness, clusters of gold chains and jewellery everywhere about her person and a permanent pout on her luscious purple lips. My image of Israeli women had been quite different before I arrived: I conjured up pictures of fresh-faced blond Europeans with determined eyes and smiling mouths, always unadorned and clad in khaki. But those were the Ashkenazi kibbutzniks I was thinking of, girls of Russian and Polish background, the *sabra* offspring of early Zionist pioneers. I had not known that more than half the Israelis were Sephardic Jews, exotic dark-skinned brunettes from Africa who resemble their enemies the Arabs much more than their northern European Jewish cousins (although a Sephardic Jew would curse you forever for pointing out the similarity).

The last form had been signed. "When you come to get the car, Yossi will show you everything," said Ayala, airily dismissing us and indicating her lone cohort on the salesforce, who was just coming in from lunch. Yossi looked like a lot of car salesmen, a little paunchy, a little dyspeptic, a little worried. But then in some ways he looked quite different; for example he had a pistol stuck in his belt. We had not realized that selling Volvos in Israel was such high-risk work.

"*Lehitraot*, see you soon," we sang out with the false jollity that the sight of inappropriate firearms in Israel always seemed to induce.

Now we had to get along for three months while our Volvo made its stately way from Göteborg to Haifa. We had acquired an Israeli Eldan rental car the day we arrived, but it would not do for the long term. We took it across the invisible line one evening into Arab East Jerusalem to have dinner at the sumptuous American Colony Hotel, and as we drove up, the hotel's Palestinian car jockey was instantly at our side. "We have a few parking spaces *inside* the building," he said nervously. "I think it would be best if I put your car there." We agreed. We didn't want the hassle of having the car trashed. He didn't want a car with Hebrew writing all over it sitting in front of his hotel. Bad for business.

It was time to call George at Petra Rent-a-Car in Arab East Jerusalem. From his grotty little office on Nablus Road, its walls covered with lurid colour photos of all the local Palestinian soccer teams the firm sponsored, George and his brother catered to the needs of those adventurers who wanted to drive in the occupied territories: journalists, visiting businessmen and a few intrepid tourists. George had a handsome fleet of black Opels with Arabic writing all over them. This seemed a more prudent choice, for as we quickly discovered, an Israeli car in Arab areas attracted stones, whereas an Arab car in Israel attracted only stares and lectures. I was subjected to a tongue-lashing every time I pulled the Petra car into the Supersol parking lot to do my twice-weekly shopping; the attendant, Uri, proud of his army service in Lebanon, took it hard that a visitor to the country would drive around in what was, to him, an open provocation. If I had had enough Hebrew to tell him we drove a Petra car so that we could safely visit West Bank Arab towns such as Hebron and Nablus, he would have been even more incensed.

Eventually, only about four weeks later than promised, our Volvo arrived in Talpiot. Pistol-packing Yossi gave us the grand tour of the

car, including the fire extinguisher and the complicated burglar alarm
system, which he seemed to know was going to malfunction immediately. "If it goes off by accident," he said, throwing up the hood and
disappearing into the bowels of the Volvo, "you turn this key here,
and pull this cord here, and then take out this fuse here." Which was
exactly what we did two days later when it set up a deafening wail in
the middle of the city.

There are many types of sound pollution in Israel, the most terrifying being the sonic booms as the Israel Air Force bombers break
the sound barrier over the West Bank to let the Palestinians know
who's in charge. But the sound of broken car burglar alarms is the
most pervasive, so common that you would be hard-pressed to react
appropriately if one went off during an actual break-in. I sat on the
terrace of the YMCA on King David Street one spring day and
watched with interest as an ear-splitting alarm went off in a Daihatsu
parked just below. The tourists sprang up in consternation; the
Israelis carried on with their drinks and conversation as if nothing
had happened.

We were prepared to take our chances living without a burglar
alarm, but our insurance agent, Doron, would have none of it. He
visited us a week after we took delivery of the Volvo and told us
sternly that in Israel high-value cars like ours required an even fanci-
er and more complicated burglar-proof system called a Bit-honit. If
we refused to comply, our already exorbitant car insurance rates
would almost double. So it was back to Talpiot to have a Bit-honit
installed, a kind of metal necklace that fit around the distributor cap,
breaking the electrical connections that would start the car. A special
jack that plugged into the dashboard would allow us to reconnect the
wires each time we wanted to move. "Now just make sure you put
the jack back into its leather case before you get out of the car,"
explained the mechanic. "If you don't, and it comes too close to
your automatic locking system on the door here, it can short out.

The leather case will protect it about ninety percent of the time." Right, we thought, as we saw our brand-new car, a marvel of Swedish engineering technology, turning into a graveyard for useless Israeli burglar alarms.

But the Bit-honit lived up to its awkward name, and it was only a few days before it got a chance to show its stuff. One December morning, when we had owned the Volvo for only three weeks, Patrick and the boys went to the parking lot to drive to school. The front passenger window of the car had disappeared in a shower of green glass shards, and the ignition system spilled out from under the dashboard in a jumble of broken coloured wires. Thieves had tried to hot-wire the car but were thwarted by the Bit-honit. Disgruntled at losing a prize Volvo, they removed the car parked next to it, which turned up two hours later in an army raid on a garage in the West Bank Arab town of Hebron.

Our car was so new that we didn't have a service garage, so we phoned Yossi at the dealership. "There are only three Volvo garages in town," he warned, "and the best is Itzhik's. Don't take it anywhere else." The bleak boulevards of Talpiot felt like a second home by now as we cruised along looking for Itzhik's garage. And there it was, with Itzhik himself, a beaming young Sephardic Jew with a riot of black curls around his cherubic face, kibitzing at the entrance with one of his mechanics. The mood of the garage was friendly and slow-moving. Itzhik hoped we weren't in a rush. Of course not, we'd just call George and enjoy the verbal cut and thrust of driving around town in another Petra car for a while.

With one window gone, this seemed as good a time as any to have the car West Bank–proofed. That meant installing plastic windows, which would not shatter if hit by rocks. Itzhik would have to subcontract that work out to A & A Auto Glass, whose proprietor sauntered down the street to discuss the job. "You can't have plastic on the front, it scratches too badly," he advised, "so we'll triple-glaze the front window. Plastic down both sides is fine, but I wouldn't put it on the back." Why not, we wondered, since it seemed to us the back window might be a common part of the car's anatomy to take a direct hit. "You need an escape route if you get hit by a Molotov cocktail," he explained laconically. "If the car goes up in flames you have to have at least one window you can smash." He then wandered off.

When we got the car back from Itzhik, something seemed to be amiss. The ignition was fixed and the plastic windows installed, but the whole inside of the driver's door was disintegrating and the upholstery kept flipping up over the gas pedal, which made driving at high speeds an unpredictable adventure. It took two more trips to the garage before everything was squared away. We would gladly have taken the car elsewhere for servicing after this dubious performance, but we were quite prepared to believe everyone who told us that Itzhik was the best in town. Besides, he was so pleasant each time we turned up, shaking his curls in genuine solicitude and offering small cups of terrible coffee while we waited. Although he had never heard of the Hippocratic oath ("First do no harm"), Itzhik did have a good bedside manner.

One day Patrick and I encountered him downtown, a little unrecognizable out of his grease-covered jumpsuit, but still beaming. "I'm just waiting for my wife, she's at the doctor's," he said, sketching a parabola over his stomach to indicate that he and his wife were making another new citizen for the state of Israel. "That's my car over there," he continued proudly, pointing to a startling purple van outrageously parked half-on, half-off the corner at one of the busiest downtown intersections. "I put on special big tires, see? Now the police can't boot me. I can park wherever I want." He was clearly delighted with himself.

Itzhik had touched a nerve. Just the week before I had parked on the sidewalk in front of the bank for two minutes. (Back home it never would have occurred to me to park on the sidewalk, but there is a certain Wild West quality to life in Israel that gets into the blood quite quickly.) Then Patrick walked in, the banking got more complicated, and it was a quarter of an hour before we emerged. The front wheel of our car was locked in the tentacles of a Denver Boot, a demonic clamping device presumably invented in Denver, with which the Israeli traffic police terrorize the entire motorized population.

Patrick became an iceberg of disapproval, and informed me frostily that since I had parked on the sidewalk, I could do whatever was necessary to extricate the car. This involved walking across town to a dingy underground garage where a cashier with a malicious grin declared that I owed 70 shekels ($30) for the boot and 85 ($38) more for the traffic ticket. "Now take this receipt," she said, pounding it viciously with her stamp, "and go back to the car. He will be around to unlock it sometime this afternoon." In fact I had an hour and a half to wait, and me with no book. I spent the time trying to pronounce every Hebrew sign on the street. It took me that long.

Having our plastic windows installed gave us a certain sense of security, but we needed more than that to feel safe travelling in the West Bank. Large Canadian-flag decals fore and aft added, we hoped, a certain "honest broker" touch, and the red Foreign Press sticker in English, Hebrew and Arabic dominated our front windshield. Most important, though, was the *keffiyeh* on the dashboard, the dramatic patterned headscarf sported on the nightly news by Yasser Arafat for the past twenty-five years, and the overarching symbol of Palestinian nationalism. (When I returned to Canada in the fall of 1993, I noticed that the *keffiyeh* has become the fashion statement of choice for an astonishing number of Torontonians. It had always enjoyed a certain grungy popularity in left-wing circles, but when I saw one around the neck of a Rosedale matron just leaving her mansion, I was reminded yet again that Canadians are among the most politically naive people in the world.)

There were different schools of thought in the foreign press community about the use of *keffiyehs* on the dashboard. Some journalists saw them as patronizing to the Palestinians, announcing a solidarity with their cause that didn't truly exist. Others thought they sent a clear but negative signal that the car driver thought all Palestinians were hoodlums. A practical group said the kerchiefs were plainly useless at high speeds, as no stone-thrower would be close enough to see them. We always kept ours on display nevertheless, preferring to have all the protection we could muster. When the car was parked in hostile territory, a couple of *keffiyehs* draped around might help it escape torching.

The long stretches of West Bank hinterland were not the places where you would be likely to encounter stone-throwers. The danger spots were the entrances and exits from Arab towns and villages, where young boys would gather waiting for Jews who had to traverse Arab communities to reach their gleaming new settlements. The Jews were immediately recognizable, not only by their trademark vans and the yellow glare of their licence plates but by the breakneck speed with which they hurtled through the narrow main streets of Palestinian towns. And the settlers weren't the only ones. Ordinary Israelis, using West Bank roads because they were the shortest distance between two points, would do the same. My haircutter, Marc, a young Belgian Jew who had immigrated in the mid-eighties, boasted to me proudly one day that he would streak through the lovely town of Jericho at 110 kilometers an hour on his way to the Jordan Valley highway.

"*C'est pas gentil, ça,*" I protested weakly in our only common language, but Marc saw no problem.

"They don't want to look at me any more than I want to look at them," he said.

Precisely. Which is why eye contact is one of the hardest things to achieve in the Israeli-Arab lands. Until we moved here, I was almost oblivious to the importance of eye contact in my daily life; yet it was something I practiced constantly and that contributed in an invisible but essential way to my sense of well-being. Walking down a street, sitting on a bus, standing in the supermarket lineup, waiting in the dentist's office, I was used to experiencing a hundred micro-encounters a day with complete strangers, wordless moments that expressed impatience, amusement, mutual commiseration or sometimes just frank admiration or curiosity. Each glance was a tiny filament in a complex web of relationships, totally superficial and yet fundamentally communal, that made me feel part of my neighbourhood, part of my city, part of the human race if it comes to that.

Israelis don't practice eye contact with strangers. If you try to engage their gaze, they simply look through you or past you. Their beautiful children will perhaps answer your look with a solemn infant stare, but never with a smile. Arabs exchange glances with each other but not with Israelis. Anyone who looks blond and of European stock is automatically assumed to be a Jewish Israeli, so outsiders like our family had a hard time making eye contact with Arabs as well. The sense of isolation the averted glance produces is profound and demoralizing, and I found myself fighting against it every day, silently willing people to answer my gaze.

In West Bank villages this was easier than on Israeli streets. As soon as we would reach the outskirts of an Arab town, we would slow down to a crawl, open all the car windows, wave to the children, salute the *mukhtars,* or village headmen, with a grave nod of the head, point to our Canadian flags, gather our pathetic scraps of Arabic and fling them in every direction. Inching our way through the Hebron market one day, we realized that we had become an object of amusement, but not derision, for the Arab sellers and their customers. Fine, we thought; if they're laughing, at least they're not angry.

Generally this worked. More than once we watched a young boy scoop up a stone when he saw our yellow licence plate and then freeze in mid-throw when we caught his eye directly. But it never paid to get too cocky. Our friend John Gray, another *Globe and Mail* reporter who was on duty in the Middle East during the Gulf War, was making his slow, friendly way through Gaza when a stone struck him on the side of the head. And Kay and Lindell, Church of the Nazarene people from Indiana who lived in the Christian Arab town of Beit Jala, took a rock through their car window one day that caught their eight-year-old son behind the ear. "It was such a shock," Kay told me later. "Even in the occupied territories, you come to think of certain routes as safe because you drive them all the time. We might expect to have trouble deep in the West Bank, but not on the main road from Jerusalem to Bethlehem."

We had seen Arab stone-throwers on the television news since the outbreak of the intifada in 1987, so we expected to encounter them when we came to the Middle East. What we were not prepared for were Jewish stone-throwers, but they exist too. Among the *haredim,* driving a car on the sabbath is forbidden, indeed an abomination, and the Jerusalem ultra-Orthodox, of the neighbourhoods of Geula and Mea Shearim, get angry if they even glimpse others less religious than themselves out using the public roadways. Through their manipulation of the Israeli political system, they have succeeded in having all public bus services suspended throughout the country from sundown Friday to sundown Saturday. Shortly after we arrived in Israel, a new highway opened to connect many of the West Bank Jewish settlements directly to Jerusalem, so that commuters could bypass several risky Arab neighbourhoods. But Road No. 1, as it is called, also skirts Mea Shearim, and the first Saturday it was open, the *haredim* turned up *en masse* to protest. The police had told them they could demonstrate behind barriers at the edge of their neighbourhood, a safe twenty metres from the six-lane highway. But the black-hatted zealots time and again broke through the police phalanx, screaming *"Shabbes, shabbes!"* and hurling stones and cinderblocks at both the police and the moving cars. By the end of the day, four policemen and five *haredim* were tending their wounds and eleven demonstrators were arrested.

The following Saturday came the media circus. Crowds of curious Jerusalemites and squads of journalists and cameramen turned up to watch Round Two. The police presence had more than doubled. We were there too, swimming at the nearby American Colony Hotel and peeping through the fence at all the action. But only a few hundred *haredim* appeared, and they stayed put behind their designated barriers and threw no rocks. During the week the strictest rabbinical court in the land, the Eda Haharedit, had nixed further violence at Road No. 1, preferring, as they said, to work behind the scenes. What they meant by that was asking the ultra-Orthodox Reichmann brothers of Toronto, who had contributed $30 million to Jerusalem's new City Hall Square, to pressure municipal politicians to close parts of the road on Shabbat. Given what happened to the Reichmann financial empire about two months later, it is perhaps no surprise that Road No. 1 remains open on Saturdays.

The sabbath barricades put in place by the police on Friday afternoons were often a puzzle for us. If they stretched right across a road, their message was unequivocal: this is a *haredi* neighbourhood, don't drive here. But at some streets, including some of Jerusalem's main arteries, barricades would protrude from both sides of the street, leaving enough space in the middle for a car to pass through. Were we allowed to drive there? Would we offend people if we did? Would we get sworn at, spat at or stoned? It was always a mystery.

Moreover, there were times when we simply got lost, not a difficult achievement in Jerusalem. One evening, very close to the end of Shabbat, we entered the city from the north, took a couple of wrong turns and found ourselves surrounded by ultra-Orthodox families, decked out in their sabbath finery, sauntering along the middle of empty, carless streets on their way home from their synagogues. The men had exchanged their usual black Homburgs for *streimels*, luxurious round flat hats made of thirteen fur pelts, a ritually significant number that could not be varied. Many had changed out of their black frock-coats or suit jackets into gorgeous gold-striped satin dressing-gowns, sashed at the waist and draped with blue-and-white prayer shawls, or *tallit*. If they wore the dressing-gowns, you knew that these men came from a long line of Jerusalemites, families that had been here doing their religious duty on behalf of Jews worldwide since long before the creation of the state of Israel, which in any case they did not recognize. The women had changed from their dowdy and shapeless daydresses into stiffer, more formal sabbath clothes that looked uncomfortable and were equally shapeless. They had replaced their headscarves with nasty, sharp-edged hats that emphasized all the worst features of their high-domed foreheads and moon-like faces. (Every *haredi* woman I ever saw looked better in her headscarf than in a hat.) Boy children were in black vests and pants with long-sleeved white shirts, their ringlets (or *peyot*) swinging under their elaborate sabbath *kipas*. The little girls all looked like Heidi, with thick braids and fussy flowered dresses almost to their ankles. We had not crossed any police barriers, but we were clearly on the fringe of a *haredi* neighbourhood, and the hostile shouts of the crowd made us feel most unwelcome. A young boy broke away from his family group and walked straight at the front of our car, daring us to run him down, until his father sharply called him away.

Officially, during our time there, forty-two streets in Jerusalem were closed to vehicle traffic on Saturdays. But there is a streak of lawlessness in the *haredi* community, which has little use for the edicts of the state of Israel or Jerusalem City Hall. You can be taken by surprise by makeshift barriers or chains, as I was one Friday, at least six hours before the beginning of the sabbath. I turned onto a narrow street near my children's school and halfway up the block I almost smashed into a beat-up metal barricade. Confused, I tried to back out onto the main street just as a patrol car pulled up beside me. The officer was fuming. "You want to get through that street?" he shouted. "No problem. Just follow me." I let him get in front of me, and then followed at a prudent distance. When we reached the spot, he leapt out of his car and threw the offending barricade viciously against the wall of the adjacent house. I squeezed past, just as he started pounding on the door. I sensed he had dealt with these particular religious culprits before.

Back in the sixties, one of Israel's most talented sculptors, David Palumbo, lost his life because of ultra-Orthodox zealots in his Jerusalem neighbourhood of Mount Zion, which is nowhere near the *haredi* enclave of Mea Shearim. Palumbo rounded a corner on his motorcycle and was decapitated by a chain that had been strung across the road. When I first heard that story, it seemed such a telling symbol of the hatred and division within Israeli society. Palumbo's strong abstract sculptures grace some of the country's most prominent locations, such as the Knesset (parliament) and the Holocaust memorial of Yad Vashem. He was a secular Zionist and modernist: he represented everything the ultra-religious *haredim* abhor. They destroyed him; not on purpose, but they destroyed him.

In spite of the problems with the sabbath barriers, though, there is something quite sublime about Saturday in Jewish Jerusalem. Even in the non-religious parts of town, normal traffic volume is reduced by about four-fifths. It is delightful to feel the city liberate itself from the tyranny of the car one day a week, delightful to hear the silence, to smell the honey-sweet Jerusalem air, to see its special golden light shimmering clear without the smog of a thousand exhausts.

But let me not wax too lyrical about this. For those Jerusalem residents who have no religious qualms about driving on the sabbath, Saturdays are also blissful days to be on the road. In fact, I learned to drive in Jerusalem on the sabbath. My early attempts to drive in that city counted among the most traumatic hours of my life. Between complicated one-way systems, a distinct lack of English signs, a road system designed like a plate of spaghetti and the unique impatience of Israeli drivers, every run to the boys' school that first week felt like a drag race to Hell. Even a year later, I had to plot every drive out in my mind before turning the key in the ignition, calling up mental snapshots of the traffic flow at each intersection to divine whether I could execute the moves I needed to get me from here to there.

But on Shabbat, lovely quiet Shabbat, I could cruise the roads at my leisure, figuring out the traffic-light patterns and the one-way streets, deciphering the Hebrew road signs, planning out the most painless routes to my regular stops: school, supermarket, fruit store, tennis courts, English bookstore, Israel Museum and the Jerusalem AppleCentre. On Shabbat I could relax enough to look around me as I glided over the hills and valleys of the modern city, which has mushroomed since the Six-Day War. How I wish I could have known this place before then, when the bare brown hilltops ringed the ancient city in dusty secrecy. Now each crest is crowned with a new Jewish neighbourhood, creating a circle of domestic fortresses that proclaims Israeli sovereignty and the determination never to let Jerusalem — which has been occupied and reoccupied at least thirty-two times over the millennia — fall to another invader.

Driving the streets of the city was always an adventure, but we were surprised to discover that the site of recurring high drama in our lives was the parking lot close to our home. Every couple of weeks, an incident in the parking lot — either politically or financially motivated — would remind us of the fault lines we were living on, between Jew and Arab, between rich and poor, between law-abiding and lawless.

Our beautiful neighbourhood of Yemin Moshe, built as it was on a steep hillside, was never designed to accommodate vehicles. Today it is ringed by a series of small parking lots where residents leave their cars and walk along cobblestoned lanes and staircases to their homes. It is a place of story-book beauty, but its location on the Green Line makes it regular prey to car thieves and petty arsonists. Our house was very close to an upper parking lot that, because of its isolated situation, attracted more break-ins and firebombings than most.

When we arrived to take up residence in Yemin Moshe, a team of Arab stonemasons was repaving a number of the walkways around our house. Their foreman, an expansive young fellow named Ali, much given to soulful serenading in our back lane during what seemed like interminable lunch-hours, drove to work each day in a natty bright red BMW, which he parked in our lot. It was rare to see a Palestinian with such an ostentatious car, and clearly the vandals who attacked it and smashed in the front windshield were confused. Surely such an expensive machine must belong to the rich Jews. In this case, the yellow licence plates yielded no clues, because all cars in the city of Jerusalem — whether registered to Jewish or Arab owners — carry yellow Israeli plates. When he discovered the damage, Ali ran to our house to call the police. He stood inconsolably in our living-room, repeating over and over, "Why did they do this to *me*? I'm an Arab!"

Most of the cars in our lot, though, did belong to Jews. Our next-door neighbours on the other side, David and Chaia, were victims of an attempted firebombing that didn't work. Frankly, it would have been better for them if it had. They walked out to the lot one morning to find their car covered inside and out with highly inflammable, very sticky industrial glue. An extinguished cigarette on the driver's seat indicated the *modus operandi* of the firebombers. They had embedded an unlit match inside the cigarette, then lit the cigarette and placed it in the glue on the car seat. In theory, by the time the cigarette had burned down enough to light the match and the car, the perpetrators would have slipped out of the parking lot, down into the shadows of the Valley of Hinnom and off to the Arab neighbour- hoods of Silwan or Abu Tor. But the match had failed to ignite, leav- ing David and Chaia with a sizable clean-up headache.

These were the Palestinian political statements in the parking lot: the smashed windshields, the firebombings. Sometimes the statement was even more direct. One day early in our stay, as I walked out alone to our car, I noticed a long-haired young man in ragged jeans sitting on the low stone wall that edged the parking lot. I closed the door and adjusted the seat, observing out of the corner of my eye that he was crossing behind my car into the bushes. As I backed the car up towards the bushes, I was treated to the sight of the young man in my rear-view mirror, squatting down and defecating. He had positioned himself accurately to give me a perfect view.

Moments like these were always difficult. On the one hand I wanted to spring out of the car and tell the fellow that I wasn't an Israeli, that I had nothing to do with oppressing him or his people, that my husband and I were journalists trying to observe the situation dispassionately and report on it honestly. Quite apart from the con- versational difficulties inherent in the situation, however, I didn't want to convey the message that it was wrong to take a shit in front of neutral foreigners but all right to do so in front of Israelis. As usual, I put the car in gear and drove away.

One dusky winter evening, as Patrick was walking through the lot with Gabriel and Sam, they met an elderly Israeli gentleman who was having considerable trouble controlling the enormous German shepherd he had on a leash. The dog suddenly spotted one of the myriad street cats that always hung around our neighbourhood scrounging in the fairly opulent garbage bins. The shepherd lunged at the cat's neck and with two swift shakes of his head, dispatched the scruffy little animal. Our boys froze, appalled at the speed and violence of the act, and alarmed as well by the owner's impotent fury at the dog. He kicked it viciously in the ribs and stomach but could not make it stop tearing the cat to pieces. At this point, as if in a surrealist nightmare, a Palestinian appeared in the parking lot on horseback, shouting in Hebrew at the Israeli. The dog owner shouted back with equal vehemence, just as he managed to yank the German shepherd away from the cat's bloody carcass and out of the parking lot. The Palestinian turned to Patrick and the boys and said, "Do you know what I said to him? I said that dog is a menace and you should put him down. And do you know what he said to me? He said somebody should put *you* down." Then he rode off swiftly into the dark. Gabriel and Sam buried the little cat.

These political confrontations provided the main theatre in the parking lot, yet there were many other dramatic incidents that were based on simple business concerns. Car windows were regularly smashed and radios removed by teams of professionals who could glide in and out of the parking lot in two minutes. Some of the residents took suitable precautions. Every time we met Avraham going to or from the parking lot, he was carrying his car radio in his hand. We thought this practice hilarious and never did it ourselves, but the general level of paranoia about car thievery must have affected us more than we realized.

During our first year in the Middle East, at Eastertime, we took a trip to the island of Crete, where our Greek friends were astounded to see us lock the rental car up tight as a drum each time we got out. "Why on earth are you locking it?" they asked. "Nobody here ever does." By the end of nine days, we had relaxed into a bucolic Aegean state of mind and no longer worried about the car.

Our first morning back in Jerusalem, Greek mellowness still massaging my nerve ends, I pulled into the parking lot and left the car unlocked while I popped into the house for five minutes. Five minutes inevitably stretched to ten and Patrick began to worry. We sent

Gabriel out to lock the car, and he came upon a Palestinian sitting in our front seat just about to remove the radio. Gabriel, showing more sang-froid than most eleven-year-olds in such a situation, asked the man what he was doing. The fellow jumped out and declared with a straight face, "I came into the parking lot and saw a bad man trying to take your radio. I saw that you were foreign press and I know you help my people a lot so I chased him away and I was just putting your radio back." After that inspired explanation, he wisely made his escape.

Six months later, I had my own confrontation with one of these professional petty thieves, and I startled myself by getting much more involved than was good for my health. I was reading and clipping a newspaper on our terrace one lovely September morning when I heard a prying sound, like a crowbar, and looked up through fairly dense foliage to see a fellow leaning in what appeared to be the open window of his car. I thought naively that he was the owner, that he had locked his keys in the car and had had to resort to force to get it open. It was only when he crouched down as a woman passed through the parking lot that it dawned on me that I was watching a robbery in progress.

It's a strange thing to live in the Middle East, where serious violence of word and deed goes on regularly. In some ways I became inured to it, and days could go by without my witnessing or hearing anything but the hum of normal life in our lovely, privileged neighbourhood. But then, suddenly, while doing something thoroughly peaceful and domestic like watching television with the children or mixing a salad, an image would hit my inner eye of what was happening at that very moment only a few kilometres from our house: stonings and burnings, guns and house searches, terrified Arab children, nervous Israeli soldiers, trigger-happy settlers, knife-wielding Islamic fundamentalists. The violent subtext never completely disappears, which makes life in Israel an inexorably restless affair.

In that larger context, a car break-in in the parking lot should have been negligible, but that September morning it wasn't. It seemed important, if I couldn't do anything about the big crimes around me, that I should do something about a small one. In reality, I didn't even think that coherently; I simply acted. I ran out to the parking lot, stopping just long enough to put down my scissors. If I was going to confront a criminal, it seemed more prudent to do it with moral suasion than with a weapon.

As I reached the parking lot, I saw the fellow's partner keeping a lookout exactly for someone like me. I ignored him and started for the car just as the thief was coming towards me, the car radio wrapped in a yellow plastic bag in his hand. I had time for a good long look, but I could not tell whether he was a Jew or an Arab. He was dark-haired, handsome, clean-cut, dressed in jeans and a white T-shirt, just like thousands of young men in this city on both sides of the Green Line. He stopped. I stopped. I said to him in English, "I just saw everything you did. Now give me the radio."

Was that a flicker of wary amusement in his eye? Probably. The sound of my own voice snapped me out of my heroic mood and made me realize what a dangerous fool I was making of myself. Where was his accomplice? Somewhere behind my back, very likely with a weapon in his pocket. The parking lot was deserted except for the three of us. A distant siren wailed out on the Hebron Road. Why was I trying to defend a $200 car radio that didn't even belong to me? I stood there, trying to look dignified, reproachful and menacing, as he carefully stepped around me. The two of them walked with studied ease out of the parking lot, throwing nervous glances over their shoulder from time to time, poised to bolt if I started yelling.

When I dissected the incident later over tea with my friend Helen, she said I had probably acted the way I did because I was the mother of boys. I think she was right. I expected my disapproving tone to stop this hardened criminal in his tracks and make him hand over the stolen goods. I guess I hadn't been living in the Middle East quite long enough yet.

While I was confronting the thief in the parking lot, someone stole my good scissors from our terrace.

CHAPTER 5

LTHOUGH OUR FRIEND Nachman had warned us not to mistake Jerusalem for Israel, it seemed that in the public life of the street, in the daily round of trade and commerce in West Jerusalem, the Israeli personality came through loud and clear. Nowhere are people more themselves than when they are buying and selling, especially in the Middle East.

The Lebanese are the legendary masters of the marketplace in this part of the world; no one else can touch them. During the interminable fifteen years of the Lebanese civil war, street trade went on unabated, and today, in the bombed-out streets of Beirut, it is not uncommon to see chic matrons, tottering on their fashionable high heels, picking their way over heaps of rubble to get into their favourite Parisian couturier shops on the still-standing main floors of ruined buildings.

In Jewish Jerusalem, shopping is more of an ordeal than an entertainment. In the first place there is almost nothing you would want to
buy. In the second there is almost no one who is willing to sell it to
you. The combination of expensive religious kitsch for the tourists,
startlingly ugly fashions for the locals and kosher everything in the
way of foodstuffs is enough to discourage the most determined shopper. And if you should find something you want to spend your
shekels on, it will be a serious challenge to get the two Israeli shop-
girls to stop comparing split ends long enough to acknowledge your
presence. Service has been an unknown — or if known, despised —
commodity in this fiercely independent society right from the beginning, entirely antithetical to Zionist socialist values. Israelis think service means servility, and it reminds them uncomfortably of the centuries of cringing and prostrating that European Jews had to do in
order to survive in anti-Semitic Gentile society. Now that they have
their own country, nobody is going to tell them how to behave.
Market values and the positive idea of service are just beginning to
make headway in this, one of the last socialist outposts in the world,
but generations of *sabras* are having trouble making the 180-degree
behavioural turn, especially since servility is deeply embedded in
their minds as a character trait of their worst enemy, the Arabs.

Still, families have to be fed, watered, laundered and entertained,
so it was impossible for me to get through two years in Jerusalem
without ever going shopping at all. And indeed, some of my most
interesting glimpses of Israeli life took place in the little triangle I visited at least twice a week: the Supersol, the video store two doors
away and the florist stand on the street in front of them both.

One of the few drawbacks to living in Yemin Moshe was that
there was no useful shopping within walking distance of our house.
Just to get out of our valley on foot required a daunting climb of 104
steps, and when we reached King David Street we were surrounded
by fancy hotels and the sort of trade that clusters around them: car

rental agencies and high-priced art galleries and antique shops. To purchase food and drink we had to fire up the Volvo and drive a kilometre to the Supersol at the top of Agron Street. Unlike North American supermarkets, this one did not have separate parking areas for suppliers and customers. Its tiny parking lot was always filled with swarthy Sephardic Jews with short heavily muscled legs and barrel chests shouting friendly curses at each other as they offloaded huge semis filled with crates of lettuce and flats of Kinley, the ubiquitous Israeli soft drink; ordinary car drivers had to squeeze between, and sometimes under, these enormous vehicles to find a parking spot. Like so many other things in Israel, parking at the Supersol started off for me as a nightmare but soon became a sporty challenge, especially after I made friends with Uri, the parking lot attendant.

Uri looked like a desert creature, one of those lizards that adopts sandy colouring and remains motionless to protect itself from predators. He had perfected a slouch inside his tiny parking booth that allowed him to dispense tickets and collect shekels without moving anything except his forearm. Even his long narrow eyes appeared to remain closed during these transactions. Supersol customers got an hour of free parking if they presented their grocery receipt with their time chit; Uri would not acknowledge by so much as a grunt or a head movement whether you had made it within the time limit. You would just wait, eyes straight ahead, either for the barrier to lift or for a leathery brown palm to present itself from the booth, silently but imperiously demanding two shekels.

About my twentieth visit to the Supersol, however, I must have crossed over some mysterious line that separates the stranger who deserves no more attention than a twig from the casual acquaintance. I thought perhaps I was over the time limit, so when I handed in my chits I looked enquiringly at the side of Uri's sleek, close-cropped head. Slowly he swivelled, stared provocatively at me and said, with a sneer that I think was meant to be a smile, *"Ma at rotsa? Odef?"*

("What are you waiting for? Change?") It took me a few seconds to realize that an Israeli had just made a joke. For my benefit. I was thrilled: I drove home with a grin on my face so wide it hurt. Only later did I realize how pitifully starved for affection I must be feeling after three months in Jerusalem without seeing anyone crack a smile.

After that, Uri and I were friends. I developed the habit of walking over to his booth for a chat after I had parked my car. Sometimes I even brought him some home baking; I felt that good about him. For his part, he never charged me extra ("Just this once," he always warned). He was a good person for me to practise my Hebrew on because he spoke not a word of English, a rarity in cosmopolitan Jerusalem.

Uri's family were from Morocco, part of the huge wave of North African Jews, known colloquially as the Sephardim, who came to Israel in the middle to late fifties, after centuries of low-level anti-Semitic harassment in their Arab host societies. While the Holocaust survivors, Ashkenazim from Europe, had tended to settle disproportionately in the Mediterranean coastal city of Tel Aviv, many of the African Jewish refugees gravitated towards Jerusalem, making it a predominantly Sephardi town. The Sephardim, who soon made up half the population of the new Israel, spoiled the plans of the idealistic Zionist pioneers from Poland and Russia. Those Europeans had envisaged themselves building a nation in the modern Western mode, democratic, socialist, pluralistic, secular, free at last of the shackles of ingrown Jewish tradition that had accrued through centuries of outside persecution. But the Sephardim had lived — first in Spain and, after they were expelled in 1492, in various North African countries — under the domination and influence of the Arabs, so what they brought to Israel was much closer to Arab culture than to European Judaism. The Ashkenazim tried to suck and shame that enemy culture out of their dark-skinned cousins: over three decades the Israeli school system has effectively wiped out Arabic as a second language among the Sephardim, a terrible loss when you think how valuable that skill could be in building bridges between Israel and the Arab world, should real peace ever come. In 1994, in the expansive new atmosphere of the peace process, Arabic has finally been declared a compulsory subject for Israeli schoolchildren. But it is much harder to re-establish something valuable that has been lost than to preserve it in the first place. Still, the Sephardi character of Jerusalem remains strong, and, like all ethnic groups in this last decade of the twentieth century, the North African Jews of Israel are insisting more and more that space and respect be given to their music, their stories, their religious customs and political attitudes.

Uri truly hated the Arabs. He had been permanently crippled while on duty during the 1982 Israeli invasion of Lebanon (hence his sedentary parking lot job), but that didn't seem to be the source of his hatred. "War is war." He shrugged philosophically. "We have to defend the state." My Hebrew wasn't up to pointing out the fine distinction between most of Israel's wars, which were defensive, and the Lebanon invasion, which was clearly aggressive. Even if I had been linguistically capable, there seemed to be little percentage in alienating a new friend.

No, the source of Uri's hatred was family folklore. He explained to me, painstakingly slowly, that he came from a family of seven boys and three girls, and that he, the youngest, was the only one to have been born in Israel. His older brothers had regaled him with their bitter stories of being regularly beaten up and spat upon by Arab schoolchildren back home in Morocco. "The Arabs hate us, they will always hate us," he declared. "That's why we can never trust them."

Even though we were pals, it would never have occurred to Uri to help me when I came struggling back to my car after shopping, my arms being steadily lengthened by the dead weight of six or seven loaded grocery bags in each hand. (I had tried using a shopping cart, but that was even worse, because the Supersol, like everything else in

Jerusalem, was built on a hill, and I found that the slope down to the parking lot turned a heavy cart of groceries into a dangerously uncontrollable missile.) Uri would just wave and smile at my struggles.

After about six months, I cottoned on to the fact that, for an affordable seven shekels ($3), the Supersol delivered. Huge burly mongrels would prowl the corridor at the bottom of the check-out lanes, snatch up the heavy red plastic cases full of groceries and swing them onto their shoulders. Two hours later, with a deafening pounding on the front door, they would stomp in and unceremoniously dump out my groceries in a heap on the dining room table. (I learned from experience to carry the eggs home with me.) They never expected a tip. Sometimes they would gulp a couple of glasses of cold water on the hottest days, then shout "*Shalom!*" and stomp out, leaving a pungent male aroma in the air.

Even though the Supersol was seedy and none too hygienic by glistening North American standards, I enjoyed going there. It was always luxuriously air-conditioned, for one thing, and it was one of the most multicultural hang-outs in town. The only identifiable group of Jews that didn't shop there was the *haredim*, who had their own supermarkets. From the moment you walked in and automatically opened your purse to be searched by the elderly pensioner at the door, a symphony of languages greeted your ear. Hebrew, Arabic and English, of course, but also Spanish, Greek, Dutch and German, Amharic, Russian, Portuguese and Italian. Jews come from everywhere (even Wales!), and although their children are forged quickly into Israelis through the medium of Hebrew, their immigrant parents and grandparents struggle with it all their lives and feel most comfortable when they can lapse into the language of their own distant childhood, decades and continents, sometimes a Holocaust away from their new desert home.

The best one can say about Israeli food is that it is, by and large, healthy and low in cholesterol. Kosher meat, because it has had all the blood drained out of it by ritual slaughtering methods, is invariably bland and tasteless, so many Israelis seem to have moved gradually to a poultry-and-vegetarian diet. (It's as hard to find a non-kosher butcher in Jerusalem as it is to find a kosher one in most North American cities.) Kosher cheeses, made with a vegetable substitute for rennet, manage to look like the whole range of European cheeses from Emmenthal to Camembert, but they all taste like wet wax. Israelis eat a prodigious amount of fruit, vegetables, tuna, yoghurt and what they call salads, dipping-foods made from chickpeas, tahina, eggplant and olive oil served with mounds of fresh pita. Falafel and shawarma are the snack foods of choice, heavily slathered with tahina, hot sauces and pickles. The taste Israelis crave is salt. They sell and consume more varieties of pickles and pickled vegetables than I ever believed existed. When I think of what indiscriminate amounts of salt do to the metal casings of North American cars, I picture Israeli stomachs as hopelessly corroded by the time their owners reach forty. But then they drink lakesful of cold water as well. Perhaps that helps.

There is no such thing as Israeli cuisine. There is simply food, the fuel you insert to keep the human engine running. This is a legacy of early days on the kibbutz, when everyone was too busy draining malarial swamps to have the time or leisure for the fine arts of the kitchen. And like all the rougher aspects of Israeli life, this necessity for plain food was converted into a virtue. Fancy meals were part and parcel of the decadent European society these clear-headed Zionist pioneers had left behind. I had not expected to find Sachertorte a regular staple of the Israeli menu, but it seemed reasonable to expect a decent bagel, some yummy cheese blintzes, potato latkes, noodle pudding, borscht, all the East European Jewish comfort foods that I remembered from my grandmother's and aunts' kitchens. But they were nowhere to be found in Jerusalem, a deeply oriental town. Eventually we got a line on a bakery in the *haredi* neighbourhood of

Mea Shearim that produced a chewy, salt-studded bagel that would
not shame your table in New York or Montreal, but it was a search.

At first, as a dutiful guest in a new country, I sampled all the local
versions of the staples my family could not live without: Israeli
peanut butter, Israeli cornflakes. Gradually we switched to Skippy
and Kellogg's, and at the check-out I noticed that many Israeli customers had also put taste before nationalism, which allayed my guilt
somewhat.

The dairy aisle of the Supersol was intimidating, with a daunting
array of milk-based products that I could never properly identify.
Whenever I tried to elicit explanations from fellow shoppers, I got
shrugs and no help. At the cheese counter, there were a dozen white
cheeses swimming in brine, all looking like feta, but only one of
them tasted like feta, as I learned by trial and error. Stuffed grape
leaves in the delicatessen section looked appetizing but turned out to
be starchy, boring and a little nasty.

There were some treats at the Supersol. Bread was government-
subsidized and cheap, and the supermarket bakery turned out wonderful crusty baguettes and delicious eggbread and sesame loaves. Citrus
fruits were plentiful, and in the winter their price plummeted so low
that it was cheaper to indulge in fresh-squeezed orange and grapefruit
juice than to buy frozen. And once, just once, I found a plastic container of dates from Ein Gedi, a sublime oasis near Jerusalem; I felt like
the Queen of Sheba when they melted on my tongue.

But it was never the food that made shopping at the Supersol
interesting: it was the company. There were my favourite check-out
cashiers, Chaia and Pnina, cheerful and helpful *sabras*, hanging on
miraculously to their good humour as one surly Israeli customer after
another shoved her groceries down the line. There was Shmooli, the
garrulous Argentinian behind the meat counter who doled out my
constant supply of chickens — the only meat that tasted just as good
koshered as unkoshered — with a generous dollop of Spanish conver-

sation, a language so much easier and more pleasant to speak than Hebrew. I could see from the body language behind the counter that Shmooli was not popular with his fellow workers; he was both arrogant and lazy. But he knew how to smile, and that counted for a lot with me.

Frank ran the back of the store — cheese, meat, deli. He was a handsome bearded American from Los Angeles, always kitted out in a jaunty Greek sailor's cap instead of a *kipa*. He was too competent and accomplished for his job, which left him constantly frustrated with the somnambulistic performances his fellow workers turned in. "Look at her, she's asleep at the machine," he complained quite loudly in English to me one day, pointing to a Sephardi co-worker with her mountain of hair pulled back in a sloppy kerchief, slowly slicing smoked turkey with a dreamy look on her face. "She's getting married in two weeks and she's completely useless," he carried on. "Not that she was any use before she got engaged either."

Frank was divorced, and devoted to his two daughters, who were often hanging around his counter. In the state-run school system, Israeli students go to class a grand total of four hours a day, from eight in the morning until noon, so they are around cluttering up their parents' lives most of the afternoon. I found this shocking: if there was one thing I thought would be an automatic given in the land of the Jews, it was respect, even reverence, for education. But in a country that has to devote so much of its energy and taxes to military matters, there is never enough money to finance an adequate school day.

Frank had a hard time remembering my name, but one day I wheeled my cart around the spice corner and his eyes lit up. "Brenwyn," he called out, "*ma schlomech*, how are you?"

"It's Bronwyn, Frank. I'm fine, thanks."

"Darn, I was sure I had it right this time. I knew it had something to do with a gun. Bren, you know."

"I'm not sure I take that as a compliment."

"In Israel you should," Frank retorted. "Here we say: take good care of your gun, it could save your life some day."

I asked for 250 grams of sliced salami and a container of hummus.

"By the way," Frank said as he filled my order, "I won't be seeing you for the next five weeks. *Miluim* — reserve duty."

You got used to this happening all the time in Israel. Every able-bodied male, after serving his three years of military service right after high school, is then required to do a month a year of reserve duty with his old unit until the age of fifty-five. Fathers often go off to barracks at the end of the weekend along with their sons — or daughters. Women serve two years with no callbacks. The reserves are the backbone of the Israeli defence system, and every man we knew disappeared from time to time, from the wiry little Moroccan who delivered our bottled water to the husband of Patrick's *Globe and Mail* assistant, who was chief economist for the Bank of Israel.

"Where will you be serving, Frank?"

"Near here. In the administered territories." This was a code that told me quite a lot about Frank's politics. "Near here" meant the West Bank, as opposed to the Gaza Strip, which was the most dangerous place for an Israeli soldier to find himself posted. "The administered territories" was one of the names for the West Bank, one that indicated the speaker was right-wing but not rabid. The rabid phrase was the biblical "Judea and Samaria," which was employed mostly by the settlers and those who supported them even if they lived within the Green Line of Israel proper. Left-wing Israelis, those who believed the Palestinians must be granted either a greater or a lesser version of an independent state, tended to call the lands in question "the occupied territories" or "the West Bank and Gaza." These were, coincidentally, the terms widely used in the international media. If you called them "the administered territories," like Frank, you were really saying "Israel administers these lands for the good of everyone involved and we damn well intend to keep it that way." Of course the Arabs had another word for the lands: Falestin.

"You must hate having to do reserve duty every year," I said to Frank, thinking like a North American.

"Are you kidding? I'm proud to serve. And I'm glad I'm serving in the administered territories. That means I'm still young enough to be useful. In a few years they'll have me on guard duty checking handbags at the Western Wall. Then I'll really know I'm over the hill."

Negotiating the aisles of the Supersol was much like negotiating Jerusalem streets, because Israelis drove their shopping carts just like their cars. They simply barrelled down the middle of the aisles, oblivious to other shoppers, and stopped, blocking all traffic, whenever something caught their fancy. If one shopper had left her cart askew across an aisle, the next would bang into it and push it in front of hers until it rolled out of her way. No one looked at or talked to anyone else.

In such an atmosphere, the occasional morsel of friendly human intercourse felt like manna from heaven. One day a blond store employee stopped me on the cracker aisle to compliment me in fluent English on the poncho I was wearing. It happened to be a favourite of mine, which I had crocheted myself many years earlier, so I was flattered by her interest. I took the occasion to ask her about some tasty Manischewitz crackers I had bought a couple of weeks previously, which now seemed to have disappeared. We were combing the shelves together and happily chatting about crocheting techniques when a female customer approached us and spoke sharply to the clerk in Hebrew. My new friend stopped chatting, looking amazed and embarrassed.

Then the customer turned to me — she was a woman of about sixty — and said in a thick northern European accent, "I told her she should be speaking to you in Hebrew. Why do you come to our country if you don't bother to learn Hebrew?"

I was too astounded to tell her what I thought of her extraordinary rudeness. Instead, I stammered that I was in fact studying Hebrew at the *ulpan,* had been hard at it for three months, but that it was an extremely difficult language to learn.

"Foreigners," she snorted as a final riposte, then turned on her heel and pushed her cart viciously around the corner.

The store clerk, a *sabra,* was clearly distressed. "Some people take this place too seriously," she said softly. "They had such a hard time fitting in when they came here, especially learning Hebrew, and they resent the fact that now more and more Israelis speak a lot of English." Our happy mood had been destroyed, and we each went our separate way.

It was at the Supersol check-out counter that I was introduced to the never-never land of Israeli economics. First of all, I noticed that all the customers paid for their groceries with plastic. Second, the clerk gave me the usual choice: all in one payment, or spread out over three? I said all in one, of course; it would never occur to me to buy my family's groceries on the instalment plan. She then informed me that my one payment would go through my VISA account three months hence. If I had opted for the multiple payments, I could have been paying for those rolls of toilet paper five months after they were all used up.

But the Supersol payment plan was efficient and businesslike compared to the usual method of purchasing food at the hundreds of small corner groceries around Jerusalem, the *makolets,* as they are known. At those, no one ever paid with cash *or* plastic; accounts were simply written down "in the book" and allowed to germinate and flower into major, staggering debts. One day my Canadian friend Helen was picking over tomatoes in the fruit store we both used, when another customer came in and handed the owner three crisp

100-shekel bills (about $150 Canadian) with a virtuous flourish. After he left, the shopkeeper pulled out the book to note the amount and laughed ill-humouredly. "Hah, he thinks he's making a big payment," he explained to Helen, "but that was about a tenth of what he owes me." He turned the book on the counter, and sure enough, the bottom line of the man's account read an incredible 3,000 shekels, more than $1,500. That's an awful lot of apples and onions.

It seems that Israelis run their personal finances along the same lines as their national economy. For decades, Israel has been the recipient of enormous amounts of foreign aid from the United States, currently totalling about $3 billion a year (plus loan guarantees for a further $10 billion). The only other country in the world that receives this much American largesse is Egypt, according to a formula worked out in the Camp David accords between Israel, Egypt and the United States. This is not to mention the generous donations to all public facets of Israeli life — education, medicine, culture, sports facilities, town planning — made privately by Jews all over the world. The effect of all this money has been to give life in Israel quite an unreal feeling; salaries are only half those of North Americans, but the standard and cost of living is almost as high as in the world's most privileged countries. Families seem to teeter on the edge of personal bankruptcy at all times, and yet never quite tumble over. "*Eehiyeh beseder*" (it'll be okay) is probably the most common phrase Israelis utter, and I sensed that they actually enjoyed performing the bravura high-wire act their financial lives have become.

Everything is designed to make it easy for you to spend money. At the video store next to the Supersol, another regular stop for us because of the mind-numbing quality of both Israeli and Jordanian television, the best deal was a hundred videos for 400 shekels, which brought the unit price down to about $1.75. Israelis probably put this "in the book"; we paid cash, of course. The effect of having a hundred videos to our credit was disconcerting: we became irresponsible profligates, checking out four or five videos for the weekend when we knew we had time to watch only two, and returning them two or three days late. We ran through a hundred videos in an amazingly short time, and then primed the pump with another 400 shekels.

It was in the video store that I really learned Israeli shopping etiquette. In the Supersol, after all, there was a certain physical logic to the check-out aisles; once I had planted my full cart in a lineup, it was difficult for even the most aggressive Israeli shopper to displace me. But in the video store, there was always a rabble in front of the counter, with people waving their selections in the harried clerks' faces and shouting for attention. It was survival of the loudest, and as a well-mannered Canadian I was ill equipped to cope. Even when I could get a transaction started, the clerk would often drop me in the middle to do the bidding of another customer more demanding than I. Usually I was simply stymied, like a timid driver waiting to turn onto a street filled with a never-ending flow of cars. I could wait half an hour at the video counter, my frustration level mounting by the minute but unable, because of my own decades of genteel upbringing, to demand the service I thought I deserved.

I had many long occasions to analyse what I was doing wrong in the video store and eventually, with the help of a sympathetic clerk, I figured it out. Where I was brought up, the unspoken contract of mercantile exchange called not only for the customer to be served in his or her proper turn but for the customer to treat the salesclerk with dignity as well. This meant, I realized, leaving a polite little space between one transaction and the next, smiling at the clerk and allowing him or her a moment to shift gears from the previous customer to me. In Israel, that polite little space was my downfall. Even when a clerk could clearly see that I should be waited on next, that tiny hesitation on my part was long enough for the next customer at my elbow to barrel in and take over the territory. In the video store one day, after I had already been sideswiped four times, the clerk shouted at me in English: "Tell me what you want — quickly! — before somebody pushes ahead of you." She had thrown me a lifeline, and after that I adapted to the Israeli rhythm and survived.

After the mayhem of the video store, I usually soothed my nerves by stopping at Shimon's flower stall before driving home. Shimon was a handsome and charming young Sephardi, always dressed in tight blue jeans and a sexy black leather jacket. He ran the stall along with his old father, whose hands shook with palsy as he wrapped the flowers. Shimon understood that selling flowers was a theatrical profession, that he was selling beauty and romance with his luxury merchandise. "Ah, those look wonderful together," he would exclaim, subtly complimenting the customer on her good eye. "Let's just try a couple of irises and some baby's breath with that — look, isn't that gorgeous?" It invariably was, and even though his suggestions usually doubled the cost of my purchases, they were always worth it.

Jerusalem was full of flower sellers, one of the things that made me feel good about the place whenever the bitterness of the politics or the rudeness of the citizens threatened to turn me against the town. I think people who value flowers are highly civilized, although I have no scientific basis for this opinion. I have always had a soft spot for the Latvians ever since I read, many years ago, that they had told the Soviet Union to shove its latest five-year plan that called for them to plant turnips and onions. Latvians had always been great flower growers and they had no intention of changing, no matter what the edict from Moscow. Israelis too have a sensuous, luxuriant love of flowers; on Shabbat no home in the country is without a fresh-cut bouquet of brilliantly coloured blossoms.

One Friday as I was starting to make up a bunch of daisies and tiger-lilies and roses at Shimon's stall, I noticed about two dozen women, dressed entirely in black, standing motionless with placards in their hands on a traffic island at the top of Agron Street. I asked Shimon who they were and what their placards said.

"Those?" he said, casting a disdainful glance over his shoulder as he hauled a new bucket of gladioli into place. "They're princesses — princesses playing at politics." This was intriguing but not illuminating. I asked for more information. "They call themselves the Women in Black," explained Shimon, "and they're out here every Friday at one o'clock for an hour. The signs say, 'Stop the occupation.' They've been coming for a long time, maybe since the beginning of the intifada. What do they know? A bunch of rich women who leave their kids with the babysitter so they can come out on the streets and demonstrate."

With my flowers in my arms, I walked up to the corner to stare at the silent protesters for a few minutes. They stood completely still and mute, eyes fixed on the middle distance. Most seemed like young matrons, between thirty and forty-five, and every one whose face I could see looked Ashkenazi. As the thick pre-sabbath traffic swirled around them, *kipa*-wearing drivers and passengers shouted angry epithets at them and shook their fists. Obviously Shimon's dislike of them was widespread in the Jerusalem population. I later learned that similar groups of women duplicated this peace vigil in other Israeli cities and towns every week, and that indeed they came from the ranks of well-educated, liberal, upper-middle-class Ashkenazi women, many of them North American transplants. After the Rabin–Arafat meeting in Washington, they announced their job was done and stopped their weekly appearances; but two months later they were back on their vigil, alarmed at the way right-wing demonstrators were taking over the Israeli street.

This is obviously a real problem for Israel. The peace-or-war debate tends to break along class and racial lines, so that by and large it is the so-called WASPs (White Ashkenazi Sabras with Pull, as they jokingly describe themselves in English) who support Peace Now, the Women in Black and *Yesh Gvul*, or There Is a Limit, a group of ex-soldiers working for peace. They are the "haves" in Israeli society, and they consistently poll more liberally on the question of making peace with the Arabs. The "have-nots" are the Sephardim, who not only can claim closer, therefore more distrustful, experience of living with the Arabs but who are also entirely unwilling to be lectured to on the morality of peace by the Ashkenazim, who in the fifties and sixties treated them like poor southern American blacks. The Ashkenazi–Sephardi split is slowly closing through intermarriage but it is still very rare to find a Sephardi Israeli who truly espouses peace.

Shimon the flower seller was about as liberal as the Sephardi Israeli working class got, and here's what he said when we started talking politics one day: "Yes, we're definitely getting close to peace. There's a new government in Lebanon, very business-oriented, they want peace. Jordan is desperate for peace with us. Syria will deal, they're desperate too, they've got no money and no Russian support any more."

That seemed to finish Shimon's analysis, but I felt something had been overlooked. "What about the Palestinians?" I asked. "After all, they are the ones on your doorstep, the ones you have to live with day by day, right here in Jerusalem."

A look of impatience crossed Shimon's face, as if to say, "Don't bother me with picky details." "Yes, yes, of course the Palestinians will come along when all the other Arab countries do, they have no choice. But they can forget about Jerusalem. That stays with us."

Nothing else quite so accurately demonstrates the Israeli approach to territoriality as the national method of standing in line. There are some semi-official situations — banks, post offices, clinics — where survival of the loudest is too anarchic even for Israelis, and they admit that a more disciplined approach is required. I discovered how it worked a couple of weeks after we arrived, when Patrick destroyed the ligaments in his ankle in a tennis accident and I was directed to an

odd medical dispensary, called Yad Sarah (the Hand of Sarah) on
Hanevi'im Street to obtain crutches for him. Yad Sarah wasn't a
building; it occupied a former railway carriage that had been permanently parked in a hospital parking lot. You could rent anything there
of a medical nature, from wheelchairs to commodes to neck-braces
to crutches. Well, you didn't exactly rent the equipment: you paid a
hefty deposit on it (in my case about $60 for a pair of crutches) but
you got a full refund when you returned it. Yad Sarah made interest
on your money, and that was what kept the charity going. You could
give them a small donation at the end, but it wasn't necessary.

Hanevi'im Street (the Street of the Prophets) is a beautiful
Jerusalem street right on the fringe of Mea Shearim, the old ultra-
Orthodox neighbourhood of the city. When I entered the Yad Sarah
railway car, there were ten people clustered in the waiting area, seven
of them *haredi* men wearing more or less elaborate costumes and *peyot*
(sidecurls). Some were sitting, some standing, but there was no way
of knowing who was ahead of whom. Nevertheless, every time the
secretary would call out "Next!" someone would move down the
railway car to the dispensary with no dispute. I was completely puzzled as to whom I was supposed to follow, although I did notice that
one of the *haredi* men, no more than a teenager, pointed back and
forth from himself to me a couple of times without looking me in
the eye. I took a seat between two other black-hats, at which point
they both got up and moved to the other side of the waiting area. A
woman from that side moved over beside me, two others exchanged
places, and the original two men were able to sit again. I was completely mortified, and I still didn't know where I stood in the queue.

Another *haredi* gentleman came in and I examined him closely. If
I didn't know who I was behind, at least I was going to be sure who I
was in front of. This was not easy, since all the *haredim* were dressed
in black hats, white shirts and black suits. My man, though, was in a
frock-coat instead of a suit jacket, and he was the only one with his

pants tucked into white knee-length stockings. I was confident I could pick him out in a crowd of two thousand *haredim*. However, two summonses later, this johnny-come-lately took himself off down the corridor, without a peep from the rest of my fellow waiters. I remonstrated with the secretary, but she said with great confidence, "No, he was next." A few heads in the waiting area nodded to confirm this. I remained unenlightened.

Now another black-hat appeared, looked around at all of us and mumbled, "*Mi acharon?*" I had just started studying at the Hebrew *ulpan,* and to my excitement I recognized the word *acharon* — it means last, as in first and last. In a flash, the system revealed itself. When you entered a waiting situation, you asked, "Who's last?" Someone would grunt or grimace in response and you knew where you stood. That's why the *haredi* teenager had been gesturing towards me when I came in, to indicate I was behind him. A further refinement appeared to be that once you had claimed your place in line, you could leave the premises for as long as you deemed suitable (depending on the number of people waiting ahead of you) and turn up again just shortly before the person ahead of you in line got called. If you came back after that person had been called, you'd be out of luck because there would be no one in the queue who would recognize you and vouch for your claim.

My friend Kathleen got into trouble because of her ignorance of this complicated Israeli custom. She was an American journalist on leave from the *Baltimore Sun* and, although slim and petite, a bit of a scrapper. Standing in an interminable queue in the main post office on Jaffa Road one day, she suddenly found a burly Israeli inserting himself ahead of her in line. When she complained, he explained that that was his rightful place, that he had claimed it twenty minutes earlier and had then popped out to do some shopping at the hardware store around the corner. She pointed out that while he had been away running his errands, she had been standing there waiting to buy stamps. She moved ahead of him, he moved ahead of her, some shouting ensued, and he pushed her into the ropes that defined the queue. In the end she had to give way and take her place behind him, but she kept up a loud running commentary on his behaviour until an Israeli woman walked across the room and said angrily to her, "Why don't you just keep quiet?"

It is tempting — though admittedly facile — to see this approach to queueing as a metaphor for the Zionist re-entry into the land of Palestine. We were here before, the Jews say; two thousand, three thousand years ago, this land was ours. Now we're back, claiming our place. Sorry if you Palestinian Arabs have to get behind us in line, but that's the way it is.

I am happy to report, though, that there are levels of chutzpah that even Israelis will not accept. One day I was in a post office line-up, down in the picturesque German Colony where I often shopped and visited friends. A woman blew in the door, breathless, walked straight to the head of the queue and asked the first person in line, "Do you think I could go before you? I'm double-parked outside." I don't think I have to tell you what the post office patrons said.

CHAPTER 6

W E WANTED AN ADDRESS TILE for the front of our house
— everyone in Yemin Moshe seemed to have them —
so we went to a tile shop in West Jerusalem, in a mall
under the city's only department store, Hamashbir. We
requested our name in English, Hebrew and Arabic, and
the clerk looked nonplussed. "We can't do that here," she
explained. "We'll have to send it over to East Jerusalem for the
Arabic. That will take two weeks, and it will cost an extra ten
shekels" ($5).

Officially, Israel is a bilingual country, Hebrew and Arabic. But, as
I have noticed in Canada, bilingualism usually means that the winners
speak one language and the losers speak two. In Israel that isn't quite
true: many Israelis are indeed bilingual, but, bowing to a more pow-

erful imperialism, their languages are Hebrew and English. The Arabs of Jerusalem tend to speak all three.

When we needed multilingual business cards printed, then, it seemed logical to go to an East Jerusalem printer. My request was simple: I just wanted plain English. But Patrick's were complicated: he wanted some with English on one side and Hebrew on the other, some with English and Arabic. He also wanted the English-Arabic ones divided into two subgroups: ones with our Jerusalem address and phone number, to give to Palestinians in Jerusalem and the occupied territories, and others with a Cyprus address and phone number to hand out when he was travelling in Arab countries that did not recognize Israel's existence. A Jerusalem address would not be well received at the Syrian or Iraqi foreign ministries, for example. This was all part of an elaborate international charade for which, one hopes, there will soon be no further need.

Armed with some vague directions from another journalist, we set off into East Jerusalem to find a Palestinian printer named Michel. Our journey was only a few blocks long, but it was an exhilarating adventure nonetheless. We crossed the invisible Green Line between West and East, skirted the north side of the Old City walls and strolled downhill towards the Damascus Gate, the most beautiful and elaborate of all the entrances to the Old City and the epicentre of Arab street life in Jerusalem. Unlike many of the other gates, the Damascus has been thoroughly excavated right down to the Roman layer, which means that it sits in a bowl many metres below street level. An amphitheatre of broad risers leads down to the gate, and merchants of all descriptions cover the steps with their cheap everyday wares. Women sit cross-legged but modest in their neck-to-toe embroidered dresses, with shiny polyester underwear and nightdresses laid out for sale on lurid scarves in front of them. Young Lotharios hawk the latest pop cassettes from Cairo, children sell the produce of their mothers' herb gardens, large sloppy bunches of aromatic mint, oregano and *maramiya* (sage), and the coffee vendors wander among the crowd, their entire coffee-making apparatus strapped to their bodies, wonderfully complicated copper constructions that make their owners look like the Tin Woodman from *The Wizard of Oz*. At street level above the gate, the taxi drivers huddle and smoke, ready to ferry passengers from Al-Quds (Jerusalem) out to the West Bank towns of Ramallah, Nablus, Bethlehem and Hebron. Just around the corner is a vast parking lot, the "slave market" where Arab day labourers congregate in the early hours of the morning, hoping to be chosen for construction or field work by Israeli builders and farmers. From high vantage points all over the area, Israeli soldiers keep a watchful eye on the seething activity below.

From the Damascus Gate we continued east along Sultan Suleiman Street, a lively extension of the outdoor market, and turned left into Saladin, the traffic-clogged main shopping street of East Jerusalem with its shiny pharmacies, glitzy shoe stores and Kit Kat, a romantic high-ceilinged shop that sold wonderful coffee, lavish sweets and such hard-to-come-by delicacies as bacon and Parmesan cheese. Down a narrow hill, and stepping carefully around an enormous hole in the street, we found Michel's printshop, a noisy, dark operation redolent of ink, just like old-fashioned printing establishments everywhere in the world. The tiny front office had a crucifix and stern family photos on the walls, plastic flowers and a shifting sea of papers on the desk and two cracked maroon leather chairs for customers. Mrs. Michel, who was never introduced by name, bustled her comfortable bulk about the room and then disappeared to make coffee. Michel was small and dapper, spoke elegant English and French, and told us he had just returned from looking after family business interests in Amman, the capital of Jordan, about forty kilometres away.

We were quickly to discover that, although the Israelis had taken East Jerusalem and the West Bank away from Jordan in 1967, most Palestinians still oriented themselves towards their former political masters, the Jordanians. They kept their money in Jordanian banks and used Jordanian dinars in their cash dealings almost as much as Israeli shekels. Many of them had family in Jordan, their school textbooks and curricula came from Amman, they got their news and entertainment from Jordanian television. The ties were demonstrably strong, and yet I never encountered any Palestinian enthusiasm for a confederation with Jordan, which was the diplomatic solution the Israelis were always trying to push. Palestinians with long memories would complain that their lives had been just as miserable under the Jordanians as they now were under the Israelis, and some felt even more bitter about the Jordanians because they were fellow Arabs, not the hated Zionists, who had treated them so badly.

Michel accepted our commission with alacrity and promised finished artwork for our approval by the following week. Then began a series of visits to the printshop, becoming steadily more absurd as every detail of the job went wrong: paper stock, paper colour, combination of languages, ghastly spelling errors in English (let alone in the languages we couldn't read), print runs, you name it. Sometimes, if Patrick was out of the country, I would pop in alone to check on the work. Sometimes we would turn up and Mrs. Michel would apologize profusely but her husband was in Amman today and no one else was empowered to make changes in the work. Finally, on the eighth visit, we picked up our boxes of cards and paid Michel's enormous bill. My cards had been printed in Arabic on the back, although I had expressly requested English only. Patrick's English-Arabic cards appeared to be correct, but the first time we showed one of his English-Hebrew cards to an Israeli, he scoffed and pointed out four errors. (*Avoda aravit,* or Arab work, is now a colloquial phrase in modern Hebrew for any job that is shoddily executed, whether by Arab or Jew.) The capper to the business-card episode was that two weeks after we took delivery, Bezek, the Israeli telephone company, arbitrarily changed Patrick's office phone number, thus rendering his cards useless.

I recount this story in some detail, not just because it's an amusing tale of doing business in the developing world, but because of our reaction to it as the adventure unfolded. Patrick and I found the whole experience funny and endearing, and as each visit revealed yet another mistake, we laughed and drank another cup of coffee with the Michels and strolled home through the exotic atmosphere of East Jerusalem. On about the fifth visit, it occurred to me that if we had been treated to such a string of foul-ups on the Israeli side of town, we would have been furious and would have long since cancelled the order, stomped out and taken our business elsewhere. Why had we fallen into such a double standard of behaviour so soon after arriving in Jerusalem? Was it just because the Palestinians were victims of the Israelis and therefore entitled to our unquestioning sympathy no matter how incompetently they might behave? Certainly that was part of it, but there was more. The Israelis always try to portray themselves as Western in their values, their politics and their approaches to business and culture. Although Israel seldom makes it onto anyone else's list of the Western developed nations, its own lists of social and economic barometers always have Israel right up there nestled alphabetically between Germany and Italy.

This progressive self-portrait is crucial to Israeli well-being, because it is the key that opens the door to United States government aid and to private donor support from all over Europe, North America, Australia and South Africa. As Patrick liked to say, "Israel presents itself as if it were just a little offshore from Long Island." When you come to Israel with that kind of propaganda build-up, you naturally expect life to be carried on at the same level of efficiency and public morality as back home. You do hold Israelis to a higher standard than their Arab neighbours; you can't help it. They themselves have primed you to do so.

The repeat visits to Michel's printshop also taught us a lot about the rhythm of East Jerusalem street life under the arbitrary and capricious rule of the intifada. It wasn't enough that long-suffering East

Jerusalemites had to live under the oppression of Israeli occupation, with its constant military presence, its arrests, seizures and house demolitions; the lives of ordinary Arab citizens were also controlled and circumscribed by the shadowy revolutionary committees within their own community who claimed to represent "the voice of the intifada." Although the most photographed image of the intifada since 1987 has been Palestinian youths hurling stones at Israeli troops, other aspects of the uprising have had just as deep an effect on people's lives. One of these has been a tax revolt, with Palestinians withholding millions of shekels from the Israeli authorities, arguing with considerable evidence that very little of that tax money ever gets delivered back into the West Bank or Gaza in the form of services. This has turned many formerly law-abiding small business owners into criminals, some of whom have been hauled off to serve prison sentences as a salutary example to others.

Another major impact of the intifada was the philosophical edict that, as long as their boys were being killed by Israeli soldiers and settlers or tortured in Israeli jails, the Palestinian people must mourn communally for them. In practical terms, this meant no one could visibly have any fun — wedding parties, baptisms and other forms of social celebration, even innocuous family pleasures like going to the movies or the beach, were forbidden from 1987 until about the end of 1992.

The most profound economic effect of the intifada came in the form of strikes. Strikes involved the "voluntary" closing of all shops and public gathering places, such as banks, schools and restaurants, whenever the intifada committee deemed it appropriate. I could never understand how this hurt the Israelis; it seemed to do nothing but cripple the local Palestinian economy. When we arrived in Jerusalem in the summer of 1991, shops in the Arab part of town opened only in the morning. By one o'clock, the heavy metal shutters rolled down, covered with Arab graffiti and clumsy Israeli military attempts to blackwash over them. Young *shebab,* the teenaged frontline soldiers of the intifada, ran along the crowded shopping streets of East Jerusalem and the Arab sections of the Old City, banging on the shutters and shouting at tardy shop owners to get a move on. Any reluctance on the part of these small businessmen to close up could quickly be interpreted as a lack of sufficient solidarity with the Palestinian cause, and the deadly possibility of being fingered as a collaborator with the Israeli authorities. Late in 1992, with the Madrid peace process sputtering along, the intifada leadership began easing up on the local merchants. Shops were allowed to stay open until three, then five o'clock. After the Rabin–Arafat meeting in Washington in 1993, all restrictions were removed and nightlife came back to a town that had not seen it in six years.

There were also whole days of strike that had to be observed, and some still are, even in these hopeful days of peaceful possibilities. The eighth day of every month was strictly observed as a strike day, commemorating the anniversary of the start of the intifada. And many other times throughout the year we would find East Jerusalem shuttered and deathly quiet, on days that marked particularly tragic events in the Palestinian community's never-happy history. Also, if a new tragedy occurred, the death of a Palestinian at the hands of an Israeli soldier or settler, the town would seal itself up for one, two, sometimes even three days in a row.

It was always impossible to get Palestinian businesspeople to express their true feelings about all these shop closures and strikes. They were afraid for their lives if they registered any protest. But on one of my many visits to Michel's printshop, I got to observe the coercive process first-hand. On this occasion, Michel had instructed me to come after two o'clock. As this was in the days of the one-o'clock curfew, I raised a questioning eyebrow.

"It's all right," he said with irritation. "We have been designated a factory by the intifada leadership, so we are allowed to stay open until four, not one o'clock like the shops. But when you come, you will find the shutter pulled three-quarters of the way down. Just duck underneath and come in."

I followed his instructions and turned up on the designated day. As he and I were discussing the latest problem with the business cards in the gloom of a front office that was now operating with no daylight from the street, there was a loud banging on the shutter and a boy of about seventeen ducked underneath and came up shouting. He was a nasty-looking piece of goods, swaggering and greasy and arrogant, and although I could not understand a word he said, it was clear that he considered Michel guilty of a major infraction of the rules. Michel began arguing back, obviously making his point about his legal right to be open, but the *shebab* didn't know about such fine distinctions in the categories of commercial establishments. He grabbed Michel by the arm and began pulling him. Michel yanked his arm away, looked at me in acute embarrassment and then ordered the fellow to go outside and continue the discussion on the other side of the shutter. Now I could no longer see but I could hear, and the shouting continued for another five minutes. Finally Michel returned, his eyes ablaze and his hands shaking with anger. For a prosperous middle-aged businessman to be dressed down by such a punk must have been devastating enough; for a Christian Arab to be taking orders from a Moslem was another layer of insult, since the Christians view themselves very much as the aristocracy of Palestine; and to have it all happen in front of a foreign woman was more than a traditional Palestinian of Michel's upbringing could stomach. The humiliation loosened his tongue a little.

"It is *all right* for me to be open," he insisted. "He is completely wrong. I have a ruling from the United Leadership. He can't do this to me. Every day I pray for peace so I won't have to listen to people like him any more. You can come next Tuesday — we will be open *all day!*"

❖

If the faultlines in West Jerusalem ran between Ashkenazim and Sephardim, and between secular and religious Jews, on the east side of town there were profound fragmentations as well: between Christian and Moslem Arabs, and between supporters of Yasser Arafat's secular PLO and supporters of the Islamic fundamentalist group, Hamas. It seemed to me that Arabs and Jews barely had the time or energy to hate each other when they were all so preoccupied with hostile divisions within their own neighbourhoods.

Decades of North American pop Christianity had prepared me for encountering Christians in the Holy Land. But somehow I expected them all to be — oh, I don't know — jolly Irish nuns and priests. What had not occurred to me was that most of them would be *Arab* Christians, largely Greek Orthodox but also some Roman Catholics and even Protestants. We visualize distant parts of the world in such broad, clumsy strokes, full of blurry generalizations and simplistic dichotomies; up close, the realities are invariably more complicated and more interesting. Edward Said, for example, the Columbia literature professor who is one of the world's most eloquent spokesmen for the Palestinian cause, is the son of a Baptist mother from Nazareth and an Anglican father from Jerusalem.

What turned out to be even more intriguing than the presence of Arab Christians in Jerusalem was their increasing absence. A Holy Land without Christians? It seems unthinkable but it is happening. Ever since 1948, and even more since the loss of Jerusalem and the West Bank in 1967, Palestinians have had two choices: stay and suffer, or emigrate. By and large, the Moslems have stayed and suffered and the Christians have emigrated. They have had more money and fewer children than the Moslems, more education and transportable skills and a sense of connection to the wider Christian community outside the Middle East. This has been true as well of the Armenians, a very ancient Christian community in Jerusalem who have always been more emotionally aligned with the Arabs than with the Jews.

One winter day when I was shopping in a tiny grocery store in the Armenian Quarter of the Old City, the elderly couple who ran it began reminiscing about the old days as they sat huddled in their overcoats behind the cash register. "You know all the tourist shops along David Street?" the man asked me. "Well, they all used to belong to Armenians. I had many cousins, and two brothers, who had shops over there. Now they are all gone. Only my wife and I are left from the whole family."

"Our children are in Chicago," the woman confirmed, nodding sadly.

"In 1967 the Armenian community here in Jerusalem was about thirty thousand. Now we're down to three thousand. There's no point in staying here, no future for you if you're Christian. When my brothers sold their shops, they wanted at least to sell to Arab Christians, but all the Arab Christians we knew were planning to leave too. They had to end up selling to Moslems. That whole area — the part they call the Christian Quarter — it's all Moslem now."

Another day we were browsing through wonderful antiquarian prints of the Holy Land by the nineteenth-century English lithographer David Roberts at Rami Meo's shop inside the Jaffa Gate. There was an enormous traffic in fake Roberts prints in Jerusalem, but Rami's reputation was impeccable. We had already purchased three Roberts from him but we were tempted to buy more; they were the perfect romantic expression of how this nervous and complex place had looked in simpler times, as a sleepy and exotic outpost of the Ottoman Empire.

Rami finished with another customer and came over to say hello. "I'm afraid I won't be seeing you again for a while," he said. "I have decided to take my family to Australia and we leave in three weeks." We were amazed and asked him why. Of all the Arab Christians we knew in the Old City, Rami was one of the most highly respected and well established. He had the enviable reputation of a political

moderate who was known to broker disputes within the Arab community. His business appeared to be doing well, except for the
inevitable loss of income from strike days. "I am just very tired of all
the trouble," he explained. "I want my children to lead a normal life."

Certainly by the time we arrived in Jerusalem in 1991, Palestinian
life had hit rock bottom. Huge numbers were still living in refugee
camps, the third and fourth generations to do so. Those lucky
enough to own land in the West Bank were hemmed in by hundreds
of Israeli restrictions that forbade them to develop their holdings or
build homes or additions for their expanding families. The heady
early days of the intifada were long over, leaving a society bereft of
thousands of its young men who had been killed or deported or were
in Israeli jails. Traditional family structures had been undermined by
the power of the teenage thugs who now ruled the streets. The orgy
of collaborator killings that had gone on for five years had frozen the
entire community in fear, with little possibility of free expression of
opinion or pragmatic exploration of peace with the Israelis. The local
economy was in a shambles, lawlessness was rife because Arab policemen had all resigned in 1988 in solidarity with the intifada, schools
and universities were closed for months or years at a time.

The *coup de grâce* — entirely self-administered — had been the
Palestinians' ill-conceived decision to back Saddam Hussein in the
Gulf War. Israelis, and much of the rest of the world, will not easily
forget the television scenes of Palestinians dancing on their rooftops
in celebration as Saddam's scuds sailed overhead on their way to sow
mayhem in Tel Aviv. For much of the Western world, the word
"Palestinian" has been synonymous with "terrorist" since the airplane
hijackings of the 1970s, so this latest political alignment on their part
confirmed a negative stereotype. But the worst repercussion for the
Palestinians was economic: over the years, hundreds of thousands of
West Bankers had emigrated to the Gulf states, particularly Kuwait,
where they had attained a high standard of living and a great deal of

respect in academic life and the professions. Those successful offspring of indigent Palestinian villagers and refugees made life a great
deal more bearable back home by sending generous monthly support
payments. But once the Palestinians living under Israeli rule aligned
themselves with the quixotic Iraqi dictator, Kuwait summarily
bounced all of its Palestinian residents out of the country as enemy
aliens, thus cutting off one of the most important sources of income
for the occupied territories. The Arabs of Palestine, one couldn't help
feeling, have raised to the highest of art forms the cutting off of the
nose to spite the face.

I met one of these benighted Kuwaiti Palestinians one day in East
Jerusalem, still reeling from the disastrous events that had overtaken
his life. My friend Helen and I were poking around the Palestinian
Pottery, a delightful ceramic studio and showroom run by an
Armenian family called Balian who had been brought to Jerusalem
many decades earlier, before Israel was born, when the British
Mandate was still in place. The British military governor of
Jerusalem, Sir Ronald Storrs, had taken on the great civic project of
completely restoring the exterior of the Dome of the Rock, which
was clad in thousands of hand-painted ceramic tiles, many of them
destroyed after two hundred years of wear and weather. Storrs
imported three Armenian families of ceramicists to do the work,
which took many years, and afterwards the families stayed and
opened commercial establishments that continue to produce beautiful, flowery folk-art designs of Armenian extraction. The Palestinian
Pottery is a misnomer — it should be called the Armenian Pottery —
but the canny owners of the shop are not about to disabuse tourists of
the notion that they are somehow supporting the Palestinian cause by
buying their pretty artifacts.

The day Helen and I were there, a handsome moustached fellow
of about forty came in with a large sack and began talking urgently in
Arabic to the clerk behind the desk. As he talked he drew various

large objects from his sack and unwrapped them on the table. They were strange, modern, semi-abstract ceramics that resembled mushrooms; one was a cylindrical lamp with ugly, bulbous wart-like projections along its length. The colours of these creations were also quite singular: acid yellow, puce, slate grey. They made me think of the worst excesses of what, back home in the sixties, we used to call crunchy-granola pottery, earnest artistic statements made by vegetarians who wore only natural fibres and bare feet while they worked.

The fellow's ceramics couldn't have been more different from the delicate traditional pottery being sold in the shop, but it was clear he was trying to get the clerk to take some of his pieces on consignment. It was also clear he was meeting with no success. We began chatting with him in English, and he told us his story. His name was Abdallah and he had been kicked out of Kuwait after fifteen years of teaching art there in the state school system. Before that he had done his art training in London, where he had become imbued with the modern Western idea of art as self-expression, an idea that, as well as giving us Picasso and Henry Moore, has been responsible for prodigious amounts of terrible pottery and paintings.

"They do not understand this here," Abdallah sighed, looking askance at the clerk, whom he seemed to have decided was a lost cause anyway. "All art in Palestine must reflect the traditional cultural values of the group, the tribe. Individuality is nowhere. If we do not move beyond this provincialism, we will be left behind." It was too bad his own work was such a poor example of his shining ideals. "I have opened a school," he continued, "in Nablus, where my family comes from. I will try to impart these progressive ideas about art to the children there. It is a beginning." He drew me a map of Nablus, a grim town about an hour's drive north of Jerusalem in the West Bank, and marked his studio on it. I promised to come and visit some day. I was curious to know whether he could attract even a single student in a place as political and dangerous as Nablus, but I am ashamed to say I never had the nerve to go. It was an odd thing: there were incendiary parts of the West Bank, such as Hebron, that we loved to visit, although Israelis thought we were mad to go there. But there were others, particularly Nablus and Jenin in the north, hotbeds of revolutionary activity for both the PLO and Hamas, that sent a cold shudder through me that kept me strictly away.

Given the absolute wreckage their society had become, economically, educationally, psychologically and emotionally, it was extraordinary how much pleasure we could derive from meeting and visiting with Palestinians in East Jerusalem and the West Bank. They were not easy people to spend time with — the Israelis, for all their gruffness, made for more relaxed companionship — but they had a charm and gracefulness that could be very seductive. Like all Arabs, the Palestinians raise hospitality to the level of a religion, going to elaborate, sometimes embarrassing, lengths to entertain visitors. This is part of a desert code of behaviour that often seems to have a great deal more to do with the honour of the hosts than with the comfort of the guests. How many lengthy hours did we spend in draughty Arab parlours, all similarly furnished with large plush chairs or couches lining the outer walls, the affiliation of the family blatantly displayed in photos of Yasser Arafat or tapestries of the Dome of the Rock hanging on the bare pale-yellow walls? How many identical afternoon collations did we consume, always appearing in the same order and rhythm: first, sticky fizzy orange drinks, then half an hour later tiny cups of coffee and glasses of water, followed in thirty minutes by large bowls of fresh fruit and nuts, then by some sort of sweet pastry, and finally by hot glasses of mint tea? Two visits in a single afternoon could finish you off.

The talk that accompanied such highly structured hospitality tended to be formulaic as well. One day Patrick and I drove north out of Jerusalem to see what had happened to Abed, a personable fellow we had come to know at our local picture framer's in West

Jerusalem. Abed worked for the Israeli owners of the shop, and we had had numerous interesting conversations with him about art, his life in the West Bank and his political views (very moderate) on the whole Arab-Israeli situation. After a month of intense violence in the spring of 1993, the Israeli authorities sealed off the occupied territories so that none of the thousands of Palestinian workers who regularly crossed into Israel every day could get to their jobs. Abed was out of luck and out of a paycheque. Sometimes there were closures of just a day or two, sometimes a week. The closure during the Gulf War had lasted forty-two days and inflicted great economic hardship on all the Palestinian families who depended on their Israeli incomes to make ends meet.

This current closure had lasted five weeks already and showed no sign of being over, and when I was in the framer's one day I asked his Israeli co-worker, Menashe, for Abed's home phone number so we could see how he and his family were getting along. It turned out he had no telephone, and Menashe, who had been working with Abed for three years, didn't know his last name, but he was able to tell me the name of Abed's village, Sinjil, which was just north of Ramallah, about half an hour's drive out of Jerusalem.

We arrived unannounced and made our way to the centre of Sinjil, which sat perched on the side of a broad slope of the Judean Hills, its boxy houses gazing out over a typical West Bank landscape of rocky terraces, delicate olive groves and, on distant hilltops, the new white presence of Jewish settlements. At the *diwan*, or local coffeehouse, we inquired after Abed, but the young fellow we spoke to shrugged his shoulders. "Which Abed?" he asked. "There are six of them in this village."

"Abed who works at the picture-framing shop in Rehavia," we explained, and the young man's eyes widened with interest and respect.

"Ah, that's my cousin Abed! Come, I will take you to his house."

We were met at the door by Abed's slim young wife, his two-year-old son and his stout leather-faced mother. A little flustered at the unexpected company, they ushered us into the living-room, sat us down and disappeared into the kitchen. The cousin explained, after a flurry of Arabic with the women, that Abed had gone to the Israeli civil administration office in Halamish, a nearby settlement, to make yet another inquiry about the status of his application to return to work in West Jerusalem. "He has to go almost every day," the cousin explained, "sometimes two, three hours. But until now, no luck."

While we waited for Abed's return, other male relatives began filtering in from the village lanes. Word had gotten around that Abed had foreign visitors. Cousin after cousin arrived, young and old, then Abed's brother and eventually Abed himself, a little breathless but self-possessed. He wasn't conventionally handsome, with his long, thin face, toothy smile and receding hairline, but he must have been considered a good catch because he had managed to snag a real beauty from the next village as his wife. They had been married four years, he was twenty-eight, she was twenty-one, and they already had their first two children. Because of the demographic battle between Palestinians and Israelis, having a large family was just about the best thing you could do for your social status in the West Bank, and Abed was proud of his.

"I come from a very big family," he said. "My grandparents had six daughters and two children. Among them they have over one hundred children." His hand swept around to include his relatives in the living-room plus all the others out there in the streets of Sinjil.

Calling daughters "daughters" and sons "children" was absolutely standard in even the most progressive Palestinian homes. Abed's wife and mother shared the hosting duties, ferrying the dishes and glasses back and forth and taking turns perching on the arm of a sofa for a few moments, to indicate, I think, that this was a fairly modern Arab home in which the women were allowed out of the kitchen (although, since neither of them spoke any English and all the men did, we couldn't communicate beyond the language of smiles).

"My employers are doing their best to get me a permit to return to work," Abed explained, when we asked how things were going, "but of course the Israelis say that picture framing is not an essential industry, so I have a low priority." We asked how many people in the village had been affected by the lengthy closure of the territories. The men conferred and argued in Arabic, then Abed's cousin Ali spoke.

"There are five thousand people in Sinjil, and about three hundred of them worked in Israel before the closure. Only twenty of those have been able to get permits to cross the Green Line in the last five weeks."

If you can't go back, we asked Abed, how much financial hardship will you suffer? Can you get similar work in the West Bank? He shook his head. "There are some framing shops in Ramallah and East Jerusalem, but there are no openings. Besides, I earn three times as much working in Israel as if I did the same work here." He was earning about $900 a month before the closure. It took him four hours to commute to work and back each day — first in one *service* , or multiple taxi, from Sinjil to Ramallah, then in another *service* from Ramallah to the Damascus Gate, then on an Israeli bus (Jerusalem is served by separate Arab and Israeli bus lines) to the framing shop.

What had really upset the Palestinians about this most recent closure was that it comprised all of Jerusalem, including what they clearly regarded as their part of the city. The Israelis had drawn a selective line around Jerusalem that managed to include a lot of the new hotly contested Jewish settlement areas within the city's municipal boundaries and to exclude many of the older well-established Arab neighbourhoods. This was another aspect of the demographic battle for the city that had been waged ever since the Israelis took control in 1967. And whenever there was political trouble, Jerusalem would be sealed off with heavy roadblocks on all the roads that funnelled in from its natural Arab hinterland to the north, east and south. Israelis from the West Bank settlements, with their yellow-plated cars, sailed through the roadblocks with a wave of a soldier's hand. Only Palestinians with permits to work in Israel were allowed through, and there were precious few of those issued in times of tension, as Ali had told us. For people like Abed's family in the village of Sinjil, it was like living in a satellite that was cut off from the mother ship.

What was so important about Jerusalem, I wanted to know. Did they go there to shop? No, no, said the women, there are much better shops in Ramallah. Well, then, was the family religious? Is it important for you to be able to pray at the Al Aqsa Mosque on the Haram? It is nice to be able to pray there, said one of Abed's cousins, because it is such a holy place. All over the Islamic world we say that one prayer at Al Aqsa is worth five hundred prayers anywhere else. (This explained why an Egyptian tour guide we had met on a Nile cruise a couple of months earlier, when he learned we lived in Jerusalem, gave our son Sam a handwritten prayer and asked him to deliver it personally to the Al Aqsa Mosque.) Still, it was clear that Abed's was not a very devout family, and most of the men shook their heads at the suggestion that the pull the city exercised on them was a religious one.

"It is just ours," Abed said finally, opening his hands in an expression of obviousness and certitude. "It has been the centre of our lives for hundreds of years and it still is and it always will be."

After two hours of what felt much more like an interview than a conversation, Abed and Ali offered to take us out for a stroll around the village. It was easier to talk outside the confines of the living-room, but as guests we never lost the sense of words and opinions being carefully weighed before being spoken. The afternoon sun slanted in from the west, bathing the valley below in a warm yellow glow. The fields in the valley were meticulously cultivated, but their natural bounty had been bifurcated by a new four-line highway that slashed through the valley and up the hill opposite to the Israeli settlement of Shiloh. Abed paused to make a point.

"There was no reason for them to build that road," he said. "There is a perfectly good narrow road over there at the edge of the valley, see? They could have just widened that one. But no, they left that one there and built this one a couple of hundred metres away, right across the best agricultural land we have in the village."

"Did the Israelis tell you they were going to do this?"

"Sure, they put a notice in the newspaper," said Ali. "It said if you have any complaint, you can appeal to the courts. But the people in this village have appealed before and the decision always goes against them, so what's the point?"

"The Israelis also offer to pay money for the land," continued Abed, "but no one wants to take it because it means you give your approval to the action. So they just go ahead with their bulldozers, right across our fields."

We turned away from the lip of the valley into the centre of the village, where a crumbling older neighbourhood sat picturesque and largely abandoned against a backdrop of roomy modern houses on the higher ground. "Most people have moved out of the old buildings into new ones," said Abed, underlining something we noticed wherever we went in East Jerusalem and the West Bank. For a society that had been gagged and bound for forty-five years, there was an extraordinary amount of new building everywhere we looked. What was happening here was a mirror of what was happening on the Israeli side: wealthy Palestinians abroad either helped their local family members to build new homes or else built palatial constructions for their own use during the few weeks a year they might spend in the homeland. (A smart salesman had convinced these yuppie Palestinians that the thing to have on top of your house was a miniature Eiffel Tower; the skyline of every town in the West Bank was crowned with dozens of them.) For both the Arabs and the Jews, the well-being of their communities depended to an unhealthy extent on the largesse of those who didn't live there. Abed and Ali talked reverently about a family from the village who had moved to America and become millionaires in import-export trading. They pointed out the new mosque this family had bankrolled, and the foundations of a girls' school they were building and donating to the village.

As we turned out of a narrow lane onto the main street of the village, we paused in front of some fresh graffiti, gorgeously crafted in Arabic in red spray-paint. Abed translated: "If you want to get on the geographical map, first get on the political map." It was signed by the PLO. Had Sinjil been very political during the intifada, we asked. No, no, not very political at all, was the quick and dismissive answer. This was always a common response in Palestinian conversations, but the evidence around us spoke otherwise. We passed the remains of one modern house that had been razed by the Israelis because a member of the family had been involved in an attack against the army. With gentle prodding, Ali admitted that nine other families in Sinjil had lost their homes in the same manner. In fact, we found those homeless families, mostly women and children and a few old men, now squatting in the empty old village houses down the hill. Many of them had been there five years, with no light, heat or running water, the women doing their cooking in the old *tabouns*, dome-shaped stone ovens outside the front doors of their houses.

When the men of the family were killed or imprisoned or deported, and their families rendered homeless, the rhetoric of the PLO and Hamas would glorify the mothers and wives and children as "martyrs" along with their menfolk. But these were empty political slogans. In practice, women living in Palestinian society without the protection and support of men are generally ignored and despised. As we chatted with some of the womenfolk in the ruins of old Sinjil, munching on delicious spicy flatbreads one of them had just drawn out of her *taboun,* I was remembering an autobiographical account I had read the week before in the library of the Women's Research Centre in East Jerusalem.

A woman named Mariam described how she had been married when she was fifteen; her husband had immediately been involved in an anti-Israeli Defence Force action and had been sentenced to twenty-five years in jail. Now that he had been released, she was forty-two years old and wanted children; she wanted to live a normal life after being treated, for twenty-five years, like an outcast by her society because of her manless state. She described visiting her husband in jail once a month: his brothers used to go sometimes but they didn't want a woman tagging along so they refused to take her with them. She never had enough money for a *service,* so she walked four hours alone to the jail. She would start out at three in the morning to be there for the twenty-minute visit the Israelis allowed at seven. It was never worthwhile, though, because everyone was in a huge courtyard together and there was so much shouting and screaming and wailing that she could never hear what her husband was saying. Now, to add to her misery, her newly returned husband would not sleep with her and try to conceive a son. She had heard rumours that Arab prisoners in Israeli jails were routinely sterilized at the beginning of their sentences. She surmised that this had been done to her husband and he was too ashamed to admit it to her. (No amount of research I did could uncover any truth to this rumour, but its sexual focus was absolutely consistent with the entire Palestinian symbolism of the Arab–Israeli relationship: the raping of the land, the destruction of the nation's honour, the emasculation of its men, the threat to its women's virtue.)

As I looked at the women of Sinjil, squatting and chatting in their courtyards of rubble, I wondered how many of them had stories like Mariam's. They would certainly never share them with me if they did, the shame would be too great. Mariam had told her story only to another Palestinian, a sociologist who had herself grown up in a refugee camp in Syria. There truly are limits to what we in the developed world can legitimately ask people who live in such deprivation and by such different rules to share with us. I came to feel, during my two years in their part of the world, that the Palestinians had been forced to give up not only their land, their pride and their mastery over their own lives but also their privacy. Ever since 1948, when Israel became a nation and the refugee problem began, the Palestinians have been subjected to a small army of United Nations troops, private charities, non-governmental agencies, international task forces, journalists, sociologists, politicians, anthropologists, psychiatrists and photographers who have shone bright, cruel lights into every corner of their miserable lives. The Israeli academic world has taken the Palestinians as a popular and interesting field of study as well; part of the prerogative of being the victor seems to be the right to study the vanquished. (I never encountered any Palestinian studies of Israeli life.) Much of this work has been done with the best of intentions, and yet the Palestinians are quite right when they point out that opening themselves up to the curiosity of the West has not done a thing to improve their relationship with the Israelis, which, in the end, is the only relationship that counts.

As we were making our way back to the main road through the village, Abed stopped by a shallow circle of stones with a couple of old planks of wood lying across the top. "This is the pit that people here believe Joseph's brothers threw him into after they stole his coloured coat," he said matter-of-factly, as if pointing out the nearest mailbox. "We keep it covered so no children will fall in."

The four of us stood and looked down at this nondescript spot on the earth's surface and the usual wild mix of associations and questions arose. Sunday school Bible lessons clashed with Broadway musical numbers in my mind, and I couldn't help wondering whether the Israelis knew about this place. Did they think it was the real spot of this important biblical episode, or did they have a rival contender somewhere else in the West Bank? If it had been known as a holy place for a long time, perhaps that would explain the rather odd name of the village. Sinjil sounded like a bastardization of Saint something, maybe St. Giles? Could the Crusaders have claimed this place as part of their biblical heritage ten centuries ago? Abed had pointed out on our tour that the old village mosque was built on the foundations of a Byzantine church, which would date it back to the fourth century, when Queen Helena was earmarking the local holy sites. Could this possibly be the real spot? How could you tell? Did it matter?

Our heads spinning in a confused but pleasant way, we returned to our car, said goodbye to Abed and his cousin, and made our way through the Israeli army roadblocks home to Jerusalem.

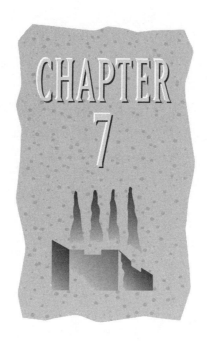

CHAPTER 7

O N A SUNNY FEBRUARY MORNING Avraham came over to prune our grapevine. Our next-door neighbour, who had been a *kibbutznik* for seventeen years, was always giving me tips on how to cultivate the luxurious semi-tropical garden our landlords had left us to care for, but I was too nervous to tackle the grapevine alone. It was actually Avraham's grapevine, which he had trained, over a decade and a half, to branch both left and right so that it shaded the whole front of our house as well as his. The bark of the vine was getting dried out and flaky, and Avraham kept threatening to pull the whole thing out and start a new one. Thankfully, he never got around to it as long as we lived there.

While he pruned I made coffee, and when he was finished we sat on our terrace and watched the tiny bee-eaters swoop and dart, poking their long sharp beaks into the few early spring blossoms they could find, their iridescent green throats throbbing as they drank. Avraham and I had developed a warm neighbourliness by then, but this was the first time I had the leisure to hear his story. Every immigrant to Israel had a story, many of them unbearably tragic, and we soon learned not to stop the flow of daily life by inquiring about too many of them. There seemed to be an unspoken pact among Israelis not to let their personal pasts swamp their lives, but instead to adopt as a communal past a broad tapestry painted in bold, inspiring colours, a heady mixture of biblical romance and military heroism. This was easier for the native-born *sabras* than for the immigrants. One day in the English-language daily, the *Jerusalem Post*, a group of Israeli teenagers was asked what historical period they would like to return to; they all said either 1967, the year of Israel's most resounding modern victory, or the time of the First Temple of Solomon around 900 B.C. The intervening 2,800 years appeared not to exist for them.

But Avraham loved his personal story and told it with great relish. He was from a family of Polish Jews, who fled to Russia when Hitler invaded Poland in 1939. They moved from one agricultural commune to another, finally ending up far south in Uzbekistan, near the city of Tashkent. Life was miserable, but at least the family was alive and together.

Meanwhile, the Poles, under British auspices, had set up a Polish army in exile, headquartered in Tashkent, largely manned by Polish refugees who had fled to Russia like Avraham's family. In 1943 this Polish army established an orphanage there for the hundreds of Polish children wandering the Russian countryside, and Avraham's parents told their thirteen-year-old son to go there and declare himself an orphan. "They thought I would be better taken care of there, and would get some schooling, and maybe I would be able to help them out too." Every week his parents would come to visit surreptitiously, and Avraham would smuggle tins of British bully beef to them through the fence.

One night in 1943, after he had been in the orphanage for two months, all the children were suddenly awakened at midnight, dressed and packed onto a train for Krasnovodsk, on the Caspian Sea. Avraham's parents knew nothing about his abduction and the camp authorities knew nothing about the existence of Avraham's parents. "I was going crazy on the train," he told me. "I had to get back to my parents. When the train stopped for a while in Samarkand I escaped, but the Uzbeki police found me two hours later, stealing fruit in the Samarkand marketplace. I was starving! They put me right back on the train." Soon they reached the Caspian Sea and the two hundred children were put on board a military ship bound for Iran. A massive clandestine rescue operation was in progress.

When the ship landed in Iran, representatives from the Jewish Agency were waiting on the shore to pick out the Jewish children and send them on to Palestine. In Avraham's batch, only a dozen or so were Jews, but they were soon joined by hundreds of others who were being spirited out of Europe. In the end there were 780 of them, gathered in a holding camp in Teheran, and eventually they set sail in another British ship for a long and tortuous voyage to Palestine, via Karachi in India, then Aden, through the Red Sea and the Suez Canal to Alexandria, and thence by train up the Palestine coast to Haifa.

"I think all the Jews in Palestine were in Haifa that day to welcome us," Avraham recalled. "A Jewish millionaire in India had outfitted us all on our stopover in Karachi, from our shoes up to these little British pith helmets, and that's what we were wearing when we stepped off the train. This was 1943, remember, by which time everyone in Palestine had learned about the death camps in Europe, and I think the arrival of hundreds and hundreds of orphaned European Jewish children gave great hope to the Jews here in the darkest days of the Holocaust. We became known as the Children of Teheran, and all Israeli children read about us in their history books."

Every kibbutz in the land took a few of the children, and Avraham went to Ashdot Ya'akov, a beautiful, rich, well-established kibbutz just south of the Sea of Galilee. He remained there until he was thirty, bringing his bride, Tamar, a *sabra* from Jerusalem whom he met in the army, to live there with him and give birth to their two children. He was able to re-establish contact with his parents as soon as the Teheran rescue operation was completed, but after the war they returned to Poland instead of joining him in Palestine.

"They were from Wrocslaw, which is a big city," he explained. "The Polish Jews who tried to return to small villages after the war were met with fierce anti-Semitism and local people who were afraid the Jews would demand their property back. But in the big cities, the Communists kept things under control and they protected the Jews, so my parents had no big problems. Years later, though, they did move to Israel, and my mother is still alive here, down in Tel Aviv."

At this point, Avraham hurried next door to find a Hebrew book about the Children of Teheran. I could not read the text, but there were the photos of hundreds of little ones in their pith helmets, huddled on a station platform, squinting dazedly into the blinding Palestinian sun. I later found an English translation of the book. What Avraham had described as a rather larky *Boys' Own* adventure had in fact been an unmitigated nightmare, with hundreds of sick and malnourished children, traumatized by war and the loss of their families, violently ill and constantly weeping on the long sea voyage, with suicide attempts, lice, scabies and vicious quarrels the normal order of the day. To Avraham, though, it had been the exciting prelude to a long and happy life in Israel.

I have seldom met anyone as intelligently cheerful and optimistic as Avraham, and I quickly came to view him as the perfect Israeli:

brave in war (he had fought in four of them) but dovish in his politics, full of warmth and good humour but never taking any crap from anyone, competent at everything physical and manual but a lover of good music and art and literature, quick, thoughtful, crazy about his family and strong as an ox. I could not believe that fortune had set us down right next door to him.

Tamar we did not see as often. While Avraham was semi-retired and always on the lookout for good gossip and conversation in the neighbourhood, she was principal of a school for emotionally disturbed teenagers; she returned from work at two o'clock every afternoon largely wrung out and preferred to remain quietly in her cosy house. Her calm dignity was an absolute contrast to Avraham's garrulous and opinionated *bonhomie*, but there was no question of their utter devotion to each other. One day as she was watering the roses, her conversation turned, as it often did, to her husband. "You know, I have had this polio hip since I was small and there are many things I cannot do around the house, so Avraham does them — a lot of the cooking and cleaning and shopping. And he has never, not once, even in the middle of our worst fights, ever complained about all the extra work. I am a very lucky woman."

It was a blessing that we had Avraham and Tamar on one side of us, because some of our other neighbours were not so pleasant. Half a block away lived the Matars, who simply refused to talk to us once they learned we were journalists. They were Orthodox Jews from the United States, with a son living out in a West Bank settlement. Ruth operated an exclusive little jewellery studio and shop out of their home, all her pieces incorporating Judaic symbols or archaeological elements designed to appeal to the well-heeled Jewish tourists from North America who came to Israel looking for their roots. There was such a high demand for this kind of artwork, expensive, well executed and highly chauvinistic in content, that I always felt it skewed the output of Jerusalem artists in a depressing manner. It was almost impossible to buy non-religious art in West Jerusalem, and yet it seemed to me that the artists who created the silk prayer shawls, the silver menorahs, the Chagall mezuzzahs and the biblical lithographs were acting entirely according to commercial, not religious dictates. In their own lavish way, they were as narrowly nationalistic as the Palestinian artists working a kilometre away in East Jerusalem on their olive-wood crucifixes and local flowered pottery. So much for art as a universal language.

Two doors from us lived another religious American couple, Martin and Rosalie, who were more civilized than the Matars but difficult to spend time with. They were the first people on the street to invite us in, and over coffee in their beautifully appointed sunken living-room Martin held forth on the history of Yemin Moshe, the problems with the Arabs (lazy and untrustworthy), the problems with the Israeli Jews (godless and socialist), the glories of the Negev Desert south of Jerusalem where they had built a retreat, and their hostile relations with the neighbours because they had had the temerity to dynamite the bedrock under their house to make more living space. Martin also recommended various expensive kosher restaurants around town but steered us away from the luxurious Mishkenot Sha'ananim, which was right in our neighbourhood. "The fellow who runs it doesn't keep the Shabbat laws," he explained. "He opens on Saturday night the minute Shabbat is officially over, but that means his staff have had to break the sabbath and come in to work two or three hours earlier. That's not good enough."

Martin and Rosalie had lived for many years in Israel, although he still acted as a consultant on broadcasting issues to the Federal Communications Commission in Washington. He was clearly a man of rigid moral character who was used to being listened to with gravity. He had been in his political element in Israel ever since the Likud government had taken power in 1977, bringing its right-wing and religious agenda to the conduct of the country's affairs. Martin had advised the Ministry of Health on the contentious issue of Israeli abortion legislation, which he considered far too liberal. During the 1982 Israeli invasion of Lebanon, he gave an interview in which he said that abortions had resulted in the loss of twenty army divisions since the creation of the state, a statement that indicated succinctly what he thought about both state security and Israeli womanhood. He was not a popular figure among the country's feminists.

As we left their house that first day, Martin gave us a copy of his recently published book, *Access to the American Mind: The Damaging Impact of the New Mass Media,* which turned out to be a well-written rant against all the ex-hippies who run the television industry in North America. Articles by him would sometimes turn up in the *Jerusalem Post,* the right-wing English-language daily owned by Canadian press baron Conrad Black, commenting on the Arab–Israeli conflict from the viewpoint that claimed there were no such people as the Palestinians; they were a "fabrication" of the Arab states, designed to make Israel look like an aggressor instead of a victim.

Martin and Rosalie and their adopted Israeli son, Amos, were unfailingly friendly and polite to us whenever we met on the sidewalk, and there were times when Rosalie joined me on our terrace for a cold drink and a chat. But we never invited them over formally because entertaining Martin would have been like crossing a field seeded with landmines. He was so sure of his opinions that it never seemed to occur to him how much they might hurt or offend others. One day Tamar and I were out front admiring the beautiful riot of spring flowers she and Avraham had planted and tended, although they fell technically within the communal part of the Yemin Moshe gardens. Martin walked in from the parking lot, impeccably suited and bearded and *kipa*-ed, and he and I nodded a neighbourly hello. I noticed that he and Tamar did not acknowledge each other. After he had entered his house I mentioned the dynamiting of the basement. Tamar shook her head.

"Is that why he told you we don't get along? It wasn't that. It was about fifteen years ago, when Avraham and I were first planning the garden around the olive tree here. I was working on this patch of land when Martin came by and said, 'What are you doing? You're making it so ugly!' I was so upset I went into the house and cried and cried. Since then we don't talk."

There were other neighbours on the street who didn't talk to each other. Next door to us lived David and Chaia, their exquisite daughter, Liat, their terrifying black German shepherd named Gandhi and, when they were on leave from the army, their two matinee-idol sons. David was a successful artist and graphic designer, and Chaia was a professor of Zionist history and author of several books. They were both *sabras,* he Sephardic and she Ashkenazi, and in many ways they were the picture-perfect Israeli family, handsome, healthy, cross-cultural and passionately nationalistic. Every week they went to a folk-dancing club, and young Liat was part of a troupe that performed regularly around Jerusalem and sometimes toured in Europe. "You should come with us some night," Chaia said to me one day, looking resplendent in one of the many complicated and dramatic outfits she wore every time she left her house. She had flowing dark hair, a lithe athletic figure and posture so regal it made me feel like a sloth. "It is wonderful exercise, especially for the thighs and the lungs." It all sounded a little too healthy for me, and a bit kitschy as well. After all, I came from a country where for many years the mushy ideal of multiculturalism reached its highest flowering in the art of folk-dancing — Ukrainian, Croatian, Greek and Scottish — and it was difficult to take it seriously as a leisure activity suitable for successful citizens in mid-career. But in Israel folk-dancing was an absolutely serious pursuit, one of the cultural building blocks with which the new nation had been constructed. After draining the malarial swamps all day, one was expected to *hora* by night, every twist and stomp designed to bind the young Zionists closer to each other and to the *kvutza,* the group.

But times were moving on, even in Israel, and an activity that literally every able-bodied citizen participated in through the twenties, thirties, forties and fifties had become much more discretionary by the nineties, so that only those strongly enamoured of it took part. The other enthusiastic dancer we knew was Cindy, Patrick's assistant, who made the pilgrimage to the northern town of Karmiel in the Galilee every year for its international folk-dancing festival.

As neighbours, David and Chaia were perfectly pleasant. One evening David knocked at our door and asked if I could assist him. He was being honoured at a reception up at the Jerusalem Hilton, and he was required to wear a jacket and tie. Could I tie his necktie for him? I was incredulous; how could a man of forty-five, even in the most casually dressed country in the world, not have had at least one occasion in his life to wear a tie? Israeli fashion really gave "dressing down" a whole new meaning: people turned up at weddings in shorts. On television I watched a young son giving the eulogy for his murdered father — dressed in blue jeans and a windbreaker. I tried to explain to David how to knot the tie, but he was clearly uninterested. He needed one just for tonight and had no expectation of ever needing one again.

We shared meals occasionally at each other's tables, and always chatted in a friendly manner in front of our houses, but I have to admit that David and Chaia always made me feel a little uncomfortable. Perhaps we did the same to them. They were not religious like Martin and Rosalie, but they adhered just as staunchly to their own belief system, which was Zionism. They were intensely patriotic and incredibly proud of their two handsome, arrogant sons, who they told us were both posted to "special units" in the army, they couldn't tell us where. We were to take from this that they were doing high-level espionage work. Later, an Israeli journalist told me that many parents like to make the same claim, so many that the whole country would be overflowing with spies if they were all telling the truth.

David and Chaia had security on their minds all the time and were terribly nervous about Arabs. Because of our location on the Green Line, Arab workers flowed through our neighbourhood quite regularly, and on Moslem holidays large Palestinian families would stroll our manicured pathways and climb to the beautiful fountains and gardens on the hillside above us. We also had our own staff of Arab gardeners, street-sweepers and garbage collectors who tended the whole Yemin Moshe precinct and were thought by the Israelis to have some of the cushiest jobs in Jerusalem. One day I heard shouting outside and went to investigate. It was in October, the month of the olive harvest, and on the common lawn in front of our houses there were nine or ten trees all bursting with dark fruit. David was having a tense discussion in Hebrew with half a dozen Palestinian men, a couple of whom I recognized as members of our grounds crew and the others undoubtedly brothers or cousins. Two or three women in traditional garb lurked quietly behind the trees a few metres away, with olive-gathering equipment — sticks, pails and large white sheets. Other neighbours began emerging from their houses, a couple of them joining David in his quarrel with the Arabs but most of them, like me, just watching from the fringes. I wished Avraham were there. Eventually David prevailed, the Palestinians left with their women, and another neighbour, Eva, explained to me what had happened.

"They said they have had a traditional right to harvest these olive trees for a long time, but David said they don't. He says the land belongs to the Yemin Moshe neighbourhood co-op and that we will communally pay workers to harvest the olives and then keep the profit for ourselves." Who did she think was right, I asked her. "Well, I am very liberal in my politics," she began, "but I don't want to get involved. This is obviously an old quarrel and we just arrived in the neighbourhood." In spite of David's stand, however, I noticed that over the next month individual pairs of Palestinian husbands and wives would turn up and harvest a single tree at a time and carry the bounty away with them. One Sunday morning a couple knocked on our door at seven o'clock and asked to borrow our stepladder to reach the top branches.

As residents of the neighbourhood, we were all responsible for security, which meant doing guard duty about once a month at night or on the weekend. Since neither Patrick nor I was skilled in the use of semi-automatic weapons, we politely declined and paid to have professional security guards replace us. Many others did the same, but some of the Israeli residents seemed to enjoy the work. Avraham and David were good friends and they always requested guard duty together. "It's a nice quiet opportunity to get together and talk," said Avraham, "and it reminds me of life on the kibbutz."

Another neighbour, Jessica, an Israeli who had just come back with her husband, Menachem, after living twenty years in Sweden, also signed up for the neighbourhood patrol. This rather surprised me, since she was one of the most pacifist left-wing Israelis I met. "I'm doing it to get to know my neighbours," she told me. One day I encountered her and her partner, a few tiers up the hillside, decked out in their bullet-proof vests, with their rifles slung over their shoulders. Jessica was shouting frantically into her cellular phone; it didn't seem the ideal moment to stop and chat. Later I asked her what had been going on, and she told me she had received a call that there had been a stabbing up by the Montefiore windmill, but when they rushed to the spot, there was no sign of violence. It must have been a prank. Unfortunately, it never paid to get too complacent. At eight o'clock one summer morning, an Israeli woman walking through our neighbourhood on her way to work at the Mishkenot Sha'ananim guest-house was attacked by two knife-wielding Arabs who shouted "*Allahu aqbar!*" and stabbed her a number of times before fleeing.

The worst period of tension we experienced was the whole month of March 1993, during which hardly a day went by without a terrorist attack somewhere in the country. By the end of the month, fifteen Israelis had been killed and another thirty wounded, including five students and their principal in a Jerusalem schoolyard. Yemin Moshe, like every neighbourhood in Israel, was as taut as a tripwire. Jessica and Menachem were gutting and renovating their house, and they had a large crew of Palestinians who came to work there each day. One morning Menachem was late getting to the worksite (he and Jessica were living elsewhere during the renovation) and the seven or eight workers waiting quietly on the lawn outside caused instant consternation. David burst out of his house and demanded to see all the workers' identity cards. They whipped them quickly out of their pockets and stood docilely in front of him, waiting for him to check their documents as if he were an empowered official. At moments like these, the ugliness of the occupation relationship was uncomfortably clear.

We had been living in Jerusalem a year and a half by then, and I was still having a lot of trouble telling Arab and Jewish men apart. The women were more distinguishable because of their clothing styles and hair, but the young men all dressed the same. If a fellow had a thin moustache, it was a safe bet he was Palestinian; if he had a beard or no facial hair at all, he was probably Jewish. But you could never be sure. As Patrick's assistant, Cindy, and I stood on the terrace watching David checking the workers' papers, I wondered out loud how he knew they were Arabs. Cindy looked shocked. She was an American Jew who had been living in Israel for a dozen years, one of the "modern Orthodox" who wear blue jeans but keep a kosher home and won't drive on the sabbath.

"How could you *not* know they're Arabs?" she said.

"What's different about them?" I asked, genuinely puzzled.

"They walk differently, they dress differently."

"How?"

"I don't know," she said, squirming a little. She didn't want to say "They look more scruffy," but it seemed to me that's what she meant. "They cut their hair differently," she essayed. "They often have green eyes."

Snips of hair, colour of eyes: the subtle ways Arabs and Jews recognized their enemies and the members of their own tribes. As outsiders, we never felt as confident about making solid identifications, which was nerve-racking because the penalty for mislabelling people was acute social embarrassment. In a taxi one day, wonderful wailing desert music was snaking out of the car radio, and after ten minutes I asked the driver, "You like Arab music?" "Jewish music, Madam. This is Israeli music!" he retorted, monumentally offended. Another day Patrick and I had ventured into Talpiot to the biggest toy store in town. We wanted to buy a Nintendo for our boys, since the one we had brought from Canada proved to be non-functional on an Israeli television set. An elderly salesclerk helped us find the right equipment and ushered us through the sale with a courtly friendliness that just didn't feel Israeli at all. Physically, it was impossible to tell whether he was an Arab or a Sephardic Jew, and I wasn't sure I could detect the softly trilled Arabic r in his speech rather than the heavy back-of-the-throat roll that Hebrew-speakers give to the letter. We were tempted to throw some Arabic phrases into our conversation, just to nod in the direction of his identity; but if we had been mistaken and he had been a Jew, it would have been a terrible affront to his dignity. As usual, we did nothing.

At the end of our block was a tiny Sephardic synagogue where the African Jews gathered on Friday evening and Saturday morning. In contrast to the meticulously neat gardens of all our houses, the front yard of the synagogue was a riot of flowering bushes and bougainvillaea so dense that it blocked the view of the ornate grilled windows behind. It was one of the few buildings in Yemin Moshe that had not been renovated, and its sagging doorways and rough-plaster walls over bumpy Jerusalem stone gave an impression of how much more modest the whole neighbourhood had looked at one time. It was mostly men and boys who attended the synagogue, draped in elaborate prayer shawls and intricately embroidered sabbath *kipas,* in contrast to the Ashkenazi congregation, which gathered just twenty metres down the street, North American and European women in their stiff expensive suits and extravagant hats, accompanying soberly dressed Orthodox husbands into their much grander place of worship. With impeccable timing, we always seemed to be leaving our house on Saturday morning for a day at the beach, and had to run the gauntlet of both the Sephardi and Ashkenazi congregations milling about outside their synagogues on our way to the parking lot. No matter how quietly and quickly we tried to slip through their ranks, everything about us was an affront to these religious Jerusalem Jews: our sunglasses, baseball caps and shorts, our armsful of beach mats and umbrellas, our cooler loaded with cheese and salami sandwiches. In Tel Aviv no one would have given us a second glance; in fact, they would have been piling down to the beach themselves in gear far more outlandish than ours. But we were in the holy city, where Saturday was a day of prayer and contemplation, not fun and recreation.

The two brothers who were custodians of the Sephardi synagogue, David and Avshalom, did occasional work for us at our house. David was the grounds-keeper for the YMCA up on King David Street, and Avshalom was a plumber. One day when Avshalom was at our house fixing a leaking toilet, he mentioned that he and his brother had grown up next door, and he pointed to David and Chaia's house, which was by far the grandest on the street, double the size of the others. "After 1967 they kicked us out," he said grimly, "but we didn't go away. Our family was already taking care of the synagogue, so we moved in there. Now we all live in different places around the city but we keep charge of the synagogue, so we can keep an eye on things around here."

Clearly their continued presence on the street was designed to torment David and Chaia. It was not a subject I ever felt comfortable raising with my neighbours, but Tamar filled me in on the story one day. She told me that she and Avraham had bought their house in ruinous condition right after 1967, and that it had been empty for ten or fifteen years before that. "I was glad it was empty," she said. "It would have made me feel very guilty to put people out. But David and Chaia, they displaced the Sharbaf family, and those people stay there at the end of the street just to remind them of what they did. David and Chaia really hate them. They say to me, 'Those people were offered good money to leave. Why didn't they take it?' But I say to them, 'If someone offered you good money to leave, would you take it?'"

When Eva and Eddie moved onto Pele Yoetz Street, a year after we did, things got even livelier. They were Orthodox Jews from Belgium, and their four children already spoke fluent Hebrew because they had been educated in Hebrew day schools in Europe. Eva and Eddie appeared to be "making *aliya*," the phrase that describes the migration of Jews from anywhere in the world to Israel. *Aliya* means ascent or going up in Hebrew, and generally refers to going up to the lectern on Shabbat to read from the Torah. In biblical times, it also applied specifically to going up the mountain to Jerusalem for religious festivals. So the act of immigrating is heavily overlaid with spiritual meaning, implying that the migrant is doing something blessed for his own soul by swelling the ranks of the Jews in Israel. When an Israeli decides to emigrate (usually to New York or Los Angeles) he commits the act of *yerida,* going down, with all the moral disapprobation that direction implies.

Israel loves immigrants from wherever it can get them, but it especially loves the well-heeled, well-educated ones who come from North America and northern Europe. Like all fine commodities, these immigrants are highly prized because they are so scarce. To be blunt, there are not many Jews living in the developed nations who would be willing to give up everything they have achieved to move to a scraggy, hot, ill-tempered place like Israel whose charms take a very long time to grow on you. I was amazed to learn that only about one-fifth of North American Jews have even visited Israel, let alone contemplated resettling there. There was a burst of North American enthusiasm for migrating to Israel in the late sixties and early seventies, in the joyous aftermath of the Six Day War. Shaggy young Jewish idealists, many toting guitars and hippie lifestyles, turned up on Israeli kibbutzim and some stayed permanently. Today, twenty-five years later, the main place where these back-to-the-landers make their presence felt is in the security kibbutzim established on the Golan Heights in the years after 1967, kibbutzim that will probably disappear if Syria makes peace with Israel.

But in more recent years, particularly after Menachem Begin's Likud victory of 1977 drastically changed the tone of Israeli politics from a left-wing glorification of the land to a right-wing and messianic obsession with Judea and Samaria, the only well-off Jews who have considered immigrating to Israel have come from among the ranks of the religiously committed. Which is why Yemin Moshe and other comfortable downtown Jerusalem neighbourhoods like Baka and the German Colony are now full of recent transplants from places like Westchester and Evanston, solidly upper-middle-class Jewish families who were appalled by the increasing moral rot of American cities and made a religion-based "lifestyle decision" to move to Israel.

Eva and Eddie had made the same choice when they immigrated from Antwerp, but because of their European background they seemed much more casual and easygoing about their Orthodoxy than the puritanical North Americans we met so often. Eva was beautiful, with sparkling black eyes, an infectious grin and a sexy accent that was an odd mixture of Flemish and Danish. She was an architect who had gradually completed all her Belgian projects and was now taking a year or so off before starting to drum up business in Israel. In the meantime she decorated their modest house with sure-handed flamboyance, hanging exotic sculptured birds from the living-room ceiling and swagging metres of expensive fabric around the windows. Unlike her North American co-religionists, she did not cover her hair or wear below-the-knee dresses. Her miniskirts were not the shortest, but short enough to turn shocked heads in Jerusalem, and she seemed quite oblivious to the thousand rabbinical exhortations to Jewish women to act and dress modestly. One day when I dropped in to visit, she showed me some dampness on the walls and introduced the Sephardic workman, Moshe, who was going to patch things up. "Oh, but before he starts I'll have to get all that window fabric out of the way or he'll cover it in plaster," she said, and tried to hop up on the back of the couch to pull it down. Her skirt was too tight to make the leap, so she hoisted her clothing up to her hips, the crotch of her pantihose in full view. I was amazed. Moshe was flabbergasted.

Eddie, on the other hand, made a very public display of his religious practice. Every morning on their terrace, he would engage in the elaborate daily prayer for Orthodox men, wrapped in his blue-and-white-striped prayer shawl, or *tallit,* and bedecked in the strange ritual objects of Jewish religious observance. Strapped to his forehead was a tiny black box containing a fragment of Torah scroll, and around his forearm were wrapped phylacteries, or *tefillin,* long black leather straps meant to remind the wearer of his constant bondage to God. Facing the wall of the Old City, he would fix his inner eye on the holy wall-within-the-walls, the Western Wall, one kilometre farther to the east. At first I felt I was intruding on an intensely private moment when I passed on the sidewalk in front of Eddie as he gently bobbed and recited; but he always stopped cheerfully in the middle of what he was doing to chat for a few moments about completely secular matters before returning to his devotions. The rest of the day Eddie spent in his bathing suit, stretched out on the grassy lawn under the olive trees, with business journals and religious books piled up around him, usually dozing gently.

I took to Eva immediately, largely because she took to me. Unlike most of the North American Jews who started off warmly but shut off the friendship tap as soon as they discovered I was a journalist and not one of them, Eva seemed genuinely curious about others and much more relaxed about her position as both an Orthodox Jew and a new Israeli. One Saturday morning shortly after they moved in she knocked on my door.

"Are you Jewish?" she demanded, obviously in a hurry.

I wasn't used to being asked this question point-blank, so I didn't have a stock response. "Not very," I prevaricated.

"Good, you can come and see what's wrong with my refrigerator." She hustled me down the street, talking like a machine-gun. "It always happens on Shabbat, never any other time of the week. I've got fourteen people coming for lunch in two hours, my parents-in-law who are visiting from Belgium and a whole lot of their friends, and the refrigerator has gone dead on me. I can't touch anything electrical, you see." This was the first time I had ever been asked to be a *shabbes* goy, a non-Jew who does certain tasks for Jews that their religion forbids them to perform on the sabbath. Usually these tasks involve electrical matters, a modern extension of the prohibition against kindling a fire on the sabbath. Eva was clearly more concerned about the state of her Shabbat lunch than about the fine points of my ethnic background. (I later learned from an ultra-Orthodox family that Eva had been guilty of a serious transgression by encouraging a Jew — even a half-Jew, even a non-practising, atheist half-Jew — to break the sabbath.) I fiddled with the wires and the sockets, checked the fuses, all to no avail. The refrigerator had gone into permanent catatonia, as far as I could see. Suddenly Eva remembered another fridge still sitting among the packing boxes on the upper landing. We went up, and under Eva's nervous supervision, I plugged in the second refrigerator and was rewarded with a steady purr.

Eva had to call on my services again on Passover. The first night of Pesach is the warmest and most widely celebrated family tradition in Judaism, like Christmas dinner for the Christians. In our second year in Jerusalem, we were invited next door to share the springtime holiday with Avraham and Tamar and their children and grandchildren. (None of us realized at that time that it would be Tamar's last Passover; she died of cancer six months later.) As we were making our way through the fourth ritual glass of wine and were being regaled by Tamar's quiet reading of the exodus of the Hebrews from bondage in Egypt, there was a knock at the door, and Eva's son Elisha was there with orders to track me down. I followed him along the dark path, redolent with the spring smell of roses, but we bypassed his house and continued on to the Ashkenazi synagogue. In the basement reception room, Eva and Eddie were hosting an enormous Passover Seder, but a sudden power failure had left them lightless, heatless and ovenless. They gave me a flashlight, and a gaggle of children took me upstairs to the sanctuary of the synagogue, vast and ghostly in the dark, with only the distant floodlighting on the Old City walls seeping through the tall eastern windows to steer us past the *bima,* the large raised platform in the middle of the room where the Torah scrolls are read every sabbath. I climbed onto a chair and scanned the fuse box, then pushed the large master switch with a satisfying clunk. The synagogue burst into light, and a great roar of approval floated up from below. Nothing else I've ever done has brought me so much public acclaim for so little effort.

One morning shortly after Passover, when her houseful of family guests had returned to Europe and other parts of Israel, Eva came to my house for coffee. Heady smells of lemon and honeysuckle wafted over the terrace, and the water from the sprinklers puddled in the rosebeds. A group of about twenty students from a religious high school shuffled along Pele Yoetz, flinging themselves down on the grass farther along the street to listen to their teacher tell the history of Yemin Moshe and the glorious battles of 1967. They were all girls and all dressed in an unofficial uniform of loose baggy jersey tops and long droopy skirts to the top of their ankle socks. It was the Jerusalem look, designed to make young sexy bodies appear as neutral and unremarkable as possible, and it didn't work at all. I was always amazed by the sheer animal energy of those flocks of Orthodox girls, their extraordinary hair gleaming with good health and their hips swaying with unmistakable feminine grace and female purpose under metres of shapeless fabric. Eva's teenage daughter Natalie went to a religious college and dressed like these girls, I noticed, not like her mother, who was the height of European chic.

"How are your kids adjusting to life in Israel?" I asked Eva. They had been in the country about six months.

"Quite well," she answered. "The fact that they speak Hebrew already has made the transition quite painless. But all of them are having trouble at school with the Israeli kids. It's a totally different culture." In what way, I wanted to know. "Well, they are just so tough and aggressive, even the ones in the religious school system, which is where all my kids go. If a kid beats up other children or acts like a bully in the schoolyard, and the teacher phones the mother to complain about this anti-social behaviour, the mother goes around boasting to her friends about what a *mensch* her little boy is, can you imagine?" Yes, I could imagine all too well. "And I feel sorry for my kids," Eva continued, "because they are caught between the way the Israeli kids behave and the way Eddie and I have brought them up. The other day some Israeli kids said to my Ariel, 'If you keep acting so nice and polite to the teacher, we won't be your friend.' But of course we say to him, 'You treat your teacher with respect or else.' Also, it drives Elisha crazy how the Israeli kids spit all the time." I couldn't help feeling she and her children should check out some inner-city North American schools if they thought the Israelis were tough customers.

As we continued talking that morning, I realized that most of the important things I thought I knew about Eva were wrong, whether it was her political liberalism, her easygoing religious attitudes or even her status in the country. When I asked why she and Eddie had made *aliya,* she looked at me nervously and dropped her voice.

"We haven't," she said, "we're still on tourist visas."

"Why? Don't you intend to live here permanently?"

"Yes, of course we do. But we don't want our children to have to go into the Israeli army unless they want to. When you make *aliya,* the country gives you a lot of economic support, but your kids have to serve in the military. Not that my kids won't want to," she added in a hurry, "but Eddie and I just don't think it's fair that we should force them into that decision by declaring ourselves new immigrants right now." It sounded to me like having one's cake and eating it. "Of course there is a problem for us staying on tourist visas: it's hard to get into a health plan."

I could sense with my back-of-the-head antennae that Avraham had come out on his terrace and was busying himself sweeping and weeding while we talked. "Well, whatever your official status is, I still wonder why you made the move. From the sounds of it, you and Eddie were both doing extremely well in Belgium. Why disrupt the family so much?"

Her eyes suddenly lit up in that disconcerting way I remembered from Gunther, my Christian piano tuner in Toronto. "We are here because of the prophecies," she said. "That is what makes living in Israel so special for us. The prophecies told us we must come back, and the Jews all around the world who ignore that message are really missing something important." I always found this kind of statement a conversation-stopper, and I sat there smiling politely and wondering where to go next.

"I'm a little surprised to hear you talk this way," I ventured. "I was under the impression that Eddie was very religious but that you were much more casual about the whole thing." I was remembering the hiked miniskirt but Eva shook her head vehemently.

"If anything, it's the other way around," she said, "I take all this very seriously." Her hand swept over the panorama of the Old City, encompassing thousands of years of history. "And you know what I take most seriously of all? The prophecy that says the Jews will always be alone, with the world against them. That is so true, so true." I could hear angry sweeping strokes behind me.

But Eva was just getting warmed up. In the imperceptible way that always happened in Israel, a discussion of religion instantly became a political peroration. "You know, I think it's so crazy that in the world media the Israelis are always shown as so tough and strong and the Arabs so weak. As far as I can see it's exactly the opposite. I love watching all the television discussion programs here in Israel — there are so many of them — and they always bring together Arabs and Jews. The Arabs are always so strong, so definite, so clear in their positions, and the Jews are always weak and shuffling around and looking at things from all sides."

I wanted to interject that that was precisely what I liked about the Israelis, that for them everything was an open question, that they were more democratic and less dogmatic than the Arabs. I also thought I should make the point that if the Palestinians sounded so definite in these debates and the Israelis so unsure, perhaps it was because the Palestinians had right on their side and the Israelis knew it. However, a mixture of cowardice and curiosity kept my mouth shut, and Eva was off in another direction.

"We are so different from the Arabs, there's no way we can ever integrate." I agreed completely with this statement, but the examples she chose were unsettling. "We put such a high value on education and they don't, they are not an intellectual race at all. And we believe so strongly in saving life while they believe in killing for their beliefs. Jews are survivors, but that doesn't mean they want to be heroes. If I have to fight to defend myself or my family, of course I will, but the Arabs? They showed an Arab boy on television throwing stones and then they interviewed him and asked, aren't you afraid of what the soldiers will do to you? And he spread his arms wide and said, 'Let them shoot me.' He would become a hero, a martyr, an important person by dying that way. A Jew would never do that."

I wasn't sure she was right. I had just written an article about how the Holocaust had influenced Israeli culture, and I had been struck by the Israeli emphasis on the tens of thousands of Jews who, in the face of impossible odds, resisted the Nazis. The number of these Jewish fighters paled by comparison with the six million who perished more passively, but in the culture of memory in Israel they were given equal weight. There seemed to be a strong psychological need among Israelis to see their European progenitors as warriors rather than victims. The heroes of the Warsaw Ghetto filled the same need for Israeli Jews as the "martyrs" of the intifada did for Palestinians.

So what was Eva's solution to the Arab–Israeli problem? She paused a moment in her stream of words, and then resumed. "Only three things can happen here. Either we leave, and of course that won't happen; or they leave, and I wish with all my heart that that would happen but I am coming to accept that they won't; or we give them some land in the West Bank and build a wall between us. It's not what I want, because the prophecies say we must come back into all the land, but I think it is the only hope for peace."

I thought this was an admirably pragmatic position for someone of Eva's beliefs to come to. If you stripped away all the racist slurs and the prophetic utterances, she really hadn't ended up very far from the sensible and unsentimental position of the Israeli Peace Now movement: you make peace with your enemies, not your friends. What was more disturbing was her belief in the prophecy that the Jews would always dwell alone, because a country that believes that soon allows itself to make its own rules, to live as a pariah in self-imposed exile from the community of nations. That would be the bleakest and most dangerous of all futures for Israel, but Eva's views on the subject are shared by a disturbingly large number of Israelis, both religious and secular.

As she headed back home to make lunch for her younger children, Avraham poked his head between the potted plants and snarled in disgust. "If she didn't come from Europe, I would call her a JAP," he muttered. "You know? A Jewish American Princess. A JEP, that's what I'll call her." The religious Jews, like Eva and Martin, pushed Avraham's button the way no Arab ever could. He had fought so hard for many years for the secular socialist state of Israel he had grown up in, and to watch the religious Jews daily increasing in number and influence drove him crazy. And there were plenty of Israelis who shared *that* sentiment too. An American I knew who had spent twelve years on a kibbutz in the Galilee told me that when you checked out one of the kibbutz cars for the weekend and went to get it tanked up with gas, a sign over the pumps read: "Hit a religious Jew, get 100 kilometres free."

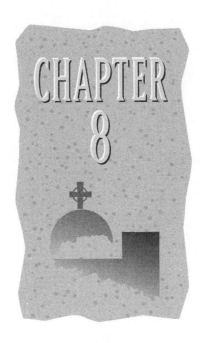

CHAPTER
8

OME THINGS ARE NOT meant to be. I went to the *ulpan,* one of
the network of hundreds of language schools dotted around
Israel, and dashed myself against the stern and unforgiving rock
of the Hebrew language four hours a day, four days a week for
five months. In the end I gave it up as a bad job and admitted
defeat. But my time there introduced me to another segment of the
Jerusalem world, one of the strangest and most intriguing of all, the
international Christians.

I had picked my *ulpan* simply on the basis of proximity to my
house, so without giving it any thought I ended up at the YMCA on
King David Street. Most *ulpanim* in Israel are designed to handle new
Jewish immigrants from all over the world. They are a key factor in
the resettling process, what the Israelis refer to rather graphically as

absorption, a word that always conjured up for me an image of Polish, Kurdish and Brazilian Jews being sucked up into a large porous sponge. Recently the overwhelming number of *ulpanim* have catered to immigrants from the former Soviet Union, almost half a million of whom have come to Israel in the past five years, fearing a rise in anti-Semitism at home. The other, much smaller but highly distinctive immigrant wave has been the Falashas, the twenty thousand Ethiopian Jews who were dramatically airlifted out of that war-torn country by an Israeli rescue mission. The *ulpan* is the government instrument by which these disparate Jews are moulded into incipient Israelis. It teaches not only Hebrew language but Israeli culture: history, holidays, customs and attitudes. In short, it teaches nationalism and it does a very good job of it.

But the *ulpan* at the YMCA was a different animal, given the Y's Christian affiliation. Because of the special peculiarities of Jerusalem society, it had an eclectic student body. In my class, for example, two of us were foreign journalists, eight were either Christians or messianic Jews, one was an American Jewish novelist spending a year in the city, two others were Jews from the United States there to study or spend part of the year with their children and grandchildren, one was a Greek boy from the Old City and four were Palestinians. The only Jewish immigrants in our group were an American mother and daughter who whined incessantly for months, learned absolutely no Hebrew and then mysteriously disappeared one day, probably back to North America. They didn't look like potential Israeli material to me.

The Palestinians were brave, I thought, to enter a situation dominated by English-speaking foreigners. Two of them turned up only sporadically, but the two who stayed the course were an interesting pair. Her name was Amal, and she wanted to become a nurse in the Israeli health system. She planned to spend a year on language study before enrolling in the nurses' training program at Hebrew University. Over coffee on the YMCA terrace during our break one day, she told me in her halting breathy English that she had to get out and make a profession for herself because of her disastrous family situation. She was the seventh of a family of eleven girls, a misfortune of almost unspeakable magnitude in Palestinian life. Rather than sit around waiting for whatever dregs her parents would be likely to find for her in the way of suitors, Amal was quietly taking her life in her own hands. She was by far the best Hebrew student in the class, but her shyness was so painful that I often wondered how she would fare among a pack of robust, self-confident Israeli nursing students.

Her male counterpart in the class was Samer, who wanted to become a goldsmith. "I have to study Hebrew," he told me, "so I can apprentice myself to one of the Jewish goldmakers because they are the best." Goldsmithing sounded so medieval to me, a strange profession for a young man to hanker after, but Samer explained how crucial it was to Palestinian society. "When people marry here, the boy must pay a price for the girl. These days the usual price is around 3,000 Jordanian dinars" — $5,000. "Then the girl takes that money and buys gold jewellery with it. That's why the shops in the Old City are always full of girls with their mothers buying gold." Samer lived in Ramallah, just north of Jerusalem, and there were many days when he was late or couldn't make it to class at all because the roads from the West Bank were clogged with roadblocks or sealed off by the Israeli army.

The dominant group in the class were the fundamentalist Christians and messianic Jews, who turned out, in Jerusalem at least, to be two sides of the same coin. The Christians came from all over the map, but predominantly from the southern United States. In our class we also had one from South Africa, one from Sweden and two from Switzerland. These are Christians who take the words of the biblical prophecies and of Revelation absolutely literally: although they can distinguish between the earthly Jerusalem and the heavenly one that is supposed to float down from on high at the End of Days to gather up the righteous, they do believe that by physically being in the earthly Jerusalem and somehow lending their support to the movement of Jews back to Israel they will help bring about the Second Coming of Jesus Christ. Revelation specifies that 144,000 Jews, 12,000 from each of the twelve tribes, must return to Israel in order to get Armageddon started, and there are already well over four million Jews in residence in the country with no sign of anything happening, but the Christians seem to believe the more the merrier. They also believe that Christianity has, over the centuries, moved too far away from its roots in Judaism and that only by practising a more Judaicized Christianity in Zion itself will the prophecies be fulfilled.

The messianic Jews, or Jews for Jesus, as most of the world calls them, are few in number in Israel but increasing rather rapidly in the United States and in England. They are Jews who accept that the Messiah their rabbis are always waiting for has already come, in the person of Jesus. They worship as Jews, keeping all the Jewish holidays — at least the ones that Jesus would have kept in his time — and they don't celebrate Christmas. What the Israelis hate about them is that they proselytize, albeit subtly and with little fanfare, among the young, the poor and the disaffected of the Israeli Jewish community.

In fact the Israelis are uncomfortable around the entire question of Christianity. On the one hand, there are the large traditional churches, like the Greek Orthodox, the Roman Catholic and the Anglican, who minister primarily to the Palestinians, so the Israelis see them as political foes. Only in 1994, forty-six years late, did the Vatican finally agree to recognize the state of Israel. On the other hand, the Protestant Christian fundamentalists, who number some forty million in the American Bible Belt alone, are crazy about Israel and want to assist in the great work of Zionism because they believe it brings them closer to the End of Days. Theologically, this puts them on the same wavelength as Jews like my neighbours Eva and

Eddie, who are awaiting the Messiah for the first time. The problem is that, according to the Christian scenario, once every Jew in the world has been gathered in to Zion, the Messiah will return and all those Jews will instantly convert to Christianity. This differs drastically from the Jewish script for the great day, which involves the restoration of Solomon's Temple on the Temple Mount and the procession of dead Jewish souls out of their graves and in through the now-sealed Golden Gate in the wall of the Old City. (The shady Jewish tycoon Robert Maxwell, who died mysteriously in 1992, bought himself a front-row grave on the Mount of Olives opposite the eastern Old City walls so that he can be one of the first through the gate when the Messiah comes.)

The Israeli government flirts constantly and dangerously with these fundamentalist Christians because they represent significant political and financial clout in the United States. A little Christian pressure here and there on key congressmen has done wonders for backup support for the Jewish lobby on Capitol Hill. The Israeli telephone company, Bezek, panders quite shamelessly to both religious Jews and Christian Zionists around the world. First it established a fax service so that Jews could fax prayers to be folded up and placed in the cracks in the Western Wall by an observant *kipa*-wearing employee of the phone company. Then in the spring of 1993 they set up a Jerusalem prayer hotline so that supplicants can call long distance and get an all-purpose Christian at the other end of the phone to pray with them from the Holy City, which is thought to be in the same area code as God.

In one sense, the Israelis would say, this is just smart marketing. We have religion to sell so we might as well sell it aggressively. An enormous percentage of Israel's tourist dollars come from its Christian pilgrimage tours. But the courting of Christian fundamentalist support seems all wrong for a country that rails against Islamic fundamentalism among its Arab neighbours and generally detests its own black-hat zealots in the *haredi* community. Unfortunately, throughout its short history Israel has been largely isolated from the rest of the developed world, and that isolation has forced it into awkward alliances with unsavoury groups: those white South Africans, for example, who are quick to draw a parallel between their struggle against black rights and Israel's struggle against the Palestinians, or a whole string of unpleasant Central and South American dictatorships that have been steady customers for Israel's military industries. One of the most beneficial side effects of peace in the region will be Israel's ability to widen its circle of friends.

My Toronto conversation with Gunther the piano tuner was the only one I had knowingly had with a messianist before I came to Israel. Now, in my *ulpan,* I seemed to be surrounded by them. There was Ron, a New York Jew who had made *aliya* twenty years earlier with his wife and who had accepted Jesus (or Yeshua, in Hebrew) as his personal saviour while he was working as a shepherd on a kibbutz in the Galilee. It didn't take long before the kibbutz booted him and his family out because of their beliefs, at which point they moved to the northern Israeli town of Tiberias, a hotbed of Christian activity because of Jesus' prominent association with the area around the Sea of Galilee. Here Jesus walked on the water, divided the loaves and the fishes, preached the Sermon on the Mount. Ron and Aliza began to get heavily involved with messianic Judaism there, but they also continued to be persecuted by Jews hostile to their ministry. "They followed our kids home from school," Ron told us one day. "They poisoned our dog. We had to get out of there. And besides, we felt we were needed more here in Jerusalem."

By the time I met them, they were running a busy little social-work agency, sponsored by all the Protestant churches in the city and by whatever donations they could cobble together from supporters around the world. Their clients were mostly from the ranks of deluded believers, either Christians or Jews, who had felt the impulse to make their way to Jerusalem but who had no means of sustaining themselves once they got there. "God will provide" was the prevailing philosophy of these spiritual waifs, and of course every time somebody competent or compassionate stepped in to help them they saw it as prima-facie evidence of the rightness of that belief. Ron and Aliza ran interference for these people with the Israeli immigration authorities and helped them scrounge food, clothing, shelter and jobs. They themselves lived in a rather spiffy ranch-style bungalow in Mevasseret Zion, one of Jerusalem's new satellite communities. They told me a parish of their Christian supporters in Florida had undertaken to pay for their car and their rent.

Ron and Aliza knew it was more than their lives were worth to proselytize openly on the streets of Jerusalem, so they were using the classic approach of religious groups everywhere: help the needy and hope to snag a few souls in the process. But they had one novel method I hadn't encountered elsewhere. Because of the religious drawing power of Jerusalem, there were Christians around the world willing to come and work in the city in exchange for mere room and board and the chance to learn Hebrew. Ron had brought three such women with him to the *ulpan*. (We quickly dubbed them his harem.) Agnes and Erna were pale, serious Swiss girls in their twenties; Stella was a cheerful widowed grandmother from Cape Town. All of them were doing live-in domestic work for Jewish families for free, their only concession being the morning time off to attend Hebrew classes. In two of the families, they were caring for Down's syndrome or handicapped children, so their jobs were far from easy. The idea, as Ron explained it to me, was a kind of passive proselytizing: "We hope that the Jews will appreciate the special level of spiritual commitment these people bring into their homes and will gradually begin to see that it comes from their belief in Yeshua." It just looked to me like a cheap way for an Israeli wife and mother to get herself some dedicated full-time help.

Then there was Bradley, a lean, keen young Christian from North Carolina who wore a small Star of David around his neck to indicate his solidarity with the Jews of Israel. He was having a terrible struggle with Hebrew, worse than any of us, and every time our good-natured Israeli teacher, Racheli, would put him on the spot and make him pronounce a sentence, his face would flush a truly alarming red and his whole body would oscillate from stagefright. One day at coffee I gently asked him why he was putting himself through this ordeal.

"It will help me to serve the Lord's plan," he said. "I am here to help the Israelis any way I can, and if I can speak their language I can do so much more for them." Then he blushed and lowered his voice as if about to tell me an amorous secret. "Also, I have made a personal commitment to translate the entire Bible from the original Hebrew. But I'm still a long way from my goal." I'll say; Bradley could hardly tell an *aleph* from a *gimel* after two months of classes.

One day, Bradley wasn't there any more. Another student, Dennis, the English pastor of a small Protestant congregation in Jerusalem, filled me in on his whereabouts. "He's gone to Russia," he said.

"Russia?" I was astounded. "Why? How?"

"He went with Operation Exodus."

I continued to look blank.

"It's a Christian rescue operation for Jews. Some Christian businessmen have hired a boat at Haifa — this is its third voyage — to bring Jews who want to get out of Russia and immigrate to Israel. They go through the Mediterranean and up the Bosporus through the Black Sea to Odessa to pick them up. They're hoping to bring about five hundred on this trip, I think." He looked at the date on his watch. "They should be on their way back by now."

Bradley never returned to the *ulpan*, but shortly thereafter I ran into him at a political lecture at the Zionist Confederation Centre

near my house and I insisted he join me for coffee afterwards. I had
to understand why he had been off to the ends of the earth corralling
Jews. Bradley never went anywhere without his well-thumbed Bible,
so he was able to literally quote me chapter and verse.

"Here it is in Isaiah 60:8–10," he began. "'Who are these that fly
along like clouds, like doves to their nests?'" That's the Jews, he
explained. "'Surely the islands look to me; in the lead are the ships of
Tarshish bringing your sons from afar, with their silver and gold, to
the honour of the Lord your God, the Holy One of Israel.'"

"Okay," I said, "I get the reference to the ships. But where does it
say that Christians have to get involved in bringing the Jews here?"

He flipped the pages confidently. "Isaiah 49:22. 'This is what the
Sovereign Lord says: "See, I will beckon to the Gentiles, I will lift up
my banner to the peoples; they will bring your sons in their arms and
carry your daughters on their shoulders."'" So far so good, but Bradley
had a further scriptural point to make. "The Bible even tells us we
have to rescue them from Russia, from the north. Look here, Isaiah
43:5–6." The verses read, "I will bring your children from the east and
gather you from the west. I will say to the north, 'Give them up!' and
to the south, 'Do not hold them back.'" I noted that all four points of
the compass seemed to have been included in the passage, but Bradley
was convinced. "Why would it say to the north, 'Give them up?' It's a
prophecy of glasnost, of the destruction of the evil Communist
empire. The Jews couldn't get out before — now they can!"

As it happened, some Israeli journalists had been taken along on
this odyssey, so I was able to read a full account of the trip the next
week in the *Jerusalem Post* magazine. It seemed that the Jewish
Agency, historically the official body responsible for bringing Jews
to Israel from all over the world, wanted nothing to do with this
Christian scheme. But Israel's minister of absorption at the time, an
ultra-Orthodox Sephardi named Yitzhak Peres, saw it as a way to
swell the ranks of Jews in Israel and wasn't too fussy about who paid

the bill. He did, however, send along a watchdog team of ten *haredim* and a group of modern Orthodox Jewish volunteers to keep an eye on the Christians and messianic Jews on board and make sure they didn't proselytize. The voyage was fraught with tension, although the secular Russian immigrants appeared to be largely oblivious to the religious storm swirling around them and slept most of the way to Haifa. The article was entirely about the Christian initiative, but I noticed that the magazine printed no pictures of the thirty Christians on board, only of intense *haredim* and smiling immigrants.

The *ulpan* wasn't the only place I got a heavy dose of Christians. Our children attended the Anglican School, the only English-language educational institution of any size in Jerusalem and one of just two in all of Israel. It was housed in a building of extraordinary beauty on Hanevi'im Street, constructed in a graceful semicircle around a lovely front garden of olive trees, flowering bushes and towering pines. Although beautiful, the place had been built in 1896 as a hospital and was hopelessly out of date in terms of educational facilities or even basic comforts. Through the chilly Jerusalem winters, the students shivered in dank, stony classrooms where, my children complained, the teachers kept tiny bar-heaters snuggled up tight beside their own desks.

We weren't thrilled about sending our boys to a Christian private school, but we had no choice. And if it had to be any church, at least the Anglicans sounded familiar, low-key and civilized. My father's family was Anglican, I had been surrounded by Anglicans growing up in Toronto, I had even spent a delightful day once upon a time in the palace of the dean of Canterbury and the only thing remotely religious he had done was slip my friend and me little prayer cards as he gave us a tour of his famous cathedral. We felt assured that we would not have to spend the next two years fighting a rearguard secular action against dogma.

So we were more than a little surprised, the first day we visited the school, to find etched over the central portal the words "The London Society for Promoting Christianity Among the Jews." This sounded more blatant than we had bargained for. Sure enough, like so many things in Jerusalem, the Anglican School was not quite what it seemed. It was an offshoot of an obscure Anglican missionary society founded in England in 1809 by a group of evangelists who believed that the End of Days was fast approaching. The stunning events of the French Revolution encouraged them in this belief. Over the next years, these fervent evangelists raised money and got themselves to Jerusalem, where they built Christ Church, the oldest Protestant church in the Middle East, just inside the Old City walls opposite the Tower of David. Immediately these Christians began ministering to the miserable and poverty-stricken Jews they found there, and by the end of the nineteenth century they had built a hospital on Hanevi'im Street. The Jews, somewhat alarmed that their community's medical needs were being served by Christians, quickly initiated medical services and a hospital-building program of their own.

After the 1948 War of Independence, the hospital was converted to an international school, which now caters to about three hundred children from forty-five countries and with thirty mother tongues. It is not a particularly popular institution in Jerusalem because its students are drawn from a number of subgroups the Israelis neither like nor trust. Almost half the families work for the United Nations, an organization the Israelis view as being completely pro-Arab. Fifteen percent of the students are from Palestinian families who see an English education as a ticket out of despair for their children. Most of the foreign journalists and diplomats based in Jerusalem send their kids to the Anglican School. And then there are the Christian families from a huge variety of sects, many living in the West Bank and ministering to the local Arab population. Although the school no longer receives funds from what is now called the Church's Ministry Among the Jews, it still lives in their buildings and is run largely by evangelical teachers, most of whom have never been connected with the Anglican Church proper in their lives.

And it still has that extremely inappropriate name etched over its portal. The impropriety was noted in 1992 by the Archbishop of Canterbury himself, who must have had it drawn to his attention that he was still the titular head of this diplomatically embarrassing branch of the Anglican Church that existed in Jerusalem for the sole purpose of converting Jews. He quietly withdrew his patronage from the sect, leaving its Jerusalem followers devastated.

One day Patrick and I walked over to Christ Church in the Old City to see how the canon was taking the bad news. He showed us around the church, which was a masterpiece of the double message, designed to make Jews feel right at home. It was square like a synagogue, rather than oblong like a church. The wooden reredos at the front resembled the ark that holds the Torah scrolls, and written on it in Hebrew were the Ten Commandments, the Lord's Prayer and the Apostle's Creed, just to keep everybody happy. The altar bore a large handsome menorah, and the cross depicted in the stained-glass window looked more like a tree. A very small traditional cross was displayed near the back, and the canon explained that until 1948 the church never contained a real cross, which is, after all, a highly off-putting symbol for most Jews. But when the city was divided, the Jordanian army swept through the sector it controlled, destroying every synagogue in sight. Its soldiers burst into Christ Church and were about to lay waste to it when the church staff rushed in with a cross and persuaded the Jordanians that, appearances to the contrary, this really was a Christian church. Since then, a cross has always been kept handy, just in case.

It wasn't long before our children started coming home from the Anglican School singing those infectious little songs:

Who's the king of the jungle? — oo — oo
Who's the king of the sea? — walla — walla — walla
Who's the king of the universe
And who's the king of me?
J – E – S – U – S – yes!
He's the king of the sea. . . .

Teachers were regularly bearing witness at the morning assemblies, and a Korean mother at the first PTA meeting got up to tell us about a miracle that had happened to her family regarding the downing of that Korean airliner by the Russians a few years ago. Religious studies seemed to take up an inordinate amount of our boys' school day, and I was getting a bit concerned.

I needn't have worried. One day our nine-year-old, Sam, casually mentioned that Melachy in his class had told him that the world was going to explode in the year 2000 and we'd all have to go and live in outer space. I asked him to go back to Melachy and get more details. A few days later, with much hilarity and head-shaking, he brought me up to date on his research. "She thinks *Jesus* is going to blow up the world when he comes back again. Melachy and Evelina and practically all the other girls in the class believe it too. But it's ridiculous, and besides it's not true. Remember after the flood, God told Noah he would never destroy the world again? So why would he go back on his word? Those girls are crazy." I realized that Sam's ability to do biblical textual analysis far surpassed mine, and I ceased worrying about the matter.

Being outsiders to both the Israeli and the Arab communities, we rather expected the school to bring a cohesive identity to our Jerusalem lives, but that never really happened. The client groups that used the school remained discrete: the UN bloc, the Christian bloc and, although it was the tiniest, the journalists' bloc.

The self-containment of the United Nations families was amazing to behold. In our son Gabriel's class there was a charming Irish sprite named Pauline who had been born in Jerusalem twelve years earlier and had lived there all her life. She spoke English with an American accent, because the majority of students at the school were Americans and she had lived among them forever. She spoke not a word of either Hebrew or Arabic and showed not the slightest interest in the community or city in which she was living. Nor did she have any meaningful connection to Ireland, except for summer visits to grandparents. She lived entirely within the artificial world the United Nations creates wherever it exists, shopping in UN stores and drawing her friends from UN circles. Her father did not work with the UN forces in Jerusalem: he had been posted to Afghanistan for a number of years and had just recently been switched to South Africa. He and his wife had decided years before that Jerusalem was the safest, most conveniently located and most stable place with a full UN infrastructure for them to raise their family. His amiable wife, Ann, lived a life of indolent luxury, with kaffeeklatsches in the morning and tennis in the afternoon. She confided to me at a school Christmas party that her husband had only two years to go to early retirement and she was dreading the day. "We haven't lived together except for holidays for the past twenty years," she said, her huge blue eyes rounding in apprehension, "and now we'll have to move back to dreary old Ireland, where we know no one, and live on his pension, and be cooped up together in the same house for the rest of our lives!" Certainly one could sympathize with the parents, but I was more intrigued with what would happen to their rootless children, who were in the Middle East but not of it and complete strangers to their home country.

Perhaps the UN would become their life as well; it was the only culture they knew. The mother of another of Gabriel's friends was Burmese by extraction but had been born and brought up entirely in the Middle East as a UN brat and had married into the UN and stayed on. Kathy had more initiative, though. She had learned fluent

Hebrew and trained as a dentist, and was now working for the Jerusalem municipality doing dental education programs in the city's disadvantaged school districts. "It's really an uphill battle working with the Sephardi Moroccan families," she told me one day when we were driving our boys down to Tel Aviv to a Guns n' Roses concert in Hayarkon Park. "I ask the kids, do you all have toothbrushes? And they'll say, yes, we have one for the whole family! Then I ask, how often do you brush your teeth? And they say, every Friday before Shabbat, when we take our showers." She sighed. "We have a lot of education to do." She sounded like an Ashkenazi Israeli.

Although the UN bloc outnumbered the Christians, it was the religious families that set the cultural stamp on the school. We would gather periodically for the universal rites of educational passage, the Christmas play, the spring concert, the summer fair, the graduation ceremonies in June, and on these occasions we would be reminded of the evangelical nature of the enterprise. Incredibly clean-cut teenagers would sing their own compositions about the joy and the difficulty of witnessing, telling the world about their personal relationship with Jesus. "I'm sixteen years old, and for the last fourteen or fifteen years my life has just been *heck*," a young guitarist shared with us one evening, "but now that I've found Jesus everything is great and I write and perform all my songs for him. This one's called 'The Prodigal Son.'" The Christmas play at the Anglican School contained none of the namby-pamby multiculturalism I'd become used to in my children's "winter festival" pageants back home in Toronto. This was Christmas straight up, with manger, Herod, star, shepherds and Christ the Redeemer. It was a touch disconcerting when we would launch into the inevitable hymns at these gatherings and certain members of the audience would close their eyes and lift their hands to heaven as we sang. It occurred to me that evangelical Christians seldom worship in mixed crowds. But Jerusalem regularly threw a mismatched bunch of us together, half the room swaying in ecstasy and the other half mumbling in embarrassment.

Messianism in Jerusalem, of both the Jewish and Christian varieties, was so prevalent that it soon ceased to be remarkable. One day when I was shopping in the Supersol, an attractive dark-haired woman of my own age approached me with a loaf of bread in her hand and asked if I spoke English. She was from Montreal, and the two of us puzzled over the Hebrew bread label, trying to determine whether it was a whole wheat loaf.

"Do you miss Montreal?" I asked, as we pawed through the bread section together.

"Well, I certainly don't miss the winters," she said.

But we were just coming off one of the coldest, snowiest winters in Jerusalem history, and I pointed out that the bad weather had followed us from Canada.

"Ah yes, but of course that's because Moshiach" — the Messiah — "is coming," she commented matter-of-factly. "It's all foretold."

During the Branch Davidian crisis in Waco, Texas, the local press discovered a Jerusalem angle to the story. It seems David Koresh had been in town the year before, trying to drum up recruits for his community. He had succeeded in snagging just one benighted Israeli, a musician, who returned with him to Texas and subsequently perished in the suicidal inferno. The *Jerusalem Post* interviewed a friend of his who recalled Koresh: "Sure I remember him," he said. "He was always spouting biblical verses about Armageddon. To tell you the truth, though, I didn't pay too much attention to him because in this town you're always running into people like that." That story gave me a whole new perspective on Jerusalem, a place where David Koresh was just a ho-hum kind of guy.

In the fall of 1992, the Canadian novelist Mordecai Richler and his wife, Florence, were in town, and we invited them to join us for a regular Jerusalem ritual: the Friday afternoon Franciscan procession of the cross in the Old City, down the Via Dolorosa to the Church of the Holy Sepulchre. First we had to run the gauntlet of the hawkers and tourist shops to climb to the top of the Via Dolorosa, where the First Station of the Cross was located inside the courtyard of an Islamic boys' school. As the courtyard gradually filled up around us with pilgrims, mostly well-scrubbed middle Americans in polyester pantsuits and golf caps, Mordecai commented, "I've spent my entire life trying to avoid people like this. What am I doing here?" By the time we had shuffled down to the Fourth Station, we had all had enough. This was clearly an event for participants, not spectators. Mordecai began lobbying for a drink, but we were out of luck. The Old City of Jerusalem is essentially a Moslem town, and few public places serve alcohol. We walked through the Moslem and Christian quarters, made our way out through the New Gate and across Paratroopers' Road to the imposing Roman Catholic Notre Dame de Paris hostel for pilgrims. There you could always get booze.

In spite of the heavy Christian presence in our lives, however, when it came to the Christmas season our family was very aware that we were completely out of step with the overwhelmingly Jewish community around us. We got a taste of what Jews in North America must have gone through for decades before most of them succumbed to the cultural pressure of the majority and began buying "Hanukkah bushes" and distributing presents. Christmas in the Holy Land felt like an obscure underground secret, a samizdat ritual, and all the more charming for that.

The first week of December, having canvassed the Jerusalem stores and found them wanting, we took a day trip to Tel Aviv to do our Christmas shopping. What a pleasure it was wandering through the sloppy but lively Dizengoff Centre, with just the usual weekday smattering of Israeli shoppers and no "Silver Bells" on the Muzak. The complete lack of Christmas hype on radio and television had also lowered our children's consumer expectations, so we bought more frugally and more contentedly than we ever had in Canada.

As we tried to leave the seaside city at the end of the day, we got caught in a flash flood that instantly submerged low-lying streets. In our sturdy Volvo we were able to make our way through deeper water than most of the cars, but eventually we were stymied as well. Every direction we tried led to either an unmoving traffic snarl or a lake. Consulting the map, we decided to try one further escape route, the road through the ultra-Orthodox village of Bnei Brak, the Tel Aviv equivalent of Mea Shearim. As we crawled through the *haredi* community, we realized that this was the first night of Hanukkah. Dusk had just fallen, and through grey sheets of rain we saw one apartment window after another begin to glow with the flames of the Hanukkah candles. Shadowy figures of men with long forelocks bent over the heads of their children as they sang the traditional blessing. In Hassidic homes, fathers caught up their babies and twirled them around in joyous dances. It was an unforgettable sight.

Now we had our presents, but there was more shopping to do. So far we had managed to resist the kitschy pull of Bethlehem, which was located in the occupied West Bank only a ten-minute drive south of Jerusalem, but as Christmas drew near we felt an over-whelming urge to purchase a hand-carved Bethlehem nativity scene. Christmas cards direct from the birthplace seemed like a good idea too. And we definitely needed some Christmas ornaments, in case we should be able to locate a tree. Besides, you can remain a snob about places like Bethlehem for only so long. Even though experts had convinced us that it was the most unlikely place (and Christmas the most unlikely time of year) for Jesus' birth, we were all curious to see it.

It was another raw rainy day when we pulled into Manger Square, paid a few shekels' protection money to a local Palestinian urchin not to break into our car, skirted the tour buses belching diesel fumes and the Israeli soldiers on watch-towers around the square, and entered the Church of the Nativity. In spite of its world-wide Christian reputation, Bethlehem is quickly becoming a Moslem town, and since the beginning of the intifada quite a surly and dangerous one at that. Six years in a row, Bethlehem was closed for Christmas by the Israeli authorities for security reasons, opening again only after the signing of the Rabin-Arafat peace proposal in 1993. Bethlehem was the only place in the Middle East where I witnessed gunfire. It has always been a devilishly difficult town for the Israelis to control because of its confusing warren of back alleys where PLO and Hamas insurgents can melt away without a trace.

The Church of the Nativity evokes the same feelings as the Church of the Holy Sepulchre in Jerusalem: skepticism and amazement. The church is indisputably old, dating from the fourth century, which makes it possibly the oldest Christian church in the world. But it is simply a gloomy cavernous barn crammed with ornate hanging oil-lamps and soot-covered wall decorations. The only detail of historical interest, apart from some good floor mosaics, is the tiny front door you have to crouch down to enter, apparently a remnant of Crusader days, when the large front door was shrunk to its present size to discourage soldiers from entering the church on horseback. At the front of the church, steps lead down to the grotto, where a four-teen-pointed star embedded in the floor is meant to mark the exact spot of the birth. Once again, as in Jerusalem, the chasm between believer and non-believer is absolute: the groups of pilgrims visiting the grotto with us were in transcendence, while we found the scene completely unbelievable and verging on the silly.

As at the Holy Sepulchre, jurisdictional disputes at the Church of the Nativity are an ongoing nightmare. Fifteen oil-lamps burn around the birth grotto: six belong to the Greeks, five to the Armenians and four to the Latin church. Two Christmases ago, a punch-out occurred at the grotto between Syrian Orthodox and Greek

Orthodox monks over the positioning of the Greek patriarch's chair. Israeli police and army officers intervened, stopped the fight and negotiated a location for the chair that was acceptable to both sides. Lord knows who will settle such disputes when the Israeli army withdraws from the West Bank.

In the first tourist shop we entered across Manger Square after visiting the church, the Palestinian family that ran it were in a serious holiday funk. "So few tourists — the intifada — it is very hard for us," said a middle-aged Arab woman as she showed us various olive wood nativity models.

"Yes, but the big problem is the tour guides," chimed in her husband. "The guides bring the tourists to the church, but then they tell them it's too dangerous to shop here in Manger Square. They say, let's all get back on the bus and I'll take you to a safe place on the outskirts of town where you can buy all the same things. And, of course, they have an arrangement with those shops so they get a big percentage of the sales. We are helpless."

As they wrapped our set of carved figures and our packs of Christmas cards, we asked about real Christmas decorations, the shiny tacky pieces of glitz without which the season wouldn't be festive in our jaded North American eyes. Their cousins' stationery shop would certainly have such things, they advised us, and gave us complicated instructions into the back streets of Bethlehem. When we set out, two things happened simultaneously: the heavens opened in another seasonal deluge, and it was suddenly closing time, with heavy metal shutters banging into place one after another. We ran through the rain to the cousins' shop, which was still half-open. The owners looked nervously at each other, torn between the prospect of the best sale that day and the wrath of the intifada committee. They stayed open for us. But their stock was pitiful and expensive, a couple of boxes of glass balls, three or four lengths of gold and red tinsel, no strings of lights. We bought everything they had and scurried back to

the car, desperately anxious to get back to the dryness and comfort of
Yemin Moshe.

The final requirement, and the most important for a legitimate
Christmas celebration, was a tree. But there was no place to buy such
a thing in Israel. Since only a tiny handful of people in the country
wanted one, there was no commercial market for trees at all. Nor
could you just stride out into the woods and hack one down, since
felling trees is illegal in Israel; this is the country that made the desert
bloom, after all. However, even in a country that virtually deifies
trees, sound husbandry dictates that forests must be culled from time
to time, so the Israeli government turned this activity into a bit of
festive public relations. If you were a foreign diplomat or journalist or
with the UN or any of the Christian churches in the country, you
received a notice to turn up on the edge of a specified forest (a different one each year) to get your free Christmas tree.

My friend Helen and I set out for the Ben Shemen forest on the
appointed day, accompanied by the usual December rainstorm. When
we arrived and bounced up the forest road to the opening where the
distribution was taking place, it became clear that this was going to be
a serious free-for-all. Crowds of Christians bunched around the edge
of the clearing, and when a truck would pull in heaped with mud-
encrusted baby pines, they would surge around the vehicle and strip
it bare. Then we would wait for the next truck. The worst were the
nuns, kitted out in gumboots and vicious elbows, who were banking
successfully on a certain degree of chivalry in the mostly male gathering. For just a second, I got a flash of how we must look to the Israeli
forest workers and soldiers who were handling the operation: an
aggressive pack of foreign primitives, fighting over the meaningless
totems of their strange, idolatrous religion.

And so we managed it, our lopsided little tree with its pathetic
decorations (plus a string of twinkle lights Patrick had managed to
dig up on a journalistic foray into Jordan) and a sparse sprinkling of

presents underneath. A Palestinian butcher shop in East Jerusalem provided a splendid turkey. On Christmas Eve we climbed up to the YMCA for a lugubrious but seasonal evening of Christmas carols, and when we stepped outside onto the Y's broad stone terrace at eleven o'clock at night, the temperature dropped those crucial two degrees and the incessant wall of Jerusalem winter rain transformed itself into soft wet snow. We walked homeward and stopped near the French consulate just at the lip of our valley. The stones of the Old City shimmered before us in a lacy white mist, and from the YMCA's bell-tower behind us the carillon wafted out the strains of "O Little Town of Bethlehem," whose lights we could see faintly glowing over the horizon to the south. Such is the power of myth over reality that it seemed like pure magic.

CHAPTER 9

M Y FRIEND RAWDA AND I had been trying to organize a visit to the West Bank village of Surif for about six weeks. Everything in Palestinian life seemed to take that long, often for no discernible reason. A foreign diplomat in Tel Aviv had advised us that if we ever wanted help, advice, information or introductions from a Palestinian, it was important to make a preliminary face-to-face visit first, simply to pay your respects and drink tea. After that, you could call up and expect help. This encrusted civility contrasted startlingly with Israeli casualness and lack of ceremony. For a journalist, the Israelis were dreamboats: you'd call them up for the first time, even very important ones, and chances were excellent they'd pick up their own phones and settle in immediately for a forty-five-minute chat.

Rawda was an Israeli Arab, born in the town of Nazareth, who had married an American Lutheran church worker. They lived in East Jerusalem with their two daughters, who went to the Anglican School. Our friendship developed in the school parking lot, particularly when we discovered that we had a common interest in Palestinian embroidery. I wanted to write an article about how this handicraft work fit into the cultural and economic life of the women of the West Bank, and I had already made one visit to the Mennonite Centre in East Jerusalem, which had been encouraging and selling this work worldwide since the fifties. The day of my visit, the head of the centre introduced me to Zena, a tall, thin, serious woman in full Islamic garb who ran the women's sewing cooperative in the West Bank town of Surif, down near Hebron. Zena spoke no English, but she indicated that I would be welcome to visit their centre and meet the village women who worked there.

Rawda had her own reasons for wanting to visit Surif. She and her husband, Greg, neither of whom were ordained, were essentially sponsored in the Middle East by a group of Lutheran parishes in the United States to do Christian education among the Palestinians. She was looking for a wholesale supply of Palestinian embroidery that she could ship to the parishes for sale at local church fairs to raise money for their mission.

Both of us were frankly nervous about travelling into the West Bank without benefit of male company. We had access only to yellow-plated cars, and to drive into the wilds of the Hebron mountains in them, even with Rawda speaking Arabic, seemed foolhardy. After several days of dithering, Rawda finally announced that we couldn't go now because Ramadan was about to start, so we could forget the whole next month. Why, I wondered? "Because during Ramadan, people don't eat anything all day and it does weird things to their heads," explained Rawda. "The very religious Moslems in particular can get quite unpredictable. Besides, Greg says no." That was that.

A month later, we started our planning again. This time we decided to hire an Arab car and driver from Guiding Star, the East Jerusalem agency that specialized in ferrying diplomats and journalists around the region and into Jordan. We could not phone Zena to tell her we were coming; there were no telephones in Surif. On a bright April morning we set out, but only after Rawda had sent me back to my closet to change from pants into a skirt. "They'll treat you with a lot more respect, which is what you want, right?"

We headed south out of Jerusalem, past the twin towns of Bethlehem and Beit Jala, past the seven-metre-high chain-link fences of the Dahaisha refugee camp (designed that way so the *shebab* couldn't throw rocks at passing cars) and onto a small and winding mountain road through several Palestinian villages to Surif. On the way, Rawda described her feelings about the political situation in her country.

"I grew up inside Israel, in Nazareth, and I always thought of myself as an Israeli Arab. We went to Israeli schools, learned Israeli history, even though we were all Arab students and teachers. Now I realize how weird it was, but at the time it seemed normal. We didn't know anybody in the West Bank or Gaza, and I certainly didn't have any sense of kinship with all those refugees. It wasn't until I moved to the United States and began meeting Palestinians that my thinking started to change. I'd introduce myself as an Israeli Arab and they'd say, 'You are not! You're a Palestinian!' and eventually I began to see that we were all the same people. It was just an accident of history whether our families fled in 1948 or stayed put. Now I feel very Palestinian and I sympathize with their cause. Except for the hate. I can never hate the Israelis the way they do because of where I was brought up."

The 800,000 Israeli Arabs, or the Palestinian Israelis, or whatever they choose to call themselves, will have the most difficult and uncomfortable choice to make when the peace process finally bears fruit and an autonomous Palestinian state comes into being right beside Israel. They can remain citizens of Israel, accepting the fact that their citizenship will always be second-class and inferior to that of the Israeli Jews. Or they can throw in their lot with the new Palestine over the border, risking political and economic upheaval for years to come and probably suffering discrimination from the West Bank and Gazan Palestinians who will view them as having been illegitimate and in bed with the enemy for the past forty-five years. I suspect most will remain in Israel. I would.

At the outskirts of Surif, our driver, Mohammed, slowed down to ask directions from a moustached teenager sitting on a rock by the roadside. The boy jumped into the car and directed us through the narrow streets of the village to the far side, where the women's co-op sat perched on the edge of a precipitous valley. The sun was dazzling, but inside the building the late-winter chill still lingered in the large draughty rooms, where a dozen women in headscarves and long shapeless dresses sorted embroidered tea-towels, aprons and cushion covers, accompanied by much rapid-fire chat and bursts of laughter. Zena came out of her office and welcomed us, interrupting the accounting work she had been doing on the co-op's computer, a new gift provided by Swedish funds. In spite of her lack of English, Zena was working with an English computer program. Someone at the Mennonite Centre in Jerusalem had shown her which keys to push in which sequence to give her the spreadsheets she needed. The village had electricity from the power grid only from five till eleven at night, but the women's centre had its own generator to run the washing machines, the irons and Zena's computer.

Tea appeared on a copper tray and we settled in for a chat. I was interested in the embroidery work, not so much for its aesthetic value as for its role in helping Palestinian women cope with their frankly miserable lives. These women were doubly oppressed, first by the Israeli occupation, which affected everyone, and second, by traditional social structures that kept them firmly under the thumb of their fathers, brothers and husbands. But through a huge network of international helping agencies that had operated in the occupied territories for decades, many women's cooperatives had been set up to keep the folk arts alive, to give the women a place to socialize outside their homes and to allow them to make a bit of money of their own.

For a few of them, the brightest ones with a little education (who often turned out to be the unmarried ones as well), the co-ops were a liberating experience. One of Zena's assistants, Souad, described what a scary thrill it had been for her to take the bus to Jerusalem by herself for the first time to do some work for the co-op. "The other passengers, all male workers, stared at me strangely. I was shy and couldn't raise my face, thinking what was going through their minds. It was a forty-minute bus trip, but to me it felt more like two hours." For most of the women in Surif, though, the embroidery work was done in their homes at night after all the other domestic chores were done, and didn't seem to have changed their lives for the better. However, Zena assured us that, modest though the co-op's income was, it was by far the most viable and successful business in Surif. The hordes of unemployed men hanging around the streets as we drove through town were testimony to that.

As we were chatting, a large, genial American named Kelly appeared in the office doorway. He worked for the Save the Children Fund, based in Amman, Jordan, and part of his job was to help co-ops like this one get out of the aesthetic rut they were in and try to market their products more aggressively. Assuredly, the handicrafts being created by the Surif women were pretty banal, stripped-down, paint-by-numbers versions of the richly ornamented work done by their grandmothers on much-loved wedding dresses and other dowry items through the nineteenth and early twentieth centuries. "The women will only work on white mijdal cotton, which we buy from a weaver in the Old City," explained Zena. The cloth had a clear weave so that a girl could learn to cross-stitch on it without much trouble.

The traditional Palestinian work was almost always done on fine black wool or cotton, but Zena said the women today refused to work on it. "It ruins their eyes. They only have a dim lightbulb to work by at night in their homes, so they want double the money if they work on black cloth."

From Kelly's point of view, the problem was that there was a glut of this ersatz-traditional handiwork on the market. "In Amman," he said, "middle-class Palestinians are always being hit up at dinner parties to buy more tea-towels to help the refugees in the West Bank, but there's a limit." And Sahir at the Mennonite Centre had told me that sales to the North American charitable market had plummeted in recent years because they were being severely undercut by the Indians and Bangladeshis. Kelly's solution, which he had already implemented successfully among the more sophisticated Palestinian community in Jordan, was to develop ambitious articles for which there was an identifiable consumer demand — rugs, lampshades, purses, bedspreads — and to get the women to work in trendy pastels instead of the strong traditional colours, especially the reds and blacks, of their indigenous culture.

Here at Surif he had the women working on quilted bedspreads, with long thin strips of embroidery in lively, delicate colours alternating with Damascus cloth, the most sumptuous fabric the Middle East produces. He took us up onto the flat roof of the co-op, where two girls were hanging finished strips of the embroidery work out to dry after they had been laundered. The work was exquisite. In the spring wind the long strips danced and floated all over the rooftop, a brilliant mobile of colours against the buff-grey backdrop of the barren West Bank hills and valleys. Then we went down three floors to the basement, where two more women were laying out pieces of fabric and embroidery on huge cutting tables according to Kelly's instructions, trying to work out the most pleasing patterns for the finished quilts. Everywhere the women seemed puzzled and amused by Kelly's instructions, which were so completely different from those for the simple tea-towels and table runners they were used to. But he was a man, and an American, and they did what he told them.

We returned to the office and I continued interviewing Zena, with Rawda translating, until we were next interrupted by our driver. We had left Mohammed waiting out in the car and hadn't given him another thought, but he had clearly decided that he had been there long enough. Never mind that he was being paid for half a day's work; as far as he was concerned it was time to go. He announced as much in Arabic to Zena and Rawda, who both stared at him with barely disguised contempt and then turned back to our discussion. Mohammed helped himself to a chair and sat glaring at the three of us, swinging his car keys noisily and consulting his fancy watch every thirty seconds. "He's humiliated to be working for women," Rawda explained. "He has to make it clear that his time is far more valuable than ours. Just ignore him."

Twenty minutes later we drew the interview languorously to a close, while Mohammed literally hopped with impatience. As we said goodbye, solemn Zena flashed me a rare smile and said quietly through Rawda, "You are welcome back here whenever you want. But don't ever bring that jerk into our village again."

Ten months later, Rawda and I returned to Surif, she to buy more potholders and I because I was curious how the bedspread project had turned out. This time I confidently drove our own car. (Doing things a second time was never a problem, once I knew what I was getting into.) When I asked about the bedspreads, Zena rolled her eyes heavenward. They had indeed produced eight of them, and had tried to sell them at a number of local trade fairs. The price was high, $500, but not out of line for the enormous amount of high-quality work involved. Not one of them had sold. "This is what comes of these special projects," Zena muttered, "fancy ideas and nowhere to sell them. We're better off sticking with what we know."

With a sense of impending financial doom, I asked if we could see the bedspreads. On the cutting-room table downstairs, the women spread them out, an orgy of lavish colours and designs. But there was a problem: Kelly had turned them into quilts with thick layers of cheap polyester filler, which made them look lumpy and heavy instead of elegant. Still, my eyes fell on the white and yellow one, and it was love. I knew it would take many hours to undo the quilting, take the thing apart, remove all the polyester and turn it into a beautiful lightweight bedspread again, but I had to have it. I have it now, glowing on my bed, and every time I look at it I remember the women of Surif and the long snakes of brilliant colour dancing in the sunlight on their roof.

I met Sama and her aunt Khadija at the Qalandiya Refugee Camp, just on the outskirts of East Jerusalem. When I was researching the handicrafts, everyone in the field said I must go to Qalandiya, where the women's centre was preserving the art form in something close to its original sumptuous state. Once again I felt nervous. I didn't know if you could just drive up to the front gate of a refugee camp and ask to come in and see the embroideries. I was advised not to enter without a representative from UNRWA (the United Nations Relief and Works Agency, which has run the camps since 1948), but none was available the week I wanted to go. I had Sama's name on a piece of paper, and I took my Sam along for protection. I figured I couldn't get into too much trouble with a nine-year-old in tow.

Conquering my fear of the unknown was the most prevalent theme of my life in the Middle East. Time after time interesting situations would present themselves, but always accompanied by a chorus of warnings about how dangerous they would be. After we had been in our house only a week, Patrick and I realized late one night that some videos were due back at the store by midnight. We argued for ten minutes about the danger of walking out of our house to the parking lot. Finally, Patrick decided he was going. I asked if he wanted me to come along (for what? for protection?). In the end we agreed I should stay home, neither of us articulating our mutual thought that our children should be left with at least one parent after the night's adventure. When Patrick came back through the door fifteen minutes later, we breathed a quiet sigh of relief, laughed at ourselves and never worried about repeating that particular escapade again. But it did nothing to alleviate the fear the next time a *new* situation came up. The refugee camps, those seething cauldrons of hatred, terrorism and despair as portrayed in the world media, ranked high on my list of fearful places.

The women's centre was just outside the barbed-wire fence, so you could visit it without entering Qalandiya itself. But after Sama and Khadija, the director of the centre, had shown us the premises and the beautiful embroideries, I asked to visit some of the camp women who were doing the actual work in their homes. We set off into the camp on foot, past the enormous security barricades made of oil barrels filled with concrete piled on top of each other to a height of eight or ten metres. These had been erected by the Israelis after the intifada started so they could more effectively control the movement of the refugees into and out of the camp.

I had always believed that the camps were prisons that restricted the refugees' freedom, but that's not exactly the case. During the day, people come and go from the camps freely to jobs or school or to shop. At night, and on days of terrorist incidents or political unrest, the Israelis impose curfew and everybody stays home. But that can apply equally to the Arabs who live in towns as to the camp dwellers.

Over the decades, many camp people have tried to move out and resume something approaching normal life. This is not easy in a traditional agrarian society where one's legitimacy as a resident of an area is measured in centuries, not years. Those whose families have always lived in villages in the West Bank and Gaza view the camp people as displaced strangers from far away, not the sort of people they want their daughters to marry. In the hierarchy of Palestinian misery, the camp dwellers are at the bottom. And yet, having lost everything, they are prepared to take more risks than their cautious West Bank cousins, and so have become the political heroes and "martyrs" of Palestine. The revolution master-minded by Yasser Arafat finds its hard-core support in the camps of the West Bank. The Gaza camps are even more extreme and have provided abundant seeding ground for the Islamic terrorist group Hamas.

In his sad and beautiful book, *The People of Nowhere,* Israeli journalist Danny Rubinstein writes that the Palestinian longing to return to the original homes they lost in Jaffa, Haifa or West Jerusalem has been slowly transmuted over the years into a longing for an independent Palestinian homeland, and that once they have that they will be satisfied. As I got to know Sama better, she indicated that that was how she and her family felt. Her father had come from the village of Libda, she told me as we walked the squalid, reeking lanes of Qalandiya, visiting needlewomen. Her mother was from Lod, where the Israelis later constructed Ben Gurion Airport. Libda no longer exists; the remarkably ugly Jerusalem Hilton Hotel, on the far western outskirts of the new city, stands on the site. "It's too bad they built the Hilton so tall," said Sama. "I can always see it no matter where I am in East Jerusalem and it reminds me of the home we lost."

Sama didn't personally lose it; she was born in Qalandiya in 1964. But such is the power of memory among Palestinians that most camp dwellers of all ages routinely say, when asked, that they are "from Haifa" or "from Jaffa," even though what they mean is that their grandparents fled from there in 1948. Yet Sama was not a mournful ideologue, determined not to set foot out of the refugee camp unless she could go back to her family home. "When we were small, our teachers always talked about return, return, return. But I have come to accept over the years that I will never get Libda back, it is part of the past. I will feel that our long struggle has been worthwhile if we can simply have a piece of land called Palestine that is truly ours."

We stopped near the top of Qalandiya to visit two cousins who embroidered for the cooperative. The inevitable orange fizzy drinks were served in the family's cramped parlour, empty of decoration except for a huge tapestry of the Kaaba, the enormous black plinth at Mecca that draws pilgrims from all over the Islamic world.

"Are there any Christians in the camps?" I asked as we watched the two veiled women bent over their needlework.

Sama hooted with laughter. "No, no, the Christian refugees were taken care of by their rich churches," she explained sarcastically, "while we Moslems sat and waited for help from all the Arab countries. Lots and lots of promises, but they have never done anything for us. That is why the camps are filled with Moslems."

I liked Sama, even though she spouted rather knee-jerk phrases about "our great leader Yasser Arafat" and "the tragic soul of the Palestinian people." Because her English was excellent (she had majored in English literature at the West Bank's notoriously radical Bir Zeit University), her job at the co-op included dealing with foreign visitors, and I felt her rhetoric was largely put on for my benefit as a representative of the foreign press. I asked if I could visit her some day at her home, after working hours, and she agreed.

I realized later that one of the reasons I took to Sama was because of her easy self-confidence, which was partly, I think, the result of her having grown up in a house without an overbearing Arab father. Her family had built a small neat house about a block outside the Qalandiya camp entrance, and she lived there with her sister and her aunt Khadija. Her mother had died when the girls were young, and her father had remarried and moved to Kuwait. When all the

Palestinians were kicked out of Kuwait after the Gulf War, he moved back to Jordan but not to the West Bank. Sama saw him from time to time, had even gone with him and her aunt recently, not on the hajj to Mecca, but on what is known as the semi-hajj, to Embra, also in Saudi Arabia. "You have to have a man in your party in order to buy the tickets," Sama explained. But essentially she and her sister had grown up in an all-female household, and she did not suffer from the giggly shyness and blandness that most Palestinian women display to the outside world.

"My aunt is a good, mature woman who always treated us well and helped us make our own decisions about important things. She has a high reputation in the Qalandiya community because she's considered an example to other Palestinians of how to make something of your life even when you've been left with nothing."

Sama was twenty-nine, a brunette with cascades of thick curly hair, and heavily made-up eyes and mouth. She was pretty in the same soft, slightly blurry way that many Palestinian women were pretty, no competition in the looks department for the dramatic beauties across the Green Line. She dressed in blue jeans and moved lithely in her body as a result of years of folk-dancing, an activity even more popular and more charged with political significance in Palestinian society than in Israel.

The day I went to visit, with the standard-issue box of chocolates as a guest offering, the family was atwitter over Sama's sister's impending wedding. Sahar was two years younger than Sama, and was marrying a fellow from another refugee camp, north of Ramallah. The family was an interesting mixture of modern and traditional. They showed me the highly posed, fussy photos of the official engagement, which had taken place a month earlier, and there was a great deal of talk about hair and the best place in East Jerusalem to get it done on the big day. On the other hand, when I asked how much bride-price Abd-el-Naser had paid for Sahar, she showed me a single gold coin on a chain around her throat. Sama explained, "The coin is a bow to tradition but really this is going to be a marriage between equals. Nobody buys anybody in this family."

Although she was obviously an active supporter of both the PLO and the intifada, Sama admitted that they had taken their toll on her and her generation. "We have really lost our youth, you know? One of my friends said to me the other day, 'Sama, when the peace comes and the intifada ends for good, we will have to go back and live these five or six years over again, because we really didn't live them at all.' She's right. Time passed and we all got older, but we had no joy. Now I see young girls on the street in Jerusalem or Ramallah, girls sixteen or seventeen, really enjoying themselves, taking care of their clothes, their appearance. To me that is a hopeful sign, that they are determined to make a life for themselves no matter what is going on around them politically. My generation is different. We are totally involved in the politics of Palestine, in the martyrdom of our people, in the blood that has been spilt. Dressing up and having fun, that's completely alien to our nature."

Sama was a virgin, and even though there was no heavy-handed male in the picture guarding her hymen, she had clearly internalized the Arab obsession with female honour. A few young women in her community were quietly murdered by their fathers and brothers every year if they stepped over that forbidden threshold and were found out. One of the reasons Arab sources give for the enormous flight of Arabs from their homes in 1948 was a widespread fear that the advancing Israelis would rape their daughters. That was how conquerors had always acted in the past, so why not now? A refugee mother in a camp in Lebanon, when asked in an interview how she would feel if her daughter was raped, said, "I would be far happier if her three brothers were killed and no enemy were able to reach her. If my daughter was raped and my honour defiled, our family would be disgraced and my sons' lives would be pointless." It seemed to be a social code of unbearable harshness, and all hinging on a hidden few centimetres of female flesh.

For the Israeli perspective, I asked my friend Nachman whether there was any substance to this widespread Palestinian fear of rape. He shook his head. "Look, all I can tell you is that in the Israeli Defence Force during the Six Day War, when we were moving into the occupied territories, we were told three things by our commanders. One, no looting. Two, don't shoot or shit in the holy places. Three, don't touch the women. There was some looting, but we left the holy places and the women alone." An Israeli academic has documented approximately twenty cases of rape of Palestinian women by Israeli soldiers since 1967, a remarkably low number for an occupying force. There could, of course, be unreported cases, especially since young women might fear for their lives if they admit the rapes to their families. But I was never convinced that there had been many; that particular darkness just didn't feel part of the Israeli–Palestinian relationship.

"What do you think of Israeli men?" I asked Sama, and her eyes flashed with appetite.

"They are so incredibly handsome," she said, the words tumbling out. "When my friends and I are waiting to be questioned at a checkpoint, we look the soldiers over up ahead of us and talk about how cute they are. Then they demand our papers, cold as ice, and bang! the romance disappears. Sometimes too, I have to tell you, I feel sorry for them, out on these checkpoints in the blazing sun or the pouring rain, while we drive through all nice and warm in our cars."

As if on cue, Sama's friend Mahmoud entered the living-room, a handsome, jaunty fellow about her age. He was a mathematics teacher by day and a poet and musician by night, and ran the folk-dance troupe that Sama used to dance in. He had dropped in to discuss some details of an upcoming dance festival on the Bir Zeit campus. As soon as he flopped onto the overstuffed couch across the room, sexual electricity seemed to fill the space between him and

Sama. Later in the conversation I commented obliquely on what a good-looking couple they made, which drew instant denials from both of them.

"He is not my boyfriend! I help him find girls and he helps me find boys, not that I need the help," Sama said, laughing. Then she sat back in her chair and looked at him long and shrewdly. "He is not a nice person but he's a good friend. You know what I mean?" I nodded. "And he needs to get married," she ended with a flourish of determination.

"So do you," retorted Mahmoud. "Twenty-nine years old, this isn't a joke any more."

When I left the house, Beatrice and Benedict were still sparring.

The lives of Israeli women seemed, on the surface, to be so different from those of their Palestinian counterparts: all of them had the liberating social experience of entering the army after high school, and huge numbers of them worked outside the home. Early Zionist propaganda films and posters invariably showed healthy blond maidens ploughing the fields and shouldering rifles just like the men, which gave the whole world the idea that Israel was a pioneer in women's liberation. Under the surface, it seemed to me, nothing could be further from the truth.

From the very beginning the system favoured the men. Once the Zionists decided to adopt ancient Hebrew as the language of their new Jewish state, for example, the immigrant males had an immediate advantage over the females because they had studied at least basic Hebrew in their European religious schools, whereas the girls had not. Although in theory all work on the early kibbutzim was to be fairly shared and deemed of equal value, in fact the women ended up in the kitchens, the laundries and the nurseries almost a hundred percent of the time. It is true that the women fought bravely alongside the men in the desperate days of 1948, but almost immediately after that their role in the IDF, the Israeli Defence Force, shrank back to that of non-combat support staff, where it has remained to this day.

One day I was having lunch with Alice Shalvi, the locally famous head of the Israel Women's Network, the largest of the country's feminist groups, and she shook her head in amusement at the inconsistencies of trying to maintain a feminist position in Israel. "I am absolutely dedicated to the cause of peace, as I believe most feminists are, and you can't imagine how ridiculous it feels for me to have to argue publicly for a combat role for women in the IDF. But without that, they will never attain anything approaching equality in this country. The entire structure of your later life in Israel is based on what you did during your army service, it's by far the most important item on your CV. Top jobs in business, education, government, what have you, go only to those who have acquitted themselves well in the elite fighting corps like the paratroopers. And since those corps are only open to men, they get all the rest of the goodies as well." Alice also pointed out that even though Israel had started out with high-minded European socialist ideals, including non-sexism, the country was almost instantly swamped in the fifties by waves of Sephardic Jews from Africa who brought with them a traditional, Arabized attitude towards women. The struggle has continued ever since.

But the place where I felt women really got the squeeze in Israel was in the battle for demographics. On both sides of the Green Line, women were the frontline soldiers in the head-counting war between Arabs and Jews, and their decisions to have more or fewer children were the stuff of grave political analysis and subtle (or sometimes not so subtle) propaganda. The Palestinian rhetoric proclaimed it flat out: women were "factories of men" and any woman who could produce eight, ten, twelve sons for the great Palestinian cause was loudly praised.

I asked Islah, a respected Palestinian feminist I knew, whether she and her colleagues were making any headway in the field of birth control. She laughed nervously and said, "It's very dangerous for us to speak publicly about birth control in this society, because of the enormous political pressure on women to have more children. The only thing we can do is talk about family spacing, driving home a message based on the health of the mother and the baby, which is something even the men can't complain about. At least that means that by the end of her baby-growing career she might end up with only nine or ten pregnancies instead of fourteen."

Even though they pay lip-service to the national goal of beefing up the population, Palestinian women seem to offer their own form of passive resistance. In a survey of the West Bank I came across, it was discovered that women breast-feed as long as they possibly can in the widespread belief that breast-feeding is a natural prophylactic.

On the Israeli side, things are even more complicated. Women are told that their prime job in the defence of Israel is creating more soldiers for the front lines. On the other hand, Israel is a far more modern place than Palestine, one where people are getting very tired of sacrificing their lives and their families to the elusive goal of national security. My friend Jane, an Orthodox American Jew who had transplanted her young family to Jerusalem, used to say to me, "None of us want to be in the Middle East any more. We all just want to be at the mall!" Israelis are desperate to lead normal lives, and there is nothing normal about bearing sons and watching both them and your husband go off to military service in dangerous places every year until they turn fifty-five.

One day in the video store, the owner, Alma, and I found ourselves alone, a rare occurrence. She was sitting behind the counter staring off into a middle distance that seemed haunting and troubling. It was during that terrible month of March 1993 when Israelis were being attacked in all parts of the country but most particularly in the ferocious slums of Gaza. Alma refocussed her eyes on me and smiled sadly. "Excuse me, I was just thinking about my boys," she said.

"They are both posted to Gaza, they are there right now. They could die." She paused. "I am so terribly frightened. Aren't you?" I had to admit I was not, and it created a wide unhappy gulf between us. This was the woman who, a couple of months earlier, had been scolding Patrick and me because we hadn't yet gone to see the Israel Philharmonic perform. When we finally did she wasn't impressed because we had seen an all-Russian program with a Russian guest conductor. "You have to see them play with Zubin Mehta or you haven't seen them at all," she laughed. She was a gentle, cultured woman who should not have had the death of her sons on her mind. But then, neither should the mothers in the Qalandiya refugee camp a few blocks away.

One day I met Galia for coffee at one of our favourite bistros, Kaffit in the German Colony. Galia had brought her two-month-old baby boy, Itai, who slept in his plastic rocker on the table the whole time. Galia was a *sabra* of Sephardic origin; her family had come from Iraq in the fifties. She was married to a Canadian Jew from Toronto; they had met in Paris and lived there for a number of years before deciding to settle in Israel.

I found this return extraordinary: Galia was cosmopolitan and well travelled, a highly educated social worker with a perfect command of English and a Canadian husband. When they decided to leave Paris, they could have chosen Israel or Canada. They had returned to Israel in January of 1991, the month the Gulf War began. People were streaming out of the country by the thousands at that time, terrified by Saddam Hussein's threats of chemical warfare against Tel Aviv. Galia's arrival with her two daughters was so noteworthy under the circumstances that the most popular Israeli newspaper, *Yediot Aharonot,* splashed their picture over the front page as a sign that not everyone was abandoning Israel in one of its darkest hours. And now here she was two years later with her brand-new son who, if Israeli history continued true to form, would find himself in barracks as soon as he left high school. Every generation of Israeli mothers has hoped and prayed that the conflict will be over before their children grow up, and every generation has been disappointed. Peace looks more tangible now than at any time in the past forty-six years, but it is impossible to imagine an Israel that is not perpetually under arms. The best hope for Galia's son is that Israel is moving towards a smaller, tighter professional army instead of the sprawling universal conscription it has now.

Galia had only two more weeks of maternity leave before reluctantly returning to her job running a special education class in a Jerusalem school for children with learning disabilities. She was about thirty, with sparkling eyes brimful of good humour and black hair styled in a chic Paris-influenced blunt cut. Her breasts were heavy with milk and, like all new mothers, no matter how involved she got in our conversation, her eyes slid constantly and worshipfully to her baby's face. As we toyed with our *café-hafook* (the Hebrew phrase for *café au lait,* literally meaning coffee upside down) I asked whether the decision she and Robert had made to move back to Israel was the right one.

"For the first year," she began, "I just hated it and I really wanted to leave again. After five years away I had forgotten a lot of the bad things about Israel. Like the way people behave here, so rude and aggressive. Thanks to Robert and his nice Canadian manners, I had my eyes opened to a whole other way of dealing with people, and it was a shock to come back to it. My kids are learning proper manners, but the children they play with, even age four and five, have already learned to demand things rudely. '*Maim,*' they'll say, 'Water!' Not 'Could I have some water?' or even 'I want some water.' Just 'water!' I hate it."

"Funny," I said. "I'm so used to it now that it doesn't bother me any more."

"Also," she continued, "there's this Israeli attitude: *eehiyeh beseder.* It'll be okay, we'll manage. Everything is *eehiyeh beseder.* You take out a huge mortgage to buy a house, you're earning almost nothing, you're overdrawn at the bank, bouncing cheques all over the place, all the credit cards loaded up, and all you can say is, we'll manage. But it takes its toll. There's a real tension in living like that, expecting everything to come tumbling down around you all the time. And always bargaining to get a better price. We don't do it as much as the Arabs, but we still do it a lot. And you're always thinking, I could have got it for less, I'll bet he was cheating me. That's exhausting too. After a few years in the West, I wasn't used to it any more and I don't like it at all."

Were there any good reasons for coming back, then? "Oh, yes." Galia smiled. "The best thing about Israel is the strength and warmth of the families. Mine is probably exceptional, but all Israeli families are very close and they help each other. It's wonderful to see. Listen to this: my husband, Robert, doesn't drive, so ever since this baby was born, my father has picked up my two girls and taken them to school. Then at lunch-time he leaves his work — he's a very successful building contractor with his own firm — and picks them up at school and delivers them home. He does all this just so I won't have to bundle the baby up and go out in the car twice a day." I had to admit this was a stunning piece of information. I could imagine a retired father in my part of the world doing such a thing for his favourite daughter, but a busy professional man in the middle of his working day? Never.

What Galia was saying echoed a conversation I had had the week before with a raffishly handsome young Jewish taxi driver who was taking me, under protest, to an East Jerusalem destination. After he bargained me up an extra six shekels for danger pay ("If I take a stone through my window the insurance company will not pay, you know, madam"), we settled in for a personal chat, and I learned that he had just returned from two years of illegally working in New York, something many Israeli young men try out after their army service. So why are you back, I asked, was it tough to find work? "No, the work was no problem, the immigration was no problem, but I missed my family too much." Come on, I thought, a cute twenty-four-year-old single guy who missed his family so much that he came home from New York to be with them and wasn't embarrassed to admit it? I hinted that I was a bit skeptical; maybe there was someone else in the picture, possibly female? "No, no," he insisted, "I still haven't met the right girl. But I just felt so lonely without my family around. They are the best people in the world. Are you married?" he asked. I replied in the affirmative. "How many people came to your wedding?" I recalled the eighty carefully chosen relatives and friends who helped us celebrate the big day. "You know how many I will have when I find a girl to marry?" he asked. "At least six hundred, and that will just be relatives. Her family and my family combined." I didn't doubt it.

Somehow the Israelis seem to have managed almost a perfect balance between the rather strung-out and remote family life of the West and the fearful and overbearingly paternalistic families of the Middle East. The women settle for second-rank jobs in the workforce instead of beating their heads with frustration against the glass ceiling as their North American counterparts tend to do. Children are given a great deal of leeway and independence, because parents are aware of how quickly they will have to grow up once they hit the army. The alienation of teenagers in the West is almost unknown in Israel because, up to this point anyway, everyone in the country has been able to agree on the common goal of national security. Thousands of families drive for hours every sabbath to have picnics at IDF camps with their soldier sons and daughters who haven't drawn weekend leave. Many young people, especially in the middle classes, tend to enjoy a "deferred adolescence," cutting loose and going on long, exotic round-the-world treks once their three years in the IDF are behind them.

All these factors contribute to family closeness, but they all have their roots in the difficult political and military situation Israel has always found itself in. If the road suddenly becomes smoother, if peace becomes a solid reality in the Middle East, Israelis might get the normality they have always craved and might live to regret it. Like the British who continually hark back to the days of the Blitz, the Israelis may find that "normal" life can never match the excitement of life on the edge, and can instead lead people into a wasteland of selfishness, consumerism and dysfunction. Of course the Israelis are as entitled to that wasteland as anybody else, but they could lose something precious in the process.

I would often walk over to the Western Wall on Shabbat evenings, where the spectacle was always made up of one part sincerity and three parts hokum. The hokum came from the wide men's section to the left, where the black-hatted *haredim* were on display, bobbing fiercely in front of the massive stones and then, on some mysterious predetermined signal, linking up into a loud and incongruous conga line that snaked around the plaza, prayer-books fluttering, ringlets swinging. Orthodox men in white shirts crowded around the various prayer tables in *minyans* (a *minyan* is the group of at least ten men required to hold a Jewish religious ceremony), but they often appeared to be checking out and criticizing each other's method of praying and chanting as much as talking to God. All of them, I cynically imagined, were playing to the gawking gallery of tourists who, even on Shabbat, outnumbered the worshippers two to one.

The sincerity, on the other hand, seemed to emanate from the much narrower women's section to the right, which was hemmed in by all kinds of male-imposed restrictions. There were no prayer shawls, no dancing and no singing on the women's side. All the ostentation and all the communal fun was the exclusive province of the men, while the women were required to keep their worship quiet, seemly and individual. In fact, nobody and nothing in Jewish religious practice required the women to be there at all, so it was only true devotion that brought them.

In recent years, feminist groups of Jewish women had tried to storm the men's section of the Wall and had been beaten back by furious chair-wielding *haredim*. Others had tried to hold their own morning prayer services on the women's side, with a *minyan* of women and with their own Torah scrolls and prayer shawls. They were repeatedly attacked, beaten and spat upon, not only by men but by traditional female worshippers as well. Once a group of them got tear-gassed for their pains.

On a typical Friday evening, though, as I leaned on the stone barricade that separated the watchers from the worshippers, the only sign of female protest was a group of twelve young women with dark manes flowing down their backs who had formed themselves into a circle, arms linked across each other's shoulders, and were gently swaying to the right and then to the left, quietly murmuring a prayer in unison. Older women in headscarves stared at them with heavy suspicion, but their protest was so subtle that no one was prepared to confront them. Hundreds of graceful swallows swooped over the floodlit face of the Wall, darting in and out and sometimes disappearing completely into the thin fissures between the massive ancient stones. The cacophony from the men's side grew muted inside my head as I strained to catch the delicate chanting of the women's circle. Their swaying was hypnotic and powerful and utterly female, and it suddenly became clear why the men of the Middle East have devoted centuries of custom and law to keeping women on the edges and under control: they are afraid of them.

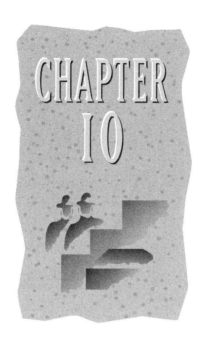

CHAPTER 10

THE JERUSALEM WORLD of Orthodox Judaism was the most interesting but also the most difficult one for an outsider to enter. Especially for an outsider like myself who, out of reticence and a desire to not get directly involved, preferred not to advertise my half-Jewishness. I had heard stories of North American Jews, especially those with young children, being subjected to extraordinary pressure from religious Jews in Israel to make *aliya*. Since this was out of the question for our family, it was simply easier not to let the subject arise at all. My identity in Israel was "Canadian journalist," and since I had neither the looks nor a name that would raise questions, Israelis all assumed I was a Gentile.

Did this fudging of my background make me feel uncomfortable at times? Yes, it did, whenever I thought of the reason for Israel's

existence in the first place, as a haven where Jews would never again
have to hide their identity in order to survive. But I knew that if I
declared my Jewishness, my life in Jerusalem would be a long series of
personal challenges, like the one my brother David faced when he
and his wife, Karen, came to visit us and found themselves sharing a
service taxi with an ultra-Orthodox gentleman one day. The conversation went like this:

> *Haredi*: Are you a Jew?
>
> David: Yes, half.
>
> *Haredi*: Which parent?
>
> David: My mother.
>
> *Haredi*: Then you're a Jew. (*Pause.*) Is your wife Jewish?
>
> Karen: No, I'm Armenian.
>
> (*Haredi* rolls his eyes in pain and shakes his head.)
>
> *Haredi*: (*To David.*) Why couldn't your mother find a Jew to marry?
>
> David: (*Startled.*) I believe she fell in love with a Gentile.

David and Karen were only visiting for two weeks. I was living there
for two years. Did I need this?

One of my main entry points into the Orthodox world turned
out to be Mark, the man designated to handle the most complicated
foreign accounts at our local branch of the Bank Leumi. Banking in
Israel is as rough and ready as most other activities, but Mark was an
accounting genius who soothingly sheltered us from financial chaos.
He was from England and had made *aliya* twenty years earlier, but his
English training was still in his bones and it made him a delight to
deal with. On the rare occasion when I would turn up at the bank to
find Mark away sick or on holiday, I was thrown into a panic knowing that I would have to trust my dealings to one of the Israeli staff.
One day, standing in line for the teller's wicket, I watched in horri-
fied amusement as the teller manually counted out fifty 100-shekel
notes for a customer, then ran them through the money-counting
machine, which registered forty-eight, ran them through again and

got a result of fifty-one, then shrugged impatiently and handed them over to the customer, who had been chatting with a friend all this time and was oblivious to the show of incompetence, both mechanical and human, that was going on with his money.

Mark was a seriously religious man, but not *haredi*. He believed strongly in the state of Israel and, although he lived in West Jerusalem, he was having a number of his six children bused out to schools in religious settlements in the occupied territories. He was an elfin creature with rosy cheeks and a wide, slightly cocky smile, a man whose high-level talent with figures would have netted him a comfortable living if he had remained in England, but who had made the spiritual decision to move to Israel. Materially, that meant that he and his large family lived in a cramped two-bedroom apartment, that he did not own a car and that he took three buses to get to work each day.

Mark was both fascinated and repulsed by the Arab countries that ringed Israel, and since we always had to make financial arrangements before going on a trip, he was privy to Patrick's Middle East wanderings to Cairo, Amman, Beirut, Damascus and Algiers. "Be careful not to let them know you've come from Israel or they'll arrest you as a Zionist spy," he always warned, even after we assured him about our two-passport system. We would bring him postcards and cheap tourist items from exotic Arab lands, major curiosities for his children and friends. (Mark's religious demeanour hid complicated inner depths. When I asked him once what he'd like me to bring him back from a one-week trip to London, he asked for the Madonna book. "We have our fantasies too, you know," he said shyly, patting the *kipa* on his head.)

Mark was the one who told us about the Palm Beach Hotel, the Mediterranean beach resort for Orthodox Jews right next to a Palestinian refugee camp in the Gaza Strip. He and his family had gone there for their one-week summer holiday. The hotel had its

own airstrip, so that religious Jews could hop a subsidized plane from
Tel Aviv or Jerusalem and thus avoid the extreme security risk of driving through Gaza. The resort catered to all tiers of religious practice,
so its beach was divided by high plastic fringes on poles that extended
several metres out into the water. There was a men's only section, a
women's only section and a mixed bathing area for more lenient families. The first time Patrick went to look the place over, he walked
out onto the terrace facing the sea where he found several men in
their shirt-sleeves and *kipas* relaxing on deck chairs and reading prayer
books while the Muzak system pumped out Frank Sinatra singing
"My Kind of Town."

One day Mark offered to take me grocery shopping at the *haredi*
supermarket in Givat Sha'ul, one of the new ultra-Orthodox neighbourhoods on the west side of Jerusalem. I could have wandered in
on my own, but I couldn't have bought anything because these
supermarkets were subsidized by the religious establishment and one
needed a membership card to shop there. The store wasn't so very
different from the Supersol. A touch more down at the heel, perhaps,
and lacking the expensive imported treats we tended to indulge in
too often, it was like the large no-frills stores that have popped up all
over North America. The main difference was that here the majority
of the shoppers were men, all dressed in variations of eighteenth-century Polish morning suits and black fedoras. As I wheeled my cart up
and down the aisles, I could feel the men I passed shrinking into the
shelves of canned peas to put as much distance as possible between
their bodies and mine. I had been in Israel about a year at this point,
and I had got past the outrage and insult I had felt the first time a
haredi rabbi refused (charmingly, I will admit) to shake my hand.
Now I just found the *haredim* curious.

I stopped in front of the toilet paper display and piled three
twenty-four-roll packs into my shopping cart. That sort of thing was
twice the price at the Supersol. Then I noticed a huge bin contain-

ing packs of individual folded pieces of toilet paper, the kind you find in those nasty metal dispensers in many public washrooms. Mark pulled his cart up alongside at that moment and explained. "On Shabbat you are forbidden to work. The definition of what constitutes work differs depending on which tracts you read and which rabbis you follow. For the strictest groups, pulling apart perforated toilet paper constitutes work."

Writing things down is also work. Orthodox Jews who want to play Scrabble on Shabbat have devised a way to keep score without writing down any numbers. Each player keeps his or her own score by turning the pages of a book to the right number. Sometimes the prohibition against writing can get downright spooky, though. One Saturday night at a concert, after Shabbat was over, my friend Helen and I overheard a young nurse telling her companion that she had got confused at work that day over a doctor's instructions about medicating a patient and ended up administering the wrong dose. "Luckily it wasn't serious," she said with a laugh.

Orthodox hospitals did operate on Shabbat, of course, because all the hundreds of commandments and regulations religious Jews are required to follow, on the sabbath or any other day, are automatically superseded by the Talmudic dictum that the most important human endeavour is saving or preserving life. Still, falling ill or needing medical help on Shabbat wasn't the cleverest thing you could do in Jerusalem. My American friend Jean, also a writer and wife of another journalist, had her first baby in Jerusalem, and it was a harrowing tale. Her excellent doctor was affiliated with Bikur Holim, one of the most antiquated hospitals in the city, located on the edge of Mea Shearim, the old *haredi* neighbourhood. She went into labour early on a Friday, and by the time she had given birth, then slept, then awakened, it was Shabbat. She was ravenous, and they brought in a tray of inedible food. Stiff and sore though she was, she got out of bed to use the communal phone in the hall to call her husband and ask him to bring her something to eat. The phones were unplugged for the sabbath. With exceptional post-partum determination, she dressed and shuffled out into the street, where she walked until she found a functioning pay phone.

When Mark and I finished our shopping (he took advantage of my car to buy ten enormous tins of his family's favourite nibble, salty green olives) we drove to his tiny flat in the pleasant residential neighbourhood of Beit Hakerem. There I met Rachel, his hand-some Israeli wife, and four of his six children, who were sitting around the dining-room table ploughing through masses of home-work. Their home was the most crowded but meticulous living space I had ever seen: every inch was crammed with books, papers, children's toys and family memorabilia, but Rachel looked as though she could put her hand on Child Number Three's report card or a bobbin of purple thread without even thinking about it. There were suitcases loaded with clothes and full cardboard boxes jammed under every available piece of furniture, and Mark had constructed over-head rafters in two of the rooms to make use of all that waste space up near the ceiling. The salon had long since been converted into a children's bedroom, and Rachel's tiny kitchen still had to stretch to accommodate two completely separate sink areas and cupboards for her different sets of dishes. All usable wallspace was covered with bookshelves, the boards bowed under the weight of hundreds of heavy religious tomes, and there was a television set, which indicat-ed that Mark and Rachel were not ultra-Orthodox. (The *haredim* are forbidden to watch public television, although screening carefully selected tapes on a VCR machine is permissible. When Israel was being outfitted with cable in 1992, none of the five private compa-nies involved wanted to handle Jerusalem, since such a high percent-age of the population could be counted on never to buy their wares. Eventually the government stepped in and forced one of the compa-nies to take the city on.)

"This is my life," said Mark, beaming as he showed me around. "With my family and my books, I'm a happy man. Every day I leave the bank behind and rush home to study Torah. It's a lifetime's work and I love it." The written Torah is the first five books of the Old Testament, Genesis, Exodus, Leviticus, Numbers and Deuteronomy, but that is only the beginning of wisdom for a serious Jew. Mark pulled down volume after volume, showing me the small square of written Torah in the middle of a page, surrounded by layers of commentaries on the text by learned rabbis through the ages. My head swam at the thought of so much nit-picking scholarship, but there was no mistaking Mark's genuine adoration of the books and the accumulated learning they represented.

Mind you, Mark did not consider himself much of a scholar. After all, he had to spend most of his waking hours juggling figures in a bank. The true scholars of the Orthodox world were the *talmidei hachamim,* literally the wise students, those men who managed (through a combination of charitable donations and working wives) to spend most of their lives inside the walls of their yeshivas, studying Torah and Talmud and listening with rapt attention to the deliberations of their rabbis.

As far as secular Israelis were concerned, however, many of the mature yeshiva students were not scholars at all, but draft dodgers. Even a sympathetic commentator on the *haredim,* Samuel Heilman, in a recent exhaustive book on the subject, noted that what the yeshiva system turns out in Israel is not so much scholars as "defenders of the faith, cultural warriors in the battle against secularity." These troops can be mobilized in an hour, to throw stones at cars on the sabbath, to burn down bus shelters that have modern billboard ads showing, for example, a woman's bare arms, to shatter the windows of the poor old Edison Theatre, around the corner from the Anglican School. The manager of the Edison tried to placate his fanatical neighbours — there were no movies shown there on Friday night — but having a modern cinema in their midst at all was anathema to the most radical, and whenever there was the slightest whiff of trouble the Edison's big lobby windows would be smashed. These *haredi* foot soldiers could also form themselves into thuggish "modesty squads," patrolling their own neighbourhoods to discourage philandering husbands and keep an eye on unmarried boys and girls. Their techniques included turning up at an offender's house at night and beating him to a pulp.

The issue that really got the *haredim* exercised during our two years in Jerusalem, however, was archaeology. All over the city, and indeed the country, archaeologists are involved in the serious business of reconstructing an Israeli cultural past. Every scrap of evidence they can find of ancient Jewish settlement helps to cement their claim to the land. Many archaeological finds, especially in the Jerusalem area, include human bones, because ancient custom was to bury the dead just outside the city walls. The Valley of Hinnom, where we lived, and the Kidron Valley that flanked the walled city on the eastern side, were mass graveyards dating back three thousand years.

To the *haredim*, disturbing human bones (especially Jewish ones) is an abomination; it means that those long-dead souls will never be able to rest quietly again until the coming of Moshiach, and who knows how long that will be? New Israeli highways have had to be rerouted around ancient graveyards at the cost of millions because of the incessant pressure of the *haredim*. And when the archaeologists, in collusion with the courts, snuck into our valley one night at two o'clock in the morning and removed some contested bones, three days of rioting ensued, with the *haredim* running amok, trashing their own neighbourhoods and setting fire to the enormous green communal garbage dumpsters that sit on every second Jerusalem street corner. We strolled downtown to watch the entertainment.

On normal, non-rioting, days, it was fun to visit Mea Shearim: it was like a real-life theme park of eighteenth-century Cracow. Its name means one hundred gates, and indeed you were constantly moving through gateways in the complicated warren of alleyways and courtyards that made up the neighbourhood. Posters greeted the female visitor everywhere, in English and Hebrew, exhorting us to dress modestly. Here's a typical message, addressed to young girls: "She who wears shameless clothes, woeful are the days of her youth. Her sins are more numerous than the strands of her hair. Covered arms, covered legs, neck and heart covered — THIS IS MODEST DRESS!" The walls of the buildings were plastered with densely printed posters in Hebrew or Yiddish, which constituted a series of outdoor newspapers in which various factions of the faithful argued out their doctrinal points or warned their communities about encroachments from the modern world or transgressions of key commandments.

A common subject of debate was appropriate head coverings for married women. In such a hot-house society, every object of clothing or adornment is deeply encoded with meaning, and a woman's head stated loud and clear whether she was available as a marriage prospect or not. Here is Samuel Heilman's translation of a wall poster on the subject:

"A Call to the Daughters of Israel: The sins of our generation have made it common lately to see MARRIED WOMEN WEARING A GENTILE WIG that is practically identical to their own hair, so that they appear to go about with — heaven forbid — uncovered heads . . . THIS IS ABSOLUTELY PROHIBITED. And even in those places that permission was given to wear a wig, no one ever imagined that Gentile wigs such as these that make women look like free women, prostitutes, heaven forbid, would be permitted. And therefore all G-d-fearing people . . . must be scrupulous not to go about with any wig but only with an appropriate head covering. AND OF COURSE TO BE SCRUPULOUS IN ALL THE DETAILS OF DRESS, IN THE WAYS THAT OUR MOTHERS DID, so that they may remain in line with the demands of modesty so as not to arouse attention and not, heaven forbid, excite the low-lifes."

It was amazing how much both Arab and Jewish fundamentalists concerned themselves with what women wore on their heads. One day I was visiting Pia, a Swiss friend who worked at the Caritas Children's Hospital in Bethlehem, a place funded and partially staffed by Swiss and German Christians. Most of the nurses were local Palestinian Arabs, but they were required to dress in standard Western nursing garb, white dresses and aprons and the classic starched white caps. This angered the Islamic fundamentalist group in the area, which insisted that Moslem women must wear the *higab,* the Islamic wimple that hides all traces of hair and is attached under the chin. A few days before my visit, Hamas revolutionaries had broken into the hospital grounds and spray-painted threats on many walls. Pia excitedly showed me her Polaroids. The graffiti said: "Hospital administrators: Let our sisters dress themselves modestly, as befits Islamic women. You have been warned. Hamas." The women themselves, whether in Bethlehem or Mea Shearim, seemed to have very little to say about all this.

There are, of course, other groups in the world that hem their members in with myriad traditional restrictions in an attempt to stem the tide of progress. The strictest sects of Hutterites and Mennonites in North America come to mind, as does the entire country of Iran. But the *haredim* are special because they are carrying on their fierce cultural war right in the midst of secular life, in busy modern cities like Jerusalem, Tel Aviv and New York. They adore the hardware of modern communications technology, computers, modems, cellular phones and satellite uplinks, but they are convinced that they can keep total control over the software that reaches their community. They manage this by spewing out a constant barrage of hatred against the values of the secular world around them and, in Jerusalem at least, they seem to be successful. Their numbers are growing rapidly, because of their high birth rate and the extremely low drop-out rate among their children.

I wanted to be open-minded and neutral about the *haredim*, but it was difficult. So much of their thinking is based on nothing but superstition and the most complex forms of obscurantism. Many of them are obsessed with a form of "knowledge" known as *gematria*, which is an elaborate number game played with the letters of the Hebrew alphabet. The numerical value of the letters in the word *sin*, for example, 17, is identical to that of the word *nut*, indicating that sin encircles and covers the soul the same way a shell covers a nut. There are billions of combinations of letters and numbers to be played with, capable of giving the player any message or result he wishes. It seemed to me about as authoritative as astrology.

A charming neighbour of ours, Lea Van Leer, the founder of the Jerusalem Cinémathèque, told me an amazing story. When she was supervising construction of the Cinémathèque, just a few minutes' walk from Yemin Moshe further down the Hinnom Valley, a delegation of *haredim* came to visit her. They asked her to please install a revolving door at the front of the new building. Why? Because the valley had a painful history of blood and death and was full of ghosts. The first part of this statement was undeniably true: the Valley of Hinnom (or Gehenna, as it is sometimes referred to in the Bible) had been the site of numerous child sacrifices to the god Moloch, back before the Jews got a firm grip on monotheism. (It always gave us a bit of a frisson to realize that our home was in the Vale of Gehenna, a synonym for Hell among fundamentalist Christians.) The *haredim* were convinced that the ghosts of those long-departed children and other dead souls would inadvertently slip in the front doors of the Cinémathèque, and if that happened, no one named Cohen would be able to enter the building. The Cohanim were the priestly caste in the time of the First and Second Temples. There are elaborate prohibitions — today — against Cohens getting anywhere near dead people, because they would thereby become impure and unable to perform their priestly functions. El Al, for example, has specially constructed double walls with air pockets between them at the back of their planes so they can transport corpses from North America to Israel and not contaminate any members of the priestly caste who may be living passengers on their flights. In any case, the *haredim* who visited Lea were convinced that a revolving door would do the trick, that it would confuse the ghosts who tried to get in to the Cinémathèque and would spin them out into the valley again. Problem solved. There is no revolving door on the Cinémathèque.

Just once I tried to research a tiny aspect of Judaic studies, and discovered how incredibly complex and deliberately obscure the whole exercise is. I was writing a newspaper article about a Jerusalem pop music group called Tofa'ah ("phenomenon"), and it certainly was that. It was a group made up entirely of Jewish women, all originally from North America, but what made it interesting was that they would perform only for all-female audiences. They were women of varying degrees of religious observance, from mildly Orthodox to wig-wearing *haredi,* and they had agreed to follow the Talmudic dictate known as the Kol Ha Isha (the voice of woman), which prohibited an observant man from listening to a woman sing. There were a couple of men at the two Tofa'ah concerts I attended, but they were working, one as an usher, the other running the soundboard. Apparently the regulation only prohibited men listening to women sing for pleasure; if it was part of their work it was kosher.

I wanted to look this regulation up for myself, but none of the musicians in the group could give me a specific reference for it. I asked Patrick's assistant, Cindy, who was modern Orthodox, but the only mention of the Kol Ha Isha she was able to find in her religious books was an exception to the rule: evidently it was copacetic for a man and his wife to sing hymns together in bed. Cindy suggested I call Adin Steinsaltz, a renowned North American rabbi now based in Jerusalem.

I phoned and left a message for the rabbi. Twenty minutes later, his assistant, Thomas, called me back and listened to my request. "Look," he said, "I can get you the exact references, but you will need commentary and analysis as well, and of course you need this for tomorrow's deadline and you're about 435th in line to get a *responsum* or commentary from the rabbi." This was not encouraging, but I said I'd like to have the exact references anyway. I didn't even know where he was going to look them up.

Forty-five minutes later, a woman lower on the totem pole called with the goods. "There are three references for the Kol Ha Isha," she said, "the Babylonian Talmud, Tractate Berachot, page 24A; Moses Maimonides in the Hilchot Issurey Bi'ah, chapter 21, halacha 2; and the Shulchan Aruch, Even haEzer number 21, sub-paragraph A." I diligently copied all this down, and then asked if she could read these references over the phone or fax them to me. "We haven't got them in English," she said curtly. "Besides, if you read them, they're very cryptic and they won't tell you much. You have to read all the commentaries on the sources. In fact I believe a whole book has been written in Hebrew on the subject of the Kol Ha Isha, but we don't have it in our library."

That evening I called Mark at home and asked for help. Sure enough, his weighty library contained the three books in question, and he looked them up for me in sequence and gave me rough translations. All three of them referred back to the Song of Solomon in the Bible, chapter 2:14, which says: "Let me see your face, let me hear your voice, for your voice is sweet, and your face is comely." From that, the Babylonian Talmud extrapolates: "A woman's voice is regarded as her nakedness because it sounds nice and it is good." Maimonides says: "It is forbidden for a man to look even at the little finger of a woman who is forbidden [i.e., anyone but his wife] and even to hear her voice is to look at her nakedness." The Shulchan Aruch continues: "A man should be careful to keep away from a for-

bidden woman, not to wink at her, regard her beauty, smell her per-
fume, watch her hanging up washing or even listen to her voice."
Well, that seemed to cover most of the bases, and it had only taken
me a full day. I still didn't quite understand how we had moved from
the sensual joy of the Song of Songs to the prurient puritanism of the
rabbinical sources, but obviously I was going to have to fill in some
blanks on my own. Undoubtedly, if I had stood in line to hear Rabbi
Steinsaltz, he would have set me straight.

This whole process was fascinating, but I also found it irritating.
It was an insider's game, made deliberately difficult and obscure so
that ordinary Jews who had to work for a living could gain spiritual
knowledge only by listening to their "betters," the fortunate elite
who could devote a lifetime to religious study. This sense that the
priestly orders were running things and must be obeyed without
question was very strong in Jerusalem, and it was easy to see why it
drove secular Israelis wild. The religious establishment, for example,
had been able to hijack the whole Israeli public transportation system
and shut it down on Shabbat. Riding the buses on early Friday afternoon, when tens of thousands of young army recruits, all armed and
kitbagged, were making a mad dash to get home to their families
before the buses stopped, was a comically dangerous experience.

Our boys had signed up to play baseball in a small league organized by the AACI, the Association of Americans and Canadians in
Israel. They played locally each week and were often invited away for
games. One day, Sam's team was invited to play an exhibition game at
Kibbutz Gezer, an idyllic kibbutz at the foot of the Judean Hills, just
where the land began unfolding generously and gracefully out
towards the Mediterranean Sea. Many of Kibbutz Gezer's members
were originally North American, hence their keenness on baseball,
and of course it goes without saying that the whole place was as secular as you could find in Israel. Their organizers suggested the
Jerusalem team come to play a game and then stay for a swim and

barbecue at the kibbutz pool. Our team's organizers turned the invitation down flat, on the grounds that many of the Jerusalem families would not countenance boys and girls swimming together in the same pool. No thought was given to the alternative way of handling the situation: letting the kids from the secular families swim and making the religious children sit on the sidelines. Instead, everyone got sidelined because the religious families said so. In far too many cases, this was the Jerusalem way of doing things.

We did not expect to make close friendships among the *haredim,* but we kept looking for opportunities to spend some time in a *haredi* home. Once again Mark came through for us. Although he and his wife lived a more or less mainstream Orthodox Jewish life, his brother Zvi (or Herschel, as he had been born in Golders Green) was a serious scholar, who lived not in Mea Shearim but in the Tel Aviv equivalent, the village of Bnei Brak. His special job in the community was sex and marriage counselling with young *haredi* men before their weddings. After a few phone calls back and forth, we were issued an invitation to join Zvi and his family for Shabbat evening services and dinner. Early in my friendship with Mark I had broken my rule about keeping my lip buttoned about my Jewishness, and now it came back to haunt me. Mark had mentioned it to Zvi, who called Patrick to say that since I and by extension my children were Jewish, they could invite us only if we agreed to stay in Tel Aviv the entire length of the sabbath, twenty-five hours. This was because, as a serious Jew, he could not be responsible for making another Jew break the sabbath, which we would obviously be doing if we left their place late on Friday evening and drove back to Jerusalem. We felt a harmless white lie was called for under the circumstances, and we invented some Tel Aviv friends who were dying to have us stay overnight. We said we could easily walk from Zvi's home to our friends' downtown apartment, but Zvi surprised us by saying it would be all right for us to drive. Why was it forbidden to drive from Tel Aviv to Jerusalem but no problem within the city itself? Because one could drive a car on the sabbath within a measurement of 2,000 cubits, or about a kilometre. We didn't ask why.

One more phone call took place before we set out from Jerusalem. This was Zvi telling me exactly what to wear. "A long skirt, and not one with a slit up the leg. A top with sleeves below the elbows. Your hair completely covered so none is showing. Patrick and the boys must be in long pants." This visit was taking place in July and the temperature was 35 degrees. Zvi didn't bring up the subject of stockings and neither did I, because I knew he would say I had to wear them and it was just too hot. I was going in sandals with my toes peeking out, my tiny measure of feminist defiance. I pulled out of my closet what I called my Mea Shearim outfit, a gauzy blue blouse and a skirt that came down almost to my ankles. I was worried about the transparency of the skirt, however, and reluctantly put a slip on under it, which clung sweatily to my legs all night. As for headwear, I tried everything we owned — the sunhats looked too jaunty, the boys' baseball caps definitely inappropriate. I toyed with the idea of wearing one of the fezes we had bought in Cairo but thought it might be viewed as a provocation. Finally I settled for a purple scarf, wrapped ultra-Orthodox-fashion around my head. By halfway through the evening my skull was itching all over with perspiration and I was dying to rip the nasty thing off.

And even with this amount of care, I was still dressed all wrong. My outfit was not unlike what *haredi* women wear during a normal day, but this was Shabbat. Out of their wardrobes came stiff suits and fussy dresses, straw boaters, glittery snoods and obviously fake wigs. I felt like the drab country mouse scurrying down the streets of Bnei Brak beside Zvi's wife, an elaborate flowery bird. Oh well, at least I hadn't dressed in red, an unforgivable *faux pas*.

We arrived at about six in the afternoon, an hour and a half before the beginning of Shabbat. Zvi met us at the door of their snug little flat in his sombre black suit and *kipa* and took us directly to the kitchen, where his wife, Michal, was putting the finishing touches on dinner. Zvi had a fullish beard but no sidelocks; he was a member of the *mitnagdim*, an intellectual sect of *haredim*, who dressed more normally than the flashy, spiritual *hasidim*. Michal had a comfortable, bulky figure after her five pregnancies, and the pale moonlike complexion of an English upbringing and a life lived almost entirely indoors. She was still dressed in her day clothes, a shapeless shift and a kerchief, and as soon as we arrived she settled us around the kitchen table with tall glasses of fresh-squeezed orange juice and huge chunks of delicious carrot cake, freighted down with walnuts and raisins.

That was the best food we would get that night, because the sabbath dinner consisted of barely warm food that had been cooked several hours before. By the time we arrived, Michal had finished cooking and had moved on to the next stage of sabbath preparation. All the pots containing the food were removed from the stove and a thin metal sheet was fitted over the whole stovetop, with the flames kept very low underneath. Then all the pots were piled on top of the metal sheet, so that the heat from the flames could be indirectly transferred to the food to keep it warm.

This was only one of the dozens of strict rules about cooking for the sabbath and festival days. The point is that nothing must be cooked once the sabbath begins; for example, you must not pour hot water over tea leaves (because that would cook them) but you can make a strong tea essence before Shabbat begins and then thin it down with hot water. I had bought a pictorial guide to the cooking laws and was astounded by their complexity. I also found myself annoyed at the way the laws were laid out, with kindergarten-style cartoons for idiots (i.e., women) to follow, all explained by a genial *kipa*-wearing bearded man. The book contained every minute detail of the how-tos, without a single word about the whys. When I asked Michal why she had a particular configuration of three pots piled on top of each other, she laughed and said, "You know, I really have no idea. This is just the way I was taught as a girl."

Zvi and Michal's five children popped in and out of the kitchen, staring at the strangers and asking their mother's help in getting their sabbath clothing organized. The three girls were in frilly frocks, which Michal proudly indicated they had sewn themselves, the two boys in the ubiquitous white shirts and black pants and vests. They wore *kipas,* and would do so until their bar mitzvahs at age thirteen, when they would receive their first fedoras.

We had brought a houseplant as a gift, but it seemed to cause more consternation than pleasure because there was literally nowhere to put it. Michal took me around the apartment and showed me how they had enclosed both their front and kitchen balconies to make more indoor living room, so now they had no outdoor space at all. "Fortunately, we only have five children," she said. "My neighbour" — she pointed at the next apartment, which had a huge unwieldy addition built out into the parking lot — "has thirteen, and we all had to support her application for that extension. You can imagine how they were suffocating in there. But we had a tough fight."

The children obviously felt cramped as well. They were showing me a photo album of their parents' trip to Toronto the previous year, and they pointed with envy to the pictures of Toronto Island park, acres of grass surrounded by a lake studded with sailboats. "We have no parks to play in," sighed twelve-year-old Chava.

"What about Hayarkon Park?" I asked, referring to an enormous Tel Aviv park only a few blocks from the ultra-Orthodox neighbourhood. The children looked at me as though I had mentioned Madagascar; clearly, they never left Bnei Brak.

Dvora, the fourteen-year-old, shifted restlessly in her pretty floral dress. "There are playgrounds here and there for the little kids," she said, "but there is nowhere for *us* to go." With that *us* she expressed the universal adolescent longing to get away from parents and siblings and enjoy the bliss of just hanging out.

As the Shabbat hour approached, Zvi went into the dining room and a low humming began. This, he explained, was their sabbath generator, which powered the minimal lighting throughout the apartment that would stay on all night. "We cannot use the regular electricity on Shabbat," he explained, "because if there was a power failure, some Jewish electricians somewhere in Tel Aviv would have to repair it and therefore we would have contributed to another Jew breaking the sabbath." Michal herded the family into the dining-room for the lighting of the candles, the two essential tapers and one little oil-lamp for each of the children. She prayed silently for a moment with her face in her hands, then gently touched each child's face, whispering "Good *shabbes*," and kissing them on both cheeks. This moment, I felt, was the climax of her sabbath.

Next we all piled outside and down the road to a modern hospital, which contained the synagogue the family always attended. This was a very special synagogue, Zvi told us as we climbed three flights of stairs, one of only two in the world that maintains the exact traditions of the famous Frankfurt synagogue from over a thousand years ago. At the top of the stairs Michal and her girls and I went to the left, the men and boys to the right. The women's section of the synagogue was an insult, a completely bare adjunct to the main action going on beyond a plywood screen running the full length of the room. There was a narrow strip of grillework at eye level, covered with a lacy white cloth, so you could peek through, which I did most of the time, ignoring the frowns of disapproval I was getting from the few women in the pews on my side. From my angle, I could not see the ark or the rabbi or the cantor, just a modern functional room full of rows and rows of desks crammed with black-and-white-clad men and boys, lost in the ecstasy of welcoming in the Sabbath Bride. The room crackled with a restless, seething energy as the men prayed, constantly in motion. The clear, sweet solo of the cantor was abruptly interrupted time and again by waves of harsh, loud chanting from the congregation.

The women's side was truly barren. We could hear everything but see nothing. There was nothing at the front of the room for us to fix our eyes on, just a blank plywood wall. It was no wonder there were so few pews there, and even fewer women. Michal looked dead tired and yawned all through the service; I suspected she had dressed up and come only because I was there. Most of the time she fiddled with her fingers, worrying over an itchy red rash she had undoubtedly developed from the harsh cleansers she used to make her home ready for the sabbath.

Once the prayers were over, the rabbi launched into a twenty-five-minute talk in Hebrew, but Zvi had planned a special treat for us. We met up with the men in the lobby and were introduced to Dr. Rothschild, a Swiss Jew who had built the hospital we were standing in. It specialized in maternity, but had pediatric and geriatric departments as well, and was one of the most modern and well run hospitals in Tel Aviv. But it was also ultra-Orthodox, so on the sabbath all kinds of special arrangements had to be made. Dr. Rothschild, a brittle little martinet of a man, was prepared to give us a tour. That is, if we could keep up with him.

For the next twenty minutes, he ran us all over the facility, up and down numerous flights of stairs because the elevators were all shut down. The corridors were dimly lit by the hospital's generator, and the doctor proudly displayed an invention of his own, a system of signalling from the patients' rooms that involved the mechanical dropping of an opaque shutter to expose a constantly burning red lightbulb.

We all threw on blue hospital gowns and zoomed through the nursery, which was full of exquisitely beautiful little Jewish babies. I tried to picture them in three years' time with wispy sidelocks and embroidered *kipas.* "Come on, come on," urged Dr. Rothschild and pushed us around the corner into the maternity ward. The labour rooms were laid out in an intelligent semicircle around a monitoring desk. We peeked into one, then barged down the hall into one of the recovery rooms where an ashen-faced woman had just given birth.

"Hasn't anybody brought you a drink yet?" shouted the doctor, storming out to the nurses' station to demand service. Next we trooped into one of the regular four-bed wards, which appeared to be standard issue except for the wig-stand at the head of each bed. A family was visiting after the prescribed hours, and Dr. Rothschild shooed them out noisily like a bunch of barnyard chickens. We screeched down another hall and into a dining-room where about forty new mothers were eating their sabbath dinner in the candlelit darkness, all in dressing-gowns and snoods, all beaming with delight over their recent accomplishments and the sudden presence of Dr. Rothschild, whom they clearly adored. The doctor stopped for a moment and looked around. "I wanted to build a hospital that would be first-class in terms of medical care," he said, "but that would also provide the human care that most hospitals in the world forget." Judging by the smiles on his patients, he had succeeded.

Zvi and Michal were sweet and gentle souls, he quietly thoughtful and she chatty and busy. They did not seem to be the intolerant radicals and blackmailers of the system that secular Israelis believed the *haredim* to be. When we went out for a late-night stroll on Rabbi Akiva Street after dinner, Michal was shocked and disgusted to see a young *haredi* married couple walking along brazenly holding hands, but neither of them expressed any views or criticism of the society outside their tight-knit little world. If they were left alone, I got the impression, they would leave others alone.

And yet I had to conclude either that they were not typical of their community or that many *haredim* may present a different face as individuals than they do collectively. Their leaders do not quite issue death threats to their political opponents like the Ayatollah Khomeini, but they curse them publicly and pray openly for their early deaths. In 1987, a tragic bus accident in the Israeli town of Petah Tikva killed many schoolchildren, and the *haredi* interior minister opined that God was visiting a terrible punishment on a town that allowed its movie theatre to remain open on Friday nights. Near Mea Shearim, shadowy groups of *haredim* threw acid onto cars to teach drivers the "beauty" of Shabbat.

And yet...people who live their lives governed by the stark fundamentals of the *haredim* can sometimes see things more clearly than the rest of us. The most heroic single act I heard of during my two years in Jerusalem involved a *haredi* woman. At the Mahane Yehuda one day, the Jewish street market just around the corner from my boys' school, an Arab terrorist drew a knife among the throng of shoppers and managed to stab two young men before fleeing for his life. The crowd of Israelis, incensed, began running after him, a number of them drawing pistols as they ran. The Arab darted across the street, running straight towards a *haredi* woman of forty who was standing at a bus-stop. Her name was Bella Freund. In a trice she sized up what was happening. She stepped directly into the Arab's path and tripped him so that he fell to the ground, and then she threw herself on top of him to protect him. The crowd kicked her, spat on her, threatened her with their guns, but they could not loosen her hold on the Arab, and she lay there until the police arrived to take him into custody. Later, when the reporters got to her, Bella Freund said: "It was very simple. If you can save a life, you do it." Her hatred of Arabs, her lifelong conditioning never to touch a man who wasn't her husband, all of it was swept aside in a split-second of truth. "I could not see a helpless man killed by a mob, whatever he had done," she said. "That's not the way I was brought up."

CHAPTER
II

H AVING FUN IN THE MIDDLE EAST sounds like an oxymoron, and I'd be lying if I gave the impression that life there was jolly. There was too much tension, too obvious an undercurrent of erratic violence for people to truly relax and enjoy their surroundings or each other. Life was fascinating, challenging and adventurous, but seldom fun.

Among Israelis, there was a grim, officially encouraged determination to have fun at all costs. After all, this was the Jewish homeland, the dream made flesh after two thousand years of exile, and no matter what the price in blood, lives, comfort or civility, Israel was cause for celebration and everyone was required to celebrate. The country always felt like a summer camp with guns, a place where roistering group activities underlined the common nationalist spirit and undermined individual doubt or contemplation. Clinging together in groups was also a constant reminder that Israelis did not feel physically safe in their hard-won land. Just after the jubilant signing of the Rabin–Arafat peace memorandum in Washington in September 1993, three young Israeli hikers went on a celebratory walk through the breathtaking scenery of Wadi Qelt, a river gorge in the West Bank linking the outskirts of Jerusalem with Jericho. They paid for their misplaced confidence with their lives when they were attacked by members of George Habash's terrorist Popular Front for the Liberation of Palestine.

On the Palestinian side, years of occupation and intifada meant that most people had simply lost the will to have fun altogether. The usual occasions that mark life's rhythms in such a tradition-bound community still occurred — births, christenings, marriages and family alliances — but with the element of joy and celebration conspicuously removed. My friend Kelly, the American who was heading up the bedspread project in Surif, described the West Bankers and Gazans as "heavy-blooded," people who took their tragic sense of themselves so seriously that they had become almost a caricature in the Arab world. He was in a position to know because his work based him in Amman, Jordan, among the Palestinians who had fled to that country either in 1948 or 1967. Those refugees, he said, felt the loss of their homeland just as keenly in the early years, but as time passed, they had become integrated into the more normal and relatively peaceful Arab society of Jordan and had learned how to reintroduce pleasure and fun into their lives. They were the grasshoppers to the West Bank's ants, and the two groups had little use for each other.

For outsiders like us, the fun came from the extraordinary freedom and privilege we felt in being able to weave in and out of two societies who lived cheek by jowl but could not communicate with each other. Before we arrived in Jerusalem, I even entertained high-flown fantasies of acting as a catalyst, bringing Jewish friends together over my dinner table with Arab friends and thereby strengthening the cause of Arab–Israeli peace. It didn't take long to disabuse myself of that notion — if anything, the Middle East dilemma has been lengthened and muddied by the presence of too many well-meaning and naive intermediaries. In the end we settled for moving back and forth, observing, listening, enjoying, and then carrying our impressions over to those who showed any interest on the other side. Sometimes that is all you can do and it is enough.

The Sultan's Pool, in the valley below our house, was a vast water reservoir for the walled city, built in King Herod's time, and now converted by the Israelis into an amphitheatre for summer concerts of rock, folk and classical music. Living in Yemin Moshe meant that our household received two free tickets to every performance, on the shrewd principle that if they didn't co-opt us we might complain about the noise. All we had to do was go up to the bomb shelter, which doubled as a rather lugubrious community centre, where members of the neighbourhood committee doled out the tickets the day before each show.

Few of the concerts interested us, so we became very popular with the neighbourhood teenagers who knew they could usually cajole an extra two tickets out of number 41. But from time to time something caught our fancy and we would head down to lie on the grassy slopes, with the walls of the Old City and Mount Zion towering, floodlit and fortress-like, above us, and one of those improbable Jerusalem moons hanging like molten gold in the dark purple sky. One night we heard a new Israeli group called Bustan ("orchard"), which combined six Jewish and two Israeli Arab musicians in a rare cultural collaboration. It was no surprise to learn that the group came from Haifa, Israel's northernmost city. Up there, many Arabs stayed rather than fleeing in 1948 and a much more peaceful and progressive relationship has evolved between the two communities. When I got to know the members of Bustan a couple of months later, their flautist, Amir, told me, "We represent the other Israel, the one you foreign media people never hear about because you live in Jerusalem." He spoke with an aggressive wistfulness that I had come to recognize as peculiarly Israeli.

Every family needs a place to go for birthdays and other special times, and ours was the American Colony Hotel in East Jerusalem. Built in the nineteenth century by a wealthy Arab with delusions of grandeur, it was designed like a gorgeous pasha's palace around an enchanting courtyard full of fountains and flowering trees. When the Arab gentleman found that none of his wives was able to give him children to fill up the palace, he sold it, broken-hearted, to an American evangelical family who started their own religious community there, just a few minutes' walk outside the Old City walls. About a century ago, they turned it into a commercial hotel, and recently the remaining family members sold it to a Swiss hotel chain. Its prices were high, its rooms poky, its Arab service friendly and slow, but it was steeped in Jerusalem history and charm and the only place in town capable of convincing us that we had been for a night out.

Jerusalem just wasn't a night town — any Tel Avivian could tell you that — and, with a couple of exceptions, whenever we attempted to go out for dinner on the Israeli side, we encountered lonely seas of empty tables. On the Arab side, the intifada meant that the streets were seriously rolled up by seven o'clock at night, so on the rare nocturnal occasion that we ventured into East Jerusalem, the only traffic we would encounter were street cats and Israeli army jeeps on patrol. Perhaps that was why the American Colony always felt so warm and hospitable: its clientele was international, made up mostly of diplomats, journalists, UN observers, aid workers, Christian VIPs, tourists intrepid enough to brave the neighbourhood, numerous local Arab politicians or academics and the rare Israeli. The place felt sophisticated and gracious; a note on the bottom of the menu let women know that if they should take a chill in the courtyard, the restaurant had a supply of wraps and shawls for the asking.

The only problem with the American Colony was a touch of politically correct priggishness among the clientele. If you were eating dinner there, you were assumed to be sympathetic to the Palestinian cause and hostile towards the Israelis. This was an unspoken assumption, but none the less marked for that, and it was one that often made me uncomfortable. It was remarkable how, in both communities, it was not Israelis and Arabs who made us squirm but their supporters from abroad. Those directly involved in the conflict from birth tended to talk very straight, trying to convince you of their position, naturally enough, but not playing for sympathy or making unspoken assumptions about your prejudice or support. But outsiders from Western countries, whether Jews or a mixed bag of observers on the Arab side, were always trying to gauge where you stood or advising you on exactly where that ought to be.

Which is why we enjoyed ourselves so much the night we took my beautiful Jewish aunts to the American Colony. They were in from Toronto, one of them with my uncle in tow, and they were old Jerusalem hands who had visited many times over the years. Earlier that day they announced it was time to go shopping in the Old City, so we walked across our valley and in through the Jaffa Gate, only to discover that it was a strike day so the shops on David Street were locked and shuttered. Not in the least dismayed, they pointed us towards the Jewish Quarter, an area of the Old City I seldom shopped in because it was so much more expensive than the Arab and Armenian sections. As soon as I had deposited them in the Cardo, a glossy underground shopping area set among Roman and Byzantine ruins, I had the feeling my presence was no longer required, which suited me fine since I am very bad at recreational shopping. I was a little concerned for my aunts' safety, since there seemed to be a higher military presence than usual in the empty Arab alleys that abutted the Jewish Quarter. It was clear, though, that they were perfectly comfortable, so once I gave them strict instructions to move only south and west through the Old City, never north and east, I left them happily spending their travellers' cheques.

I was relieved when they turned up in one piece at their hotel later in the day and we picked them up to drive to the American Colony for dinner. Once we were seated at our large corner table with two other Jewish friends, Rob and Galia, my aunts launched into a breathless blow-by-blow description of each store they had entered, each conversation they had had with the proprietors, and each bargain they had snagged. They were in full North American shopping heat, they looked glorious and their high spirits were infectious and absolutely endearing. To Patrick and me, that is. Behind us, we could feel an iceberg of disapproval building up around the restaurant, which made the dinner all the more fun.

On the Ben Yehuda Mall in West Jerusalem, it was a fancy-dress party all day long, and people-watching from the cafés lining the walking street was one of the city's chief attractions. Late Friday morning was prime time, as the commercial and social week came to a climax before the curtain of Shabbat rang down. This is where young Jerusalemites would congregate to check out the weekend's action, the parties, the gossip, the sexual partnerings. Oriental rock music belched from the coffeehouses, competing with the sidewalk artists: the serious Russian baritone singing opera, the hippie North American guitarist recycling Bob Dylan and the antic Israeli duo on trombone and xylophone. Everyone on the street was eating something, overcooked corn on the cob out of huge vats of steaming water, frozen yoghurts, falafel or the ubiquitous *baegele,* which weren't bagels at all but simply round loops of bread sprinkled with sesame seeds and sold off long wooden poles.

At my café, an incredibly handsome pair of paratroopers took a front table and began flirting outrageously with the waitress. Their noses fell straight and razor-sharp from almost non-existent bridges, giving them the look of young Roman conquerors. Having the soldiers sitting there was obviously good for business; the café filled up around them in minutes. At the table next to mine, three grizzled kibbutzniks in khaki shorts settled in with the *New York Times* and *Ha'aretz,* Israel's thinking newspaper. Two Sephardi mothers approached with their babies in strollers, the women looking like biblical Queen Esthers in their colourful snoods. Young girls from religious families paraded arm in arm, their ankle-length skirts knotted up into graceful scallops at the side. Other, more liberated girls favoured skin-tight patterned pants or black jeans with shiny red and orange blouses. One beautiful young blonde wore a bullet on a silver chain around her neck, a present, no doubt, from a warrior boyfriend. Another nubile teenager, representing a different school of political thought, sported a T-shirt that read: "Fighting for peace is like f——— for virginity." A religious Zionist pushed his baby in a pushchair, his prayer fringes hanging down from under his white shirt and tangling with the pistol stuck in his belt. A black-hat scurried by with his Walkman headphones under his Homburg, the wires interwoven with his ringlets. A pair of young army recruits, he with his rifle slung over his shoulder and she with an enormous bunch of sabbath roses, stopped for a passionate embrace in front of our tables, to the amused approval of the crowd. On his rifle strap were written the English words: Die Hard.

By two o'clock the circus was over. The mall was deserted, the cafés locked up tight, the street a polluted nightmare of falafel wrappers, Coke cans and spilled ice-cream cones. The beginning of

Shabbat, signalled by an electric foghorn up by the Russian Compound police station, wasn't for hours yet, but a magic Jerusalem broom swept all sign of life off the streets every Friday afternoon, turning it into an enchanting ghost town for wanderers of the secular persuasion.

Because Israelis had only a one-day weekend on Saturday (although it is now stretching backward to include large chunks of Friday), we soon learned not to go exploring the country's many tourist attractions or nature parks on Saturdays. Facilities were always jammed to unpleasant limits and we, unlike the Israelis, had the luxury of a free Sunday because the Anglican School operated on a Western timetable. The first time we visited the Dead Sea Water Park, a forty-minute drive down in the Jordan Valley, it was a Saturday and we could barely find a spot to lay out our towels and picnic hamper. The second time we made it a Sunday, assuming that we would have the water-slides and wavepool all to ourselves. But we had forgotten that the Palestinians had their own timetable, completely distinct from the Israelis, and this particular Sunday fell during the three-day feast of Id al-Adha, the Feast of the Sacrifice, the biggest religious festival of the Moslem calendar. This time the water park was filled to bursting with multigenerational Arab families, the men and young boys strutting over the grass in minuscule bikinis, and their wives and daughters covered from head to toe in *higabs* and long-sleeved ankle-length dresses. This was on a scorching June weekend, and the women were not about to let their cumbersome clothing keep them out of the water. Most of them, except for the oldest grandmothers, were standing under the waterfalls or sitting half-submerged in the pools playing with their babies, seemingly oblivious to the fact that soaking their dresses in water showed off the curves of their bodies provocatively. Watching the spectacle from the deep shade of a plane tree, I decided that in the hierarchy of the oppression of women the religious Arabs came off worse than the religious Jews because of their outrageous double standard. At least among the *haredim* the males were required to be just as idiosyncratically garbed and sexually circumscribed as the females.

The Dead Sea is the strangest, eeriest place in the country, a long thin stew of salts and minerals so noxious that no fish or plants can live under its grey gelatinous surface. The air around it reeks of sulphur, and through the constant heat haze you can just make out the armed hills of Jordan on the far shore. At its southernmost end, at Sodom, loom the Dead Sea Mineral Works, where potash, bromine and magnesium are extracted from its poisonous depths. The Dead Sea advertises itself as the lowest point on the face of the earth, more than four hundred metres below sea level, so to reach it from Jerusalem means a dramatic drop of twelve hundred metres through the Judean Hills in just twenty kilometres. In spite of its inherent environmental unpleasantness, we often found ourselves heading for the Dead Sea because of its major tourist attractions: the caves at Qumran where the Dead Sea Scrolls were discovered in 1948, the great Herodian fortress of Masada, an object of pilgrimage for Jews from around the world, the lush nature preserve at the oasis of Ein Gedi and the hilarious mud baths at the Ein Gedi Spa.

Swimming in the Dead Sea was an ordeal none of us was prepared to live through more than once. Signs everywhere warned bathers not to get even a drop of water into mouths or eyes, so real swimming was out of the question. All along the rocky seashore tourists waded in up to their thighs, then sat down on the superbuoyant surface, bobbing awkwardly like beachballs and laughing hysterically at the weird sensation. Locals would have nothing to do with the activity: Israeli tour guides ushered their charges down to the shore and then lounged, smoking, in their air-conditioned buses while the tourists made absolute fools of themselves.

The height of fun and foolishness was the mudbaths. We would buy day passes to the Ein Gedi Spa, which had a heavily Russian clientele and atmosphere. Perhaps it reminded the newest Israelis of past holidays in Odessa. We'd be issued a tiny locker and a thin, none-too-white towel and we'd head down a long outdoor ramp to the mud vats. The sun this far below sea level felt wonderfully warm and soothing, but it must have been hotter than it felt because as soon as we would slather on the rich black mud it would instantly begin to dry and harden into a full-body cosmetic mask. Working the mud into our hair, over rough elbows and knees, and onto each other's backs was pure, forbidden, infantile pleasure. The Israelis had thoughtfully installed a full-length mirror beside the vats; it was interesting how many people looked more fetching covered in mud. Black is a slimming colour, they say.

Secret destinations are always more fun than those shared with the madding crowd. That was why we loved visiting the Herodion, one of King Herod's magnificent fortresses just a few kilometres' drive southeast of Bethlehem through some of the loveliest Arab farmland in the West Bank. Because of its potentially dangerous position in the occupied territories, Israelis and Jewish tourists never went there, and because it was of historical importance only to the Jews, the Palestinians never went there. So we always had it to ourselves, which was a treat.

King Herod has certainly received bad press through the centuries as a paranoid despot who preferred to kill first and ask questions afterwards. Apart from his pivotal role in the slaughter of the innocents after the birth of Jesus, he also put his own wife Mariamne and his sons to death because he was convinced they were plotting to usurp his throne. In fact the Herod family tomb, where these unfortunates were buried by the later-repentant king, was just up the hill from our house, and I passed it each day on the way to my Hebrew classes.

Undoubtedly he was a thoroughly unpleasant character, but my goodness, the man knew how to build! The vast structure of the Temple Mount in Jerusalem, the elegantly terraced palace at Masada, the Tomb of the Patriarchs in Hebron, the extraordinary Roman city by the sea at Caesarea, all of these are still in place and still speak of an architectural vision of dazzling self-confidence. But the Herodion remained my favourite because of its sheer audacity. Constantly looking for better ways of fortifying himself against his enemies, Herod ordered his engineers to shear the pointed top off a good-sized mountain, then hollow it out and build a fortress in the bowl-like interior. From enormous distances in any direction, Herod's flat-topped defiance of nature is clearly visible, one of the most amazing curiosities in an amazing landscape. Up close, it was sometimes difficult to persuade the Israeli soldiers to roll back the razor wire and let us drive up to the fortress; they were not used to sightseers. Once on top, the place was a child's dream of hidden passages and ruined towers, weed-choked courtyards and mysterious storehouses. And underneath the fortress, deep in the body of the mountain, I had read that there was a complex warren of secret tunnels that had been excavated by second-century Jewish guerrillas hiding out from the Romans. When I asked the custodian if we could visit these tunnels, he gave us candles, matches and a key and let us explore to our hearts' content. It was pure Indiana Jones.

Another deserted treasure we loved to visit was Hisham's Palace, an eighth-century jewel from the Moslem Ummayad dynasty, just a couple of kilometres from the centre of Jericho. Here we would occasionally encounter a Palestinian family or two wandering through the open courtyards of a palace that enjoyed only three years of life before it was devastated by an earthquake. But mostly, as at the Herodion, we would have the site to ourselves, from the delicate double rows of limestone arches like those at the Alhambra in Spain, to the magnificent mosaic of a lion pouncing on a deer under a fruit-laden Tree of Life. Other geometric mosaics, laid out as though they had originally formed the bottom of a series of ornamental pools, lay exposed to the elements but still retaining their sensual colours and patterns after twelve centuries. No one came to see them.

This may soon change however. Jericho was named in the Arafat–Rabin peace memorandum as one of the two areas (the other is Gaza) that the Israelis would turn over to the Palestinians for self-rule, and after months of procedural wrangling, that finally came to pass in May of 1994. It was probably a happy choice. There is a laid-back quality to Jericho that always made it a favourite destination for our family drives. Perhaps because of its lushness and blessed location as a sprawling, well-watered oasis in the stark Jordan Valley, it has not been a focus of Palestinian extremism over the years. In fact, before the Israelis took over the West Bank in 1967, Jericho was a popular vacation spot with tourists from all over the Arab world, and its ramshackle streets are filled with large whitewashed villas smothered in bougainvillaea and shaded by lofty palms.

It always seemed to us that Jericho had, potentially, some of the hottest tourist attractions in the country. First there is its claim to be the oldest city on earth, a claim disputed by other Middle East locations, such as Damascus. The English archaeologist Dame Kathleen Kenyon, who did the major excavation work at Jericho, believed that the city contained the first evidence — around 8000 B.C. — of people evolving from nomadic hunter-gatherers into settled farmers. Unfortunately, the mound, or *tel*, of ancient Jericho in the middle of the town, from which Kenyon derived her evidence, is too confusing for laypersons to figure out.

Then there's the biblical account of the Hebrews first entering the Promised Land from the east, leaving behind their dead patriarch, Moses, and following Joshua across the Jordan River valley right up to the famous walls of Jericho, which they presumably destroyed. Archaeological evidence appears to back up this claim, although from a touristic point of view it's a pity there are no longer any walls on display. I couldn't help thinking that Jericho would be a good test case for developing virtual-reality tourism.

And for the Christians, there is the Mount of Temptation looming over the town, where Satan tempted Jesus to prove his divinity by turning the stones into bread. At present it's a heavy trek to the Greek Orthodox monastery at the top, one we never made, but a consortium of Palestinian-American businessmen is planning to install a cable car, like the one that has been so successful at Masada, as soon as there is a Palestinian government to give them the green light.

The other great future appeal of Jericho could be political. This is where Yasser Arafat is expected to make his home and seat of government, at least temporarily, if he returns from the exile he has lived in most of his life. Already most of the international newsgathering organizations based in Jerusalem have set up satellite offices in Jericho to cover the birth of the new Palestinian entity. It's clear, though, that the Palestinians don't want to settle down too comfortably in Jericho: for them, it is only a stepping-stone to a Palestinian state throughout the West Bank with its capital in Jerusalem. Already there is a government building of sorts in East Jerusalem, a gracious villa known as Orient House, but the Israelis refuse to recognize it as anything official. At this point, Israel's claim over all of Jerusalem remains absolute and non-negotiable.

No matter how the future pans out, though, things have nowhere to go but up for the owners of Jericho's many large and lavish garden restaurants. A testimony to earlier good times, these huge places were almost entirely empty every time we dropped in for lunch. Our favourites were the Seven Trees and the Bedouin Tent, although I'd be at a loss to tell you why. Every place in town served exactly the same menu: a wide variety of oriental dipping salads with pita, followed by charcoal-grilled chicken breasts, pork and lamb chops and spicy sausages. The Seven Trees, with an optimism I could hardly credit during the depths of the intifada, built a huge second storey, although the place must have already had ample seating for seven hundred non-existent customers. But their instinct was right: the good times are coming back, and this sleeping beauty of a town is starting to stretch.

Etti and Nachman's son, Zach, was being bar mitzvahed, and we were invited to join the celebration. We saw a lot of bar mitzvahs in Jerusalem because many of them were held in the open at the Western Wall every Monday and Thursday, the days the rabbinate decreed that the Torah could be opened and read there. Those mostly Sephardic bar mitzvahs were pure spectacle, at least half a dozen of them going on simultaneously, with fathers and uncles singing and dancing the bar mitzvah boy around on their shoulders, while his mother and sisters stood on kitchen chairs on the women's side of the barrier, ululating and throwing sweets down on the celebrants.

Zach's bar mitzvah was a different matter altogether. It was a measure of Nachman's iconoclasm towards all things Israeli that he chose to have his son called to the *bima* in a Conservative synagogue. Most Israelis simply sneer at Conservative and Reform Judaism as modern pop-religious confections from North America. Even though eighty percent of them may be secular, they feel comfortable being secular only in relation to Orthodox Judaism. As one of the country's most outspoken secularists, Matti Golan, writes: "What we prefer is the real thing to the imitation, honesty to hypocrisy...I respect Judaism too much to accept a diluted alternative." This dispute is high on the long list of irritations between Israelis and North American Jews.

The place was packed with North American Israelis when we arrived, so we had to settle for standing room behind the last pew. The synagogue was lovely but peculiar, I discovered in reading one of my guidebooks. It had been a church, purchased by the Conservative Jews from a Baptist congregation, and its altar area faced south, making it the only synagogue in Jerusalem that was not oriented towards the Western Wall. When I had mentioned this to Nachman a few days earlier, he became even more pleased with his choice. As Zach launched into his flawless and lengthy reading from the Torah, a dainty white street cat wandered in the open door behind us and began strolling up and down the aisles. The man next to me, clearly an ex-Manhattanite from his accent, quipped under his breath, "Oh boy, I can see it now. Back in New York they'll be saying there are so few Conservative Jews in Jerusalem they needed a cat to make a *minyan.*" I observed that I thought the cat was confused and was probably looking for the Reform congregation. My companion chuckled at my feeble joke and said, "Reform, hah! At the Reform synagogue they *marry* dogs and cats!"

I found this a delightful exchange, but after it was over it occurred to me that the only reason it had taken place was because the man assumed I was "one of them," a practising North American Jew who had made *aliya* as he had. For two seconds I felt part of the tribe, one of the many Jerusalem tribes, but it had a strange effect on me. Instead of arousing my desire to belong — there, in that stiff-necked Jewish city — it gave me a pang of homesickness for all my Jewish friends back home, and made me realize how terribly I missed their easy bantering wit, their warmth, their shtick. In Jerusalem I was surrounded by more Jews than anyone could hope for, but they weren't *my* Jews. With the transplanted North Americans I always felt vaguely defensive, and with the Israelis, friendships were possible but they were highly focussed friendships based on a common interest in Israel and its problems.

In two years, I cannot recall a single conversation with an Israeli (or a Palestinian, for that matter) that was not in some way connected to the Middle East problem. Partly this was my fault because I was often asking the questions, and my curiosity about Jerusalem life was boundless. But there was also a wilful myopia and self-centredness among Israelis that I found so preposterous it was almost engaging. Our friend Jackson Diehl, who worked for the *Washington Post,* had an interesting comment about this Israeli cast of mind. "My first foreign posting was to Buenos Aires," he said, "and from there I covered the whole continent of South America. Next I moved to Warsaw and reported on all of Eastern Europe. Then I came to Israel, and the comment I get from Israelis all the time is, 'What, you mean the *Washington Post* only has *one* correspondent covering all of Israel?'"

Sometimes I used the past as an escape from the overbearing present of Jerusalem, which is probably why I spent so much time at the Israel Museum. I'm a bit of a connoisseur of museums, and this one stole my heart at the first visit. It is set down like a pile of chunky white shoeboxes on a hillside, and its atmosphere is so casual and light-hearted that I often thought how delightful it would be to *live* there. I used to visit in the evening, just to cut down on the number of organized groups I would run into. Everywhere in Jerusalem of any historical or cultural or military significance, you would invariably be stampeded by swarms of (a) schoolchildren, (b) soldiers and (c) tourists. Hitting the Israel Museum at night generally meant eliminating (a) and halving (b).

There was another reason for my nocturnal visits. Before I came to Jerusalem, I thought of archaeology as a science, and a rather dry, dusty one at that, that methodically set out to classify and record humanity's common past. In Israel, though, I came to see it as romantic voyeurism, as a series of teasing, elusive glimpses into the lives and secrets of long-dead individuals who never dreamed that the results of their intensely private actions would end up encased in Lucite for the world to view and pronounce on. Somehow night-time seemed the best time to indulge such peeping-tom fantasies, and the dark silvery lighting inside the museum always stimulated this mood even further.

There was the twelve-thousand-year-old man and his dog, for example, their bones companionably curled up together and fused into the earthenware vessel that had guarded their sleep for millennia. The dog always haunted me: had the man's Stone Age family killed it so he would have company on his unimaginably long journey through time, or had it died grieving for its master? Then there was a Canaanite fertility figurine, showing in graphic detail two tiny foetuses curled up under their mother's breasts while she pulled the labia of her vagina wide open to let them out. Only four inches high, it was meant to be held by a woman during her contractions, to bring the goddess Astarte's blessing on her labour. I could hear the woman's groans, see the sweat beading on her forehead and the panic in her eyes, feel her fingers clenching around the little figurine so tightly that she might have reduced it to dust. But she didn't, and here it stands now behind glass, mute witness to that woman's miraculous achievement thirty-five hundred years ago.

Down in the city as well, there were archaeological discoveries that made me gasp with pleasure as the pungent whiff of ancient everyday life emerged from them. Most powerful was the Lithostratos, literally the stone street, hidden far below the modern Via Dolorosa and protected from harm by the Sisters of Zion, a French order. On huge brown paving stones, their edges softened and shining from use and weather, there are gaming boards etched into the stone by Roman soldiers, trying to stave off boredom as they waited to take their prisoners in for trial at the Fortress Antonia, the seat of Roman authority in Jerusalem. Christian lore has appropriated the site as the place where the soldiers stripped Jesus, robed him and crowned him with the crown of thorns, hailing him derisively as King of the Jews. Unfortunately, the floor and the games etched into it date from a hundred years later than Jesus' crucifixion, which in no way deters the faithful. But sweeping aside all the mythology, you are still left with the feisty reality of those soldiers, cursing their years of service in this godforsaken backwater of the Roman Empire, gambling away their miserable stipends and dreaming of Tuscany.

The most stunning archaeological discovery made during our time in Jerusalem was that of the Caiaphas family tomb, found by park construction workers in the Jerusalem Peace Forest just to the south of the Old City. It rocked the world of biblical archaeology because it was the first solid evidence of the existence of any of the Jewish characters involved in the story of Jesus' crucifixion. Caiaphas and his father-in-law Annas were the Sadducee high priests who wanted Jesus dead and who made a deal with Judas Iscariot to betray him.

The discovery was clearly extraordinary, but I found myself imaginatively transfixed by one small detail: inside a female skull in the tomb researchers had found a coin with Herod Agrippa's image on it, dated A.D. 42. Placing coins in the mouths of the dead was a Greek custom, representing a payment to the ferryman Charon to carry them safely over the River Styx to the underworld. The Sadducean Jews, especially those at the highest social and religious level, like the Caiaphas family, were adamant that the soul perished along with the body, that there was no afterlife. It would be shocking beyond belief for a family like that to publicly admit that they adhered to such pagan customs, and yet here was a female family member buried with a coin in her mouth. Was it her desperate last wish, whispered in her husband's ear? Or did a pagan maid of the family slip it into her mistress's mouth as she washed the body for burial? Whatever happened, it was a moment of dark, secret intimacy, now exposed — two thousand years later — to the judging and analytical eyes of the late twentieth century. The coin in the skull seemed to make a mockery of the very idea of privacy.

I'm not sure that watching television qualifies as having fun, but I have to admit it took up large amounts of our family's recreational time in Jerusalem, just as it does in Toronto. We imposed a weekend-only video rental policy on ourselves, so on weeknights we were stuck with two Israeli (both Hebrew) and two Jordanian networks (one English and one Arabic). They were all either abysmal or incomprehensible or both. The ten-o'clock news in English on Jordan TV was our only regular date, and it really had just one news story to report night after night: what King Hussein had done that day, greeting other Arab heads of state, inspecting troops, shaking hands with European Community visitors, inspecting more troops. In an absolute monarchy, one supposes, there simply are no other stories. And I will never in my life forget the tune of the Jordanian national anthem, which signed us off to bed each night at the prim hour of ten-thirty.

After our first year and a half, cable rode into Jerusalem to rescue us from televiewer hell. Now we could click from Tony Curtis in Turkish to Charles Bronson in Italian, to Robert De Niro in French, to Sally Field in Spanish, to Bruce Willis in Russian. We received three all-news channels, CNN, BBC and SkyNews, and two MTV music stations, the European and the Asian versions. On Middle East TV we could watch a tennis tournament from Dubai, the stands filled with sleek, rich Arab men identically dressed in blinding white galabias and Ray-Bans. One night on that station, we found a domestic sitcom featuring Adolf Hitler and Eva Braun and a lot of madcap SS men mugging away in Arabic to the accompaniment of a deafening laugh-track. (The lingering Arab fondness for the Nazis is a bit disconcerting.)

Mostly what we saw was cheerful junky North American entertainment mindlessly spreading the culture of acquisitiveness across the Middle East and Asia. My favourite television moment in Jerusalem occurred on one of the Turkish channels. It was a giveaway show I tuned in to near its end, a weird combination of "Talent Time" and "The Price Is Right," in which contestants first had to perform and then correctly guess the price of their prizes. Since all the prizes were kitchen appliances, I assumed that the show was normally filmed with an audience of housewives; but this week, for reasons I was incapable of divining, they were shooting it at an army base with a roomful of pink-cheeked soldiers in khaki sporting baby-blue berets. A young man, no more than eighteen, approached the microphone and launched into a wailing Turkish number that galvanized the crowd and brought him thunderous applause. He was offered two prizes for his efforts, an electric sandwich-maker and a toaster oven, and broke down in sobs when he guessed both more or less correctly and was bundled back to his seat lovingly cradling an appliance under each arm. Next, a guest star appeared from the back of the room, obviously a popular Turkish singer in a clinging white sheath coated in glitter. As she slithered and sung her way through the sea of khaki to the stage, all the young men went wild, climbing on their chairs and swaying to her sensuous rhythm. At that point the host motioned to all the winners to come forward with their prizes, and the soldiers belly-danced to the front in rapturous union with their blenders, toasters and hand-mixers.

My jaw was on the floor. The mysterious East was meeting the consumerist West in a soufflé of expectations that seemed destined to collapse.

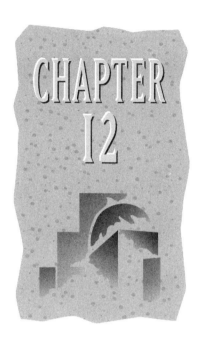

CHAPTER 12

J ERUSALEM DAY — *Yom Yerushalayim* — which occurred in late spring, was the one day of the year I preferred to stay indoors. It was a day of atavistic passions and it spooked me. I have never been to Londonderry, but Jerusalem Day made me think of the annual ritual that is played out in that bleak Northern Irish city on the Glorious Twelfth: the Protestants marching to their hollow drumbeats celebrating King Billy's long-ago triumph at the Battle of the Boyne, while smart Catholics just stay out of their way.

On Jerusalem Day, the Arabs stayed home as well, as the Jews commemorated their capture and reunification of the city during the Six Day War. From early in the morning until well past midnight, groups of schoolchildren, soldiers and veterans marched incessantly, around the Old City walls, through its narrow lanes to the Western

Wall, up one side of Mount Zion and down the other, over to Ammunition Hill and the Rockefeller Museum and the site of the Mandelbaum Gate, all key scenes of fierce fighting during those tense and terrible days of 1967. They waved thousands of Israeli flags and brandished their weapons, while helicopters hovered overhead to monitor security. The air was filled with drumbeats, military songs and the hoarse bark of bullhorns. From our terrace we had a ringside seat, plus Avraham's disgusted commentary. "This gets worse every year," he said, sweeping his arm across the whole chauvinistic panorama. "Every year more guns, more drums and more chances to stir up trouble."

Evidently it didn't have to turn out like this. Teddy Kollek, the liberal and indefatigable mayor of Jerusalem for twenty-eight years, whose term started before the Six Day War, proposed that there should be a holiday to celebrate the day the two halves of the city were officially rejoined. His goal was to tone down the triumphalist aspect of the celebration and to encourage the Arabs to participate as well. But popular opinion, encouraged by the national government, insisted on making the holiday the twenty-eighth of Iyar in the Hebrew calendar, the date the Old City fell to the Israelis. This way the day celebrates a Jewish military victory, one that drives the warring sides farther apart each year.

It was sobering to discover that the Middle East personalities we in the West most admire are all prophets without honour in their homelands. Take Teddy Kollek, seemingly the perfect mayor for such a fractious town, always trying to guarantee equality and fair treatment for his Arab and Jewish citizens alike; his work was constantly undermined by the Likud national government, which openly built Jewish neighbourhoods on the disputed lands and secretly encouraged Jewish extremists to take over Arab properties in the Old City. In the 1993 municipal election, the tired eighty-three-year-old mayor was trounced by his right-wing rival, Ehud Olmert, who reflects much more accurately the hard-line political attitudes of his Jewish constituents. Take Anwar Sadat, the president of Egypt whose historic decision to travel to Jerusalem led to the Camp David peace accords of 1979; he was assassinated by an Islamic fundamentalist in Cairo and is much reviled by Egyptians today because his peace with Israel isolated them so dramatically from the rest of the Arab world. Think of Abba Eban, Israel's first ambassador to the United Nations and author of a string of brilliant, thoughtful, liberal books on the Middle East; he was passed over time and again by his countrymen for major political positions, and was generally thought to be useful in terms of garnering Western support for Israel but otherwise old-fashioned, elitist and irrelevant. Finally, think of Hanan Ashrawi, the recent megastar of the Palestinian movement, darling of the international media because of her soft-spoken but impressively articulate presentation of her people's rights and demands; by her own admission at an international conference a couple of years ago, she is unrepresentative of her people. "First, I am highly educated," she said, "second, I am a Christian, and third, I am a woman." Palestinians do not trust her, and she fell from public view almost immediately after Rabin and Arafat signed their historic agreement on the White House lawn.

The international news outlets stick like Krazy Glue to these unrepresentative individuals who know how to talk Western mediaspeak and who generally articulate the sober, humanistic, nonextremist line we all want to hear out of the Middle East. Not only do the media thereby distort the realities of the situation but they can make things worse. The more popular Hanan Ashrawi was with "Meet the Press" in Washington, the more she became isolated at home, so her reasonable voice in the debate within her own community was effectively silenced.

It seemed important, if uncomfortable, to listen to more extreme views from both sides, which was one of the reasons I accepted an invitation to go for Shabbat lunch at Martin and Rosalie's house down the street. They were my American-born Orthodox neighbours who had made *aliya* about twenty years earlier, and who had dynamited out the bedrock under their house. I was invited for twelve o'clock sharp, and I arrived from two doors away just as other guests were turning up in their sabbath finery, having walked from all over the city. These included Esther, a religious twenty-something from New York who had been in Jerusalem for two years, worked in public relations and had the preoccupied look of the dying-to-get-married. And David, also in his twenties and also from the United States, who had moved to Israel with his family at a young age and had now completed his education and army service. He worked in the marketing end of the diamond business, and it was transparently clear that he had been invited to meet Esther. There was a mother-and-son team from Larchmont, New York, also long-time Israelis, whose names I think were Miriam and Jacob. Martin and Rosalie's adopted Israeli son, Amos, fourteen years old, rounded out the party.

We sat on a sumptuous semicircular leather couch for the first ten minutes, trying to make small talk. Miriam mentioned the trouble she was having keeping twelve-year-old Jacob occupied during the current teachers' strike, which had been going on for a week. Martin said, "Is this a salary dispute? Surely they're being paid enough." Miriam and I came up with the figures: $500 a month for regular teachers, $650 for specialists. "That can't be right," declared Martin. "It's not enough for anyone to live on." Then a happy thought occurred to him. "Of course it's not enough for a man's salary, but in Israel most teachers are women. And of course it's only a part-time job since there are just four hours of class-time a day. In fact as a second household income it's really quite good, so what are they striking about?" Miriam appealed to me: "Did he say that? Did you actually hear him say that?" She was laughing; the families were evidently old friends. I had made a resolution before I left my house that I would say as little as possible within the bounds of politeness; my tongue was clamped firmly between my teeth.

We took our places at the table for the blessing of the wine, then filed into the kitchen to wash our hands with a traditional two-handled Shabbat cup. Silently we returned to the dining-room and watched Martin carve up the *challah* loaf and pass it around. After another prayer, conversation could begin again as Rosalie shunted course after course from the kitchen to the table. For the record, we ate lukewarm chicken hearts, then lukewarm chicken soup, then lukewarm boiled chicken with cold mashed potato sculptures and cabbage salad, then a frothy non-dairy mousse of unidentifiable flavour served in huge silver goblets, then delicious homemade almond cookies and tea.

David started the conversational ball rolling by telling us stories about his work among the *haredi* diamond merchants and how he had had to learn Yiddish to converse with them. Many of the European ultra-Orthodox consider Hebrew exclusively the language of the Bible and find it an abomination that the modern state of Israel has adopted it as its official language. They use Hebrew only in their prayers and religious study and continue to conduct their daily affairs in the language of the Polish *stetls*. David recounted tales of the astounding behaviour in this arcane diamond subculture: multimillion-dollar exchanges confirmed with a handshake, dealers carrying their priceless commodity around in their pockets.

I asked him whether these merchants wore handguns to protect their property. It was an innocent question, but it swept us instantly into the heavy waters of Israeli politics. A month earlier, during a spate of terrorist attacks by Arabs, the country's top policeman, Ya'acov Terner, had called for all Israelis who owned a licensed firearm to start carrying it regularly. "It won't do any good sitting in your bedside drawer at home," he was quoted as saying. There was a predictable run on the gunshops and shooting galleries across Israel, with liberal politicians wringing their hands over the Wild West atmosphere that Terner had created.

Martin was regretful but adamant: "Rabin is doing absolutely nothing to protect us, so we have to do it ourselves. He only got into office the last time on the promise that he would never abandon Israeli security — what a joke."

David disagreed. "Having a bunch of amateurs running around with loaded guns is no way to guarantee security either. The only solution is making an agreement with the Arabs — give them the West Bank and they'll leave us alone." David spoke with the moral authority of one who had done his time as an Israeli soldier policing the West Bank. "Look," he said, "I don't want to die, and I don't want to kill Arabs. That's not what my family came to Israel for."

Esther looked uncomfortable. Her natural views were clearly close to Martin's, but David was awfully cute in spite of his progressive politics, so she had no desire to argue with him. She resorted to laughing and rolling her eyes. "Oy, politics, politics," she said. "When Israelis get together you can't escape it."

Martin had heard enough liberal claptrap at his table. With Jehovan-like thunder in his voice, he set us all straight. "What the religious Jews are doing here in Israel today — reclaiming Judea and Samaria — has a theological imperative to it. Five hundred years from now there will be new festivals in the Jewish calendar commemorating our victories." David winced in disbelief. Martin continued. "The problem is that we are our own worst enemies. We are strong but we're unwilling to use our strength. Look at the intifada — a ridiculous uprising by boys with stones that we should have smashed in two minutes. It was Rabin's fault; he was out of the country when it started and he stayed away three weeks. By the time he got back it had built and built and it was too late."

Martin's scholarly son Amos, who was sitting beside me with his long thin hands trembling in his lap, dared to interrupt. "No, Dad, I don't think it's fair to say Rabin was responsible for the intifada. Remember, it started when a Jewish truck ran down some

Palestinian kids in a camp in Gaza, and then other kids started throwing the stones."

"Be quiet," Martin snapped. "You don't know what you're talking about." Amos went chalk-white. "When it began, we should have immediately killed a large number of them and it would have stopped instantly."

"What, shoot down a bunch of Arab kids in cold blood?" demanded David. "Is that what Jews are supposed to do?"

Twelve-year-old Jacob jumped in. "I can't wait till I'm old enough to carry a gun," he said. "I'll use it on Arabs, no problem."

"No," said Martin, smoothly backtracking, "I'm saying if we had rounded up about three hundred of those kids and kept them in detention for two weeks, their parents would have wised them up good when we returned them." I was still holding my tongue, so I did not mention that thousands of Palestinian youths had indeed been rounded up, jailed and later released, with no appreciable effect on the strength of the intifada.

Now Martin veered onto a new subject: the Gaza Strip, that thirty-two-kilometre-long hell-hole on the Mediterranean jammed with 800,000 angry, desperate refugees. "We should have forced the Egyptians to take all those refugees out of Gaza when we signed the Camp David accords and gave them back the Sinai. Now we're stuck with them and they will endanger our security forever if we leave them there. What we should do is remove them from Gaza, disperse them in small groups throughout the Negev Desert and keep them under tight surveillance. They'll be easier to police in small numbers."

"That's crazy," said David. "Why would you want to bring them into Israel proper when our whole goal is to get rid of them?"

"Well, what's your suggestion?" asked Martin.

"I told you, an autonomous Palestinian entity in the West Bank."

"And just sit here and wait for them to take the whole country back again?" shouted Martin. "Never. I won't let it happen. And half the Israeli population agrees with me and won't let it happen."

My tongue escaped from between my teeth. "What about the other half of the country, Martin? Isn't their view legitimate too?"

"They are lazy cowards," said Martin.

David started smouldering. "I served for three years in the West Bank, supposedly defending this country. Now I think the practical, realistic thing is to make a clean break from the Arabs and try to live in peace side by side with them. And you think I'm a coward?"

From that point on, everyone — including myself, I'm ashamed to say — was shouting so loudly and at such hopeless cross-purposes that I could no longer follow the argument. Sometimes a verbal slugfest can be quite an exhilarating experience, sweeping politeness and hypocrisy aside in a massive air-clearing gesture. But lunch at Martin and Rosalie's didn't feel that way. The positions were too far apart for there to be any hope of constructive understanding emerging from the debate. It felt deadly, hateful and sickening.

Rosalie was the only one who had not opened her mouth during the whole meal. As the fight was building towards its futile climax, she left the table and picked up a pile of prayer books on the sideboard, which she distributed to each of us. At a signal from her, Martin stopped shouting and opened his book. Silence fell instantly around the table and the buzzsaw whisper of Hebrew prayers began. They were lengthy, at least five or six minutes, and they were competing with the electrical charge from the quarrel, which was still a hostile presence in the room. I could feel the animosity burning itself off in tiny lightning bolts that flashed and sizzled into the corners of the ceiling.

When the prayers ended, silence fell again. Then Rosalie spoke very quietly: "I have said this before. I don't think politics is a suitable subject for Shabbat lunch. It gets everyone too upset." As we pushed back our chairs and stood, I found that my knees were shaking. I thanked my hosts, made my excuses and left, as they settled in for coffee on the leather couch.

Whenever we wanted to visit the heart of darkness, we went to Hebron, a town now etched in the world's consciousness because of the events of February 25, 1994, when Baruch Goldstein stood in the corner of a mosque and mowed down dozens of Arabs at their Ramadan prayers. Long before that tragedy, Hebron was the most dangerous and volatile place in the West Bank, and sometimes we were too afraid to go there. But whenever possible we included it on our itinerary when we had guests, because it embodied more than any other place the essential dilemma and character of the Arab–Israeli conflict. Even more than Jerusalem itself.

The Bible says that Hebron was where Abraham bought a piece of land to use as a funeral plot for his wife Sarah. Since both Moslems and Jews believe they are originally sprung from the loins of Abraham, it is an equally holy place for both religions. Custom has decreed that not only Abraham and Sarah but their son Isaac and his wife, Rebecca, and *their* son Jacob and his wife, Leah (the men being collectively known as the Patriarchs), are all buried in Hebron, in deep graves that have never been precisely identified. Who cares? Herod began the commemoration of the spot with an immense fortress two thousand years ago, while inside his massive structure the usual parade of conquerors came and went: first a Byzantine church, then an Arab mosque, then a Crusader church, then a Mameluke mosque. For seven hundred years no Jews were allowed to get any closer to the tombs than the seventh step leading up to the mosque, but a tiny trickle of Jews always lived in or around the holy city until 1929, when the Arab Riots erupted throughout Palestine and about sixty Jews in Hebron were murdered.

After the Israeli victory in the Six Day War in 1967, religious Jews triumphantly reclaimed the right to live in Hebron and worship at the Tomb of the Patriarchs. Gradually, a large settlement known by the ancient name of Kiryat Arba was established on a hill overlooking the town and now houses five thousand heavily armed Jews. And in spite of the official disapproval of the Israeli government, about forty militant Jewish families resettled right in the heart of the Arab souk near the tombs. Their presence could not be more hateful or provocative to the Palestinian population, which is one of the most politically radical in the occupied territories. In most parts of the West Bank, traditional Arab villages and modern Jewish settlements keep their distance from each other, but in Hebron the communities are on each other's doorsteps, and the potential for deadly clashes is constant.

What's more, the religious Zionists established two tiny synagogues right inside the mosque, in the rooms housing Abraham's and Jacob's cenotaphs. Until the February massacre, the large central part of the mosque, where Isaac and Rebecca are commemorated, flipped back and forth between Arabs and Jews several times a week. The place was teeming with Israeli soldiers at all times, and the religious Jews were permitted to carry their M-16s into the places of worship. The water fountain in the courtyard between the synagogues was used by the Moslems for their ritual washing before prayers five times a day. But a traditional two-handled Shabbat cup sat in the fountain as well, for Jews to use on Friday evenings. Once, in front of Abraham's tomb, we watched in astonishment as two ancient men, one Arab and one Jew, prayed silently side by side to their different versions of the same Almighty. In a Holy Land so full of bogus miracles, this was the only genuine one I witnessed in two years. It will not be repeated now.

Hebron always felt hopeful and hopeless at the same time. While it was impressive to see how human beings could accommodate such gulfs in belief and understanding between themselves, there was no point in getting sentimental about it. The peace of Hebron, such as it was, was guaranteed by Israeli military power. On that fateful February morning, however, there were mysteriously only four soldiers on duty, even though it was both Ramadan and Purim, coinciding Moslem and Jewish festivals, which were bound to create more tension than usual inside the mosque. And disturbing testimony that came out at the subsequent inquiry indicated that the soldiers' standing orders were never to shoot at Jews who were firing weapons, the underlying assumption being that Jews never attack, they only defend themselves. The Israeli government was quick to condemn the massacre as the act of a "crazed, lone gunman": Baruch Goldstein was most certainly crazed, but he was not alone. He was a member of a community that largely shared his beliefs about Arabs, even if most of them didn't have the insane bravado to follow through on them.

If and when the soldiers leave, if and when a Palestinian self-governing entity, state, call it what you will, extends to the whole West Bank including Hebron, will the Arabs allow the Jews to remain? Unlikely. Will the Jews go peacefully? Unlikely. The Jews of Hebron are armed to the teeth and imbued with what is known as the Masada spirit more than anyone else in the country. That spirit is one of the most dangerous elements of Israeli culture today and could yet destroy all moderate attempts to bring peace between Arabs and Jews.

Generations of Israelis have imbibed the story of Masada with their mothers' milk, and it has had a profound effect on the national psyche. King Herod built the mighty fortress in the first century B.C., as a final refuge should the Judean kingdom be attacked by Cleopatra of Egypt. After Herod's death, when the Romans took over direct rule of Palestine, the Jews fought back against the imperial forces, but it was a doomed struggle. In A.D. 70 the Romans expelled all the Jews from Jerusalem, and a group of about a thousand Jewish "zealots" and their families retreated to the mountaintop fortress of Masada to make their last stand. After a lengthy siege, the Romans succeeded in building a massive earth ramp from their camp far below up to the very walls of the fortification, and when the Jews realized they were about to be overwhelmed within the next day or two, they made the momentous decision to commit mass suicide rather than surrender.

In one of the most interesting books I read during my two years in the region, *Civil Religion in Israel,* two academic authors chart the waxing and waning and waxing again of Masada as a dominant cultural myth for the Israelis. For the early secular pioneers from Europe, it was a sacred story demonstrating the power of human determination. They were not worried about the troubling religious implications of suicide, but rather saw the story as a historical precedent for what they were trying to accomplish: bringing the modern state of Israel into being through a sheer act of will.

In the middle period, from 1948 to 1967, under David Ben-Gurion and the Labour hegemony, the dream was that Israel should take its normal place among the normal nations of the world, so the Masada myth was discarded as defeatist and isolationist. But the place still had romantic appeal. Young Israelis scaled its heights, more as an outward-bound adventure than as an act of spiritual defiance. Thousands of Jewish volunteers excavated the site during the sixties, under the leadership of archaeologist Yigal Yadin, and among many other structures, a small synagogue was unearthed.

In the next phase of Israeli development, after 1967, when religion was reintroduced into the country's *raison d'être,* the zealots of Masada were imbued with new meaning as religious nationalists, defending Judaism against the decadence of Rome. And then, following the harrowing Yom Kippur War in 1973, when modern Israel had its first taste of defeat after a string of victories, the suicidal isolation of Masada struck a resonant new chord in the national psyche. Combined with the growing strength of the Holocaust as the other dominant Israeli cultural myth, Masada has appealed to more and more Israelis as the statement of their final political position. Golda

Meir admitted it when she said, "We do have a Masada complex. We have a pogrom complex. We have a Hitler complex."

If the final watchword on the Holocaust is "Never again," its Masada-inspired corollary is "But if it does happen again, we will control our own destiny." Masada is seen as the definitive refutation of the Jew-as-victim scenario of the Holocaust.

When we walked or drove through downtown Hebron we would always encounter small groups of these Masada-inspired Jews, striding Bonanza-like through the Arab marketplaces, three and four abreast, their M-16s slung over their shoulders and slapping against their hips. They knew they had little support for their extremism from other Israelis, but they didn't care. Their isolation from the general population made them the most potentially dangerous people in the country. A young soldier on duty in Hebron said to Patrick one day "You know, in Israel we have a saying: You can't swallow a fish that has too many bones. Hebron has too many bones."

Coming face to face with Arab extremists was something that happened rarely, mainly because the Jews were so open and voluble about their views and the Palestinians so quiet. Physical acts of Arab extremism — particularly stabbings — were in evidence every few mornings when we opened our copy of the *Jerusalem Post,* but I could never connect these bloodthirsty attacks and the reasons that motivated them with the Arabs I knew personally. Until I met Walid.

One November morning, our second year in Jerusalem, it began to rain. We knew this was bound to happen, of course, but after seven months of completely cloudless skies, we were somewhat unprepared. As water started seeping through from the atrium and trickling down the dining-room wall, I knew it was time to take action. The previous winter had broken all records for Jerusalem snowfall, and everyone in the city had suffered from leaking roofs. We had contacted our landlord a number of times during the year about making repairs, but nothing had happened. Patrick was on assignment in Istanbul; I would clearly have to take care of things myself.

Just as I was mopping up the floor, Jamila arrived. She was our Israeli Arab cleaning lady, who had been working for our landlord's family for a dozen years. She shook her head at the drips and told me not to worry. She was having leaking problems at her house too and she had a good roofer from the West Bank working over there right now. She would get Walid to phone me as soon as she got home from work. Later that afternoon he called and said he could come in two days for an estimate.

The next morning the heavens opened and the year's first deluge fell on Jerusalem. Now it was no longer a question of drips in the dining-room; I had a full-blown flood in the upstairs hall. The upper portion of the atrium simply wasn't draining, and the water was flowing in thick gurgles over the patio-door threshold, along the hall and down the stairs to the main floor. As I picked my way downstairs to see how far it had run, I caught the water just centimetres from the nest of computer wires under Patrick's desk. After flinging down every towel in the house to get things under temporary control, I phoned Walid in a panic. Could he possibly come today? He sounded perturbed because it was a strike day, which meant that he should not be working. If anyone from the intifada committee found out, especially that he was driving into Jerusalem to do work on the Israeli side of town, there would be hell to pay. Moreover, the Israelis had one of their roadblocks up, so it might take him an extra half-hour or more to drive in from Batir, his tiny village near Bethlehem. "Still," he said with eloquent simplicity, "you need me, so I must come."

He was at my door an hour later, drenched and apologetic. "I am so sorry, missus, there were lakes and puddles everywhere and cars getting stuck all over the road. Two times I had to stop and help push cars out of the way before I could get through. Now show me your problem." Any woman in distress is inclined to be favourably disposed towards a saviour who turns up on her doorstep, but Walid was a genuinely impressive person. He was thirty-nine years old, with a thin, lined face set off by deep intelligent eyes and a friendly black moustache. His voice was soft and blurry, but his English was extremely sure-footed for a man with his lack of education. Although it was undoubtedly the prospect of a substantial, well-paying job that had brought him to me, from my viewpoint here was a man who had braved political intimidation, the Israeli military and a replay of Noah's flood to help me out. I liked him instantly.

His clothes — thin-soled leather shoes, blue jeans and a cheap windbreaker — were completely unsuitable for the messy job at hand, so I rooted around and found him Patrick's yellow raingear and some rubber boots. He discovered the source of the main problem immediately, a drain in the upper atrium that was inexplicably capped with a metal disc. As soon as he punched a ragged hole through the disc, the water rushed down and disappeared. "But you have more serious problems here, missus," he said, scanning the roofline. "I have to clean out those eaves right away but I have no helper. Please find me some strong plastic bags, and then you can help me yourself." For the next two hours he worked on our red-tiled roof in the pouring rain, filling bag after bag with water-logged black sludge that must have been building up there for years. He passed the heavy, slippery bags down to me in the upper atrium and I staggered downstairs with them to the back lane. By the time he had finished, the house was a filthy mess and we were both exhausted. "I will have to come back another day when it is dry to caulk the seams," he said, "but for now this is all I can do."

We went downstairs, washed up and made coffee. Walid lit a cigarette and we began talking, with the companionable satisfaction of two people who have handled a big job together. First we compared family notes: he had been married for only four years, his wife was eighteen and they had two small babies. This seemed strange, since Palestinian men tend to marry young and Walid was almost forty. He had never been out of Israel or the West Bank, except for a couple of trips to Jordan to visit family. The most logical explanation for his lateness in marrying was a protracted stay in an Israeli prison, but I was reluctant to bring up the subject.

Walid had gone to the local school in his village for a few years, long enough to be able to read and write Arabic. But he had to leave at the age of twelve, because the family could not afford the luxury of teenage scholars. "My father was so unhappy when he had to take me out of school," he said. "He really wanted all his boys to have an education, but it was not possible. He said to me, 'If I could cut off my right hand and that would let you finish your schooling, I promise you I would do it.' But it wouldn't have helped, would it?" What an extreme, overdramatic promise, I thought, and wondered, not for the first time, why so much Arab rhetoric involved blood and dismemberment.

Walid had apprenticed himself to a Jewish building contractor in Jerusalem and had specialized in roofing and electrical work. "He was from Holland," he said, tears welling up in his eyes, "and he was the most wonderful man I ever met after my father. He taught me everything I know and he treated me like a son. He has been dead for five years now. I always mean to go and visit his wife in Rehavia, but I didn't know her well and she might not like to see me."

What was so special about this man, this Jew, I asked. "He just treated me like a person, not like part of a group he hated. He taught me to do this too, just to have a relationship with one person, not to be always thinking, Is he a Jew? Is he an Arab? Is he from my religion or not? This is where all the trouble comes from in this country, from people thinking their group is better than the other group." Talk like this was such a rarity in the Middle East that I could hardly believe my ears.

We chatted for another quarter of an hour, and then I had to change and go to an appointment. I left Walid cleaning up the mess we had made and walked out to the upper parking lot. The rain had dropped off to a steady drizzle, and the parking lot was empty except for one battered old Fiat with blue licence plates: Walid's. As I walked past it, I saw with a thud to my stomach that the driver's window was smashed. I peered into the car, and sure enough there was a gaping hole where the radio should have been. I was stunned and furious, not only at the car thieves but at myself for not telling Walid after he arrived to move his car to the lower, more secure parking lot. I had just had other things on my mind.

I rushed to the house with the bad news, and Walid looked stricken. "My new radio," he moaned, "I just bought it a month ago, a Sony, it cost me 1,200 shekels" — about $500.

"We'll call the police and make a report," I said, and went back to Patrick's office to enlist Cindy's help. She was sympathetic but reluctant to get involved. At my request she phoned police headquarters at the Russian Compound, had a brief chat in Hebrew, then hung up. "They say he has to come in and report the theft in person," she announced, looking nervously at Walid. He drew her aside and began talking to her earnestly in Hebrew, throwing embarrassed glances my way from time to time. Cindy translated: "Walid doesn't have valid papers for working in Israel, so he doesn't want to go to the police station. His last permit expired a month ago." He showed me a furry-edged piece of grimy cardboard. I asked how he had got through the Israeli roadblock this morning with invalid papers. "I was lucky," he said. "In all the rain they didn't ask to see them."

"Why aren't your papers up to date?" I asked.

"Because to get a permit I have to go to the Civil Administration office in Bethlehem and they keep me waiting at least one whole day, sometimes two. Instead of earning money I am waiting in an office. They do it on purpose to make life hard for us. Most of us, what we do is get a permit for a couple of months, then go a month or two without one, then get another one. Right now I am in Israel illegally."

"So you don't want us to report this theft to the police?"

He shook his head bitterly. "No, I would get in very bad trouble. Besides, they will never find the radio." He was probably right about that.

"What about your own insurance policy, will it cover you?"

Walid looked at me in mute misery and I understood that his car insurance payments weren't up to date either, if in fact he even had insurance. He pounded his fist softly against the door frame and said, more to himself than to me, "Why did this happen? I was having such a happy day."

I stared at him and realized what was probably going through his head. I had agreed to pay him 1,200 shekels to do the roofing job, exactly the cost of the radio he had just lost. Plus he had the window repairs to do. The whole morning's effort was financially wiped out for him. Moreover, because of his shadowy existence as an illegal Palestinian working in Israel, he had no recourse to the official channels an Israeli would have used to get compensation for his loss.

Walid was partly responsible for the fix he was in, of course. His radio was one of those fancy, self-contained units that could be removed from the car for security, so why hadn't he brought it into the house with him? And whose fault was it that his work permit and insurance papers weren't up to date? Certainly not mine. On the other hand, I knew what a ridiculous security risk the parking lot was and Walid didn't (although surely I could be excused for thinking the car thieves might take a break during the year's heaviest downpour). After the extreme effort he had made to help me out of a difficult situation, it seemed grossly unfair that he should end up with nothing.

I made a quick decision. I gave him 300 shekels to get the car window repaired, and I promised him that I would contact a friend of mine who was flying in from London the following week and ask him to purchase a new radio there. It would cost Walid about half as much without the heavy Israeli taxes. This way we were splitting the cost of the theft between us, which felt about as right as we could get it under the circumstances.

A few days later, I phoned Walid to tell him his radio had arrived, and I suggested that we could drive out to his village on the weekend and bring it to him. (Whose motives are ever as pure as we would like them to be? I wanted to get a peek at his family and his home.) Patrick had come back from Istanbul, and the next Saturday we headed down the Hebron Road and met Walid by the Bethlehem–Beit Jala intersection, the one with the full set of streetlights that never functioned. Walid had instructed us to meet him there because he said it would be impossible to find his village and house without his guidance. His scruffy little Fiat, driver's window now fully restored, was jammed with people, a couple of women in *higabs* in the back and at least four children. We kept a close eye on his car as it dodged through the West Bank traffic, since almost every other vehicle looked identical to Walid's, both inside and out.

We reached Batir and got out briefly in the main square so that Walid could show us the ancient spring that watered the town, and the long communal vegetable garden down the central valley with its neat plots of cabbages and garlic. The village was right on the Green Line, with the bare and biblical West Bank hillsides giving way to the always startling lushness of the Israeli forests.

Our caravan moved on to Walid's house, built on a steep hillside at one edge of the village. It was a square modern box with no garden in front, just trucks and building materials. As the crowd piled out of the back of Walid's car, we were introduced to his thin teenage wife and his wizened, gold-toothed mother, plus assorted babies and cousins. The formal living-room was dank and chilly, and the front door was left ajar in expectation of the steady stream of relatives who began turning up as soon as we had been seated: first Walid's father, in his best grey suit with a white burnous on his head, coming down from his apartment overhead, and then various brothers and sisters and many more babies. The usual fizzy drinks and fruit appeared, followed by a huge store-bought cake loaded down with frilly white icing and cherries. A dozen pairs of black eyes in solemn children's faces glommed on to the cake and watched its slow progress from our plates to our mouths. They were forbidden a piece, at least until after the guests left, although a couple of fathers broke off forkfuls for the diapered cherubs they were dandling on their laps.

Our conversation had the familiar stilted quality we were used to in Arab parlours. Although the primary relationship that had brought this meeting about was between Walid and myself, I found myself firmly pushed to one side as Walid and his father and brother huddled in an all-male grouping with Patrick. The usual topics were covered: a proud enumeration of all the family members, which ones were abroad, what they all did. Walid's brother-in-law was a teacher of mathematics and politics at a nearby junior college, which had only just reopened after years of closure by the Israelis during the intifada. He had worked without pay during all that time, teaching classes and giving private tutoring in his home. It was impossible to detect how willingly he had done this free teaching. We knew from other sources that Palestinian teachers had gotten the short end of the stick during the intifada: the Israelis closed their schools as hotbeds of political dissent but the pressure from within their community kept them working for no money as their "contribution" to the cause.

It was futile to expect straight talk on such subjects and we knew it. Gabriel, an Arab friend in Hebron who always guided us and our guests around the Tomb of the Patriarchs, explained one day how he and his family had managed to emerge unscathed from the deadly political games that were played out daily in his city. "I tell my sons," he said, "just keep your mouths shut. The cemetery is full of wagging tongues."

Patrick tried to nudge Walid and his relatives a little more out into the open by asking whether the family supported the PLO or Hamas. Walid's father was evidently the only one authorized to pronounce on such matters and he answered with a dismissive wave of his hand. "PLO, Hamas, they are all just politicians. We don't have anything to do with either of them. They fight among themselves and they forget the only important thing: the word of God."

Walid chimed in softly, "All we want is to live good lives and to follow the Koran, which is the word of Allah. It is very simple. The Koran says we must kill the Jews. This has nothing to do with politics."

"Do you mean all the Jews in Israel?" Patrick asked.

"No, no, all the Jews in the world," explained Walid's father. "It is written in the Koran very clearly."

As the two men sat side by side on the couch explaining these obvious facts in voices of unquestioning certitude, I realized that I understood next to nothing about the depths of hatred these groups had for each other. Our neighbour Martin would have understood what Walid and his father were talking about: here was the kind of clear "theological imperative" he could presumably relate to. As for me, though, I had been completely taken in by Walid. If required to do so in a court of law, I would have described him as responsible, intelligent, tolerant of others and honourable (honourable in my sense, not the traditional and rather brutal Arab sense of the word).

We drove home from Batir in shock, and I spent the rest of the afternoon with our English translation of the Koran, trying to find the words that would allow these apparently reasonable men to agree with the mass murder of an entire race. Of course I did not find them. The Koran, like all seminal religious texts, is a masterpiece of ambiguity; individuals can interpret it in any of a hundred ways according to their own degree of moderation or extremism. Generally the emotional tone of the Koran struck me as being one of hurt humiliation, as if Mohammed were saying, "Those people of the Book, the Jews and the Christians, how can they possibly refuse to see me as the final and definitive chapter in their story? Look how all-inclusive I am! I accept Moses and Jesus as prophets before me. So how can their followers not accept me!" The book oscillates between praise and respect for the God of Abraham on the one hand and colourful descriptions of what Allah will do to the disbelievers on the other: "Those who disbelieve Our signs We will in the end cast into the Fire: so oft as their skins shall be well burnt, We will change them for fresh skins, that they may taste the torment. Verily God is mighty, wise!" (Sura IV, verse 59).

Still, it is quite a stretch from imagining Jews burning in Hell to accepting the rightness of their liquidation from this earth, and although I looked up every reference to Jews in the Koran, I could not find one that gave people like Walid and his father direct orders to carry out such an action. Of course the out-clause for Islamic extremists is always the will of Allah. Since everything is in His hands, Allah will decide if he wants an individual Moslem to pick up a knife or a bomb and kill Jews. Personally, I thought the chances of Walid or his father getting such a command were slim; the perpetrators of such acts were almost exclusively young unmarried men with very little to lose.

I never got Walid out of my mind. Whenever the ebb and flow of Middle East politics seemed to be moving more positively — a secret diplomatic meeting leaked to the media, some conciliatory words from Yitzhak Rabin, a momentary relaxation in the tensions of the region — I would think of Walid and a shadow would pass over the sunny mood of the day. How many Walids were there in Palestine, and how many of them were prepared to act, and could anything — ever — change their minds?

One summer afternoon many months later, when I was writing on our front terrace, Walid was suddenly, silently there across the table. I had not seen him since our visit to Batir. He smiled shyly and asked if he could sit for a moment.

"Jamila told me that you are soon returning to Canada," he began. "I wanted to come and thank you for helping me last November." I nodded and waited. "I was thinking," he continued, "that when you go home, maybe you could help me and my brother apply to come to Canada to work. Everything here is so bad, there is no work, you saw the way my family lives. If we could just go and work a few years in your country, we would be able to make decent lives for our children."

I found myself responding with the hard truths about Canadian immigration that make absolutely no sense to poor citizens of the Third World: even though it looked prosperous from here in Jerusalem, I said, the Canadian economy was in terrible shape, with massive unemployment and public opinion ever more hostile towards immigrants. Unless a foreigner had either very special educational skills, or a great deal of money to start a business, or relatives already in Canada, he didn't have a prayer of getting in. Walid took all this in with philosophical calm, smiling ruefully at the way of the world and at his own unfortunate place in it. But I could not let him think these were the only reasons I would not help him.

"You know, Walid," I began, my heart pounding in my ears, "I have thought a great deal over the last months about our visit to your house and what you and your father said about the Jews. I think you should know that I am a Jew." He blinked impassively and waited for me to continue. "Do you think it is the will of God that I should die because I'm a Jew?"

"We just want all the Jews to leave Israel, to leave our land," he muttered.

"I understand that," I said, "but that wasn't what you said that day. You said that *all* the Jews in the world must be killed. Does that include me? Does that include the man from Holland who taught you everything and acted like a father to you?"

The silence seemed to go on for ever, while Walid stared into my eyes with a cool, slightly troubled expression. Finally he spoke. "In my family we follow the word of God. He knows best. He will show us what must be done. That is all I can tell you."

Then he was gone, as quickly and quietly as he had come.

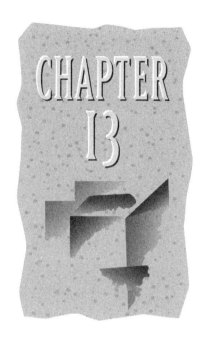

CHAPTER 13

LAUSTROPHOBIA. It became my regular state of mind from the beginning to the end of our Jerusalem stay. It is a feeling all Israelis share as they sit hunkered down on their slim dagger of Mediterranean coastline, surrounded by hostile neighbours on three sides. To the north, Lebanon. To the northeast, Syria. To the east, Jordan. To the southwest, Egypt, no longer an enemy but far from being a friend. The normal twentieth-century desire — to just get in the car and drive and see where you end up — was thwarted in Israel in every direction (although if you headed south into the Negev Desert you'd bore yourself to death long before you hit a problematic border). Nor could you pick up a phone and call someone in a town twenty-five kilometres away, if the town happened to be in enemy territory.

Perhaps this is why Israelis are some of the world's most frequent travellers, those who can afford it, that is. They are overwhelmed, two or three times a year, by the need to escape their geographical and psychological prison for a few days, to breathe free air, to turn on the news without having to deal with another stabbing, bombing or border incident, to shop without the extreme burden of high Israeli prices and taxes. The jets out of Ben Gurion Airport all streak north-west to Europe and America, leaving the Middle East behind like a bad dream.

The Palestinians would doubtless appreciate the occasional respite from their historical lot as well, but they have neither the money nor the inclination to leave. They know the Israelis would like nothing better than for large numbers of them to emigrate or evaporate, so they must be very sure before they set foot outside Israel and its occupied territories that they will be able to return home. Thousands of them who went to work in Kuwait and were kicked out of that country at the time of the Gulf War have never been able to rejoin their families in the West Bank. They stagnate over the border in Jordan, while human rights lawyers in Israel (often Jews with strong social consciences) plead for family reunification before the Israeli authorities. Occasionally they win a case.

Living in Jerusalem was doubly claustrophobic because of the city's peculiar position at the end of the steep mountain corridor that connects it to the rest of Israel. On three sides, Jerusalem is surrounded by disputed West Bank lands, although successive Israeli governments have done their best to disguise that fact by blanketing the barren hillsides with endless Jewish suburbs. But the city is also spiritually isolated from the rest of Israel by its religious concerns and the confrontational relationship between its Jewish and Arab citizens. People in Tel Aviv hated Jerusalem and could not understand how we could enjoy living there. "My friends and I never go there," said Jean-Claude, a French Jew we met when he was selling us a sofa at Kastiel, one of the world's great furniture stores in south Tel Aviv. "All those walls and stones and all that history — it smothers the life right out of you!"

We didn't agree, but there were days when it seemed difficult to draw a deep breath and we knew it was time to plan a getaway. Surprisingly, though, one of our best escapes occurred on a spring afternoon when we didn't budge from our house. It happened courtesy of Bezek, the Israeli telephone company.

The fact that we couldn't pick up the phone and talk to people in many of the surrounding Arab countries contributed immensely to the hemmed-in feeling we experienced so often. There are phone connections between Israel and Egypt, since they are officially at peace; but the Egyptian phone system is so hopelessly antiquated and overloaded that the privilege of being able to make the calls is eradicated by the frustration of trying to make them. Our first Christmas season, I tried for a week to get through to the Hilton Hotel at Sharm el-Sheik, an Egyptian resort town at the bottom tip of the Sinai Peninsula, to make a booking. In desperation, I finally drove to the Jerusalem Hilton and asked their reservations manager whether she had some more efficient way of getting through. I don't know what I thought: maybe Hilton had its own satellite link for hotel-to-hotel communication. The Israeli manager just laughed: "We can't ever get through to the Sharm Hilton. We have to use the telephone lines just like you, you know." I never could make the booking, and we never went to Sharm el-Sheik.

As for all the other Arab countries, communications were officially forbidden and physically impossible. When Patrick had to travel outside Israel for work, we had to set up elaborate procedures to keep in touch. Cyprus was the key: Patrick would often fly from Tel Aviv to Cyprus, and then take a flight into Lebanon or Syria from there. An organization called Memo in Nicosia made the bookings and requested the visas so there would be no Israeli "taint" to the arrangements. When we needed to talk, Patrick would place a call from Amman or Beirut to Memo in Nicosia, and they would get me on the phone in Jerusalem and attempt to patch us through to each other. It never actually worked, however, so we would resort to awkward three-way conversations with a stranger in the Memo office passing along whatever information needed conveying. At times like these I realized that family long-distance calls are almost never about hard facts. ("You have a dentist appointment next Tuesday," was about as incisive as they ever got.) It was the voice contact that meant something, and without that there hardly seemed any point to the exercise.

Somewhat more satisfying were our written communications through Patrick's computer. If he was sequestered in Damascus or Algiers for several days at a time, he could send personal notes to a private computer desk back in Toronto, which I could then call up and read in Jerusalem and send notes back. Even this constipated form of communicating was often thwarted by the terrible or non-existent telephone service wherever Patrick happened to be at the time. When he went into southeast Turkey and the mountains of Kurdistan, we were completely out of touch for ten worrisome days.

Likewise, there was no postal service between Israel and most Arab countries. When I wanted to send a Christmas card to my friend Kelly in Jordan, I had to send it to friends in Cyprus and ask them to stamp it and send it on from there.

I always felt indignant on Israel's behalf about these ridiculous shenanigans. The country had been very much there since 1948, but its neighbours were still carrying on the pretence that it didn't exist. If the Arab countries had to refer to it at all, half of them still called it "the Zionist entity" rather than Israel. It was true that Yasser Arafat, at a famous press conference in Geneva in 1988, acknowledged the existence of Israel and its right to exist. But Arab maps still refused to show Israel's borders, as indeed Israeli maps refused to delineate the Green Line. I found all this offensive and counter-productive.

Pretending your enemy isn't there is quite futile as a strategy for war or peace.

One day, Patrick returned from an assignment in the Golan Heights with an interesting piece of news. He had been researching a story about the Druze, a mysterious tribe of Arabs who lived in both northern Israel and Syria, their community having been bifurcated by Israel's capture of the Golan in the Six Day War. There was a romantic spot right on the contested border called Echo Valley, where Druze shepherds and their families would gather on both sides and shout tribal and neighbourly information and gossip across the no-man's-land that separated them. As one of the local sheiks was showing Patrick the scene, he remarked casually, "Of course we could phone them, but it's expensive and this is more fun."

"What do you mean, you could phone them?" Patrick asked. "There are no phone communications between Israel and Syria."

The man shrugged and said he didn't know how it had happened, but for the past few months they had been able to get through.

Back in Jerusalem, we decided to test the phone lines ourselves to see how far into the Arab world we could reach. We started with the Canadian embassy in Damascus, Syria, and got through on the first try. The diplomats at the other end were stunned and excited; they knew who Patrick was and where he must be calling from, although he was careful not to mention the country or city. After five minutes, the call was abruptly cut off as the Syrian secret police who were listening in must have finally figured out what was happening.

Patrick had the phone number of the president's office in Beirut, Lebanon, so we dialled it next and got through immediately. He spoke to a functionary, confirming a face-to-face appointment for the following week, then hung up before his interlocutor thought to ask where he was calling from.

I cannot describe how exhilarating it was to be making these calls. It was like a miracle, after a year and a half of imprisonment in the hot stuffy closet of the Israeli–Palestinian conflict. We began scrambling around the office looking for more phone numbers to call in other Arab countries. Patrick needed to make a hotel reservation in Algeria, something he would normally have asked the Memo office in Cyprus to do. He direct-dialled the Al-Ghezeir Hotel in Algiers and was put straight through to the reservations desk. Unbelievable. Next, I tried to reach my friend Kelly in Amman, Jordan, but we were stymied by the electronic beeping we were used to encountering on all Arab calls. It occurred to us that the Israelis would be least likely to open the lines to Jordan, because that would provide excessive comfort to all the Palestinians who had relatives in that country.

I unearthed a complete list of the Canadian embassies in the region, and we began dialling them all. First we tried Baghdad and got a cultured English-accented female voice telling us that all the circuits to the country we were dialling were busy, which could have been true or else the standard kiss-off to calls coming from the Zionist entity. Next we phoned Riyadh, in Saudi Arabia, and got directly through to the Canadian ambassador, who nearly fell off his chair when he figured out where we were calling from. While we stayed on the line, he tried placing a call back to us on another line but was politely informed by a Saudi recording that he must have misdialled. "Oh well, one way is better than no way," he said, and we hung up and continued our marathon. In Teheran, we dialled straight through to a message machine at the Canadian embassy, and when we tried Tripoli, in Libya, we got a busy signal.

We had racked up a multi-shekel phone bill, but it was worth it just to feel that momentary normalcy of being able to make direct contact with neighbours in the surrounding countries. Later, when Patrick talked to a spokesperson at the Bezek telephone company in Jerusalem, he found that the Israelis had been quietly opening the international lines to the Arab world since shortly after the Madrid

conference of 1991 that launched the current Arab–Israeli peace initiative. "Every once in a while," she explained, "the authorities in
one of the countries will close us down for a time. But they open up
again." When we told Israeli friends about our phone marathon, their
faces lit up in astonishment and pleasure. "You should try it yourselves," we would urge them, but they would say, "Yes, but we don't
know anyone to call in the Arab countries," which was true, and sad.

Israelis affected indifference to the Arab world around them, but
they were full of curiosity about it. For many years, one of the rites
of passage for Israeli males has been to sneak across the Jordanian border and visit Petra, the stunning two-thousand-year-old city of the
Nabateans that lies hidden in the soft sandstone folds of Wadi Moussa
(the Valley of Moses), three hours' drive south of Amman. The Israeli
army believes that some boys who went missing many years ago may
have been murdered. These days they tend to get nabbed by
Jordanian soldiers, after which they cool their heels for a few days in
an Arab jail cell, endure some humiliation in the press of both countries and have hell to pay when they are delivered back to their families. But nothing stops more of them from trying the feat.

We visited Petra legally but with the usual difficulty that accompanied any attempt to cross an Israeli border. We had applied for
Jordanian visas and entry permits well in advance and we got a car
from the East Jerusalem company Guiding Star to drive us through
Jericho and across the West Bank to the Allenby Bridge, the only place
along the Jordan River where we were allowed to cross the border. No
one with an Israeli passport was permitted entry. Palestinians had a second bridge farther north for their exclusive use, but many of them
crossed at the Allenby Bridge as well, being subjected to much rougher
treatment than foreigners when they returned to the West Bank.

After a peremptory check of our documents by the Israelis, we
piled onto a Jordanian bus, which carried us, with disappointing
anticlimax, across the Jordan River. My image of the Jordan was

always of a gentle, slow-moving but ample river, with wide green banks, rather like the Nile. The trickle that ran under the wooden planks of the ten-metre-long Allenby Bridge wouldn't have caught my attention if I was out for a Sunday drive in Ontario! Up near the Sea of Galilee, where the Jordan flowed south, it was indeed a wide and graceful river, with beautiful curves that have been appropriated by Christian sects to carry out genuine Jordan River baptisms. But with the Israelis siphoning off most of the water into their underground aquifers to irrigate the country, what was left by the time the river met the Allenby Bridge was pitiful: another biblical myth shattered.

A sign just after the bridge read: "Smile! You're in Jordan now," a good-humoured dig at the grumpiness and bad temper of the Israelis. We did start smiling, although an hour later, after being kept waiting in a series of unbearably hot rooms and having our papers scrutinized by one mystifying layer of Arab officialdom after another, the smiles were wearing a little thin. On the Israeli side, most of the hoops one had to jump through seemed to relate more or less heavy-handedly to state security; in Arab countries, the bureaucratic striations always felt like make-work projects for the educated unemployed.

Guiding Star had arranged for a rental car to be waiting for us on the Jordanian side, and once we were released from the border compound we headed south through the desert to Petra. The political problems that have plagued Israel and Palestine for the past hundred years have spread like a stain throughout the Middle East, and no country has been more harmfully sideswiped than Jordan. Unblessed by oil, and parched beyond endurance by massive Israeli water diversion projects, the country has also been unable to develop a viable tourist industry because of its proximity to "the problem." At Petra and at Jerash, the remains of a Roman city an hour north of Amman, the country contains two of the most magnificent archaeological treasures in the world, but no one comes to visit them. There is no country in the region as desperate for a Middle East peace as Jordan.

For us, the emptiness of Petra was one of its greatest charms. It is a city carved out of rosy sandstone cliffs at about the time of Christ by a gifted civilization called the Nabateans. The most miraculous thing about Petra is its position at the end of a twisting mountainous defile, about a kilometre long, so narrow and complicated that it completely masks the location of the magnificent city. Moses' brother, Aaron, is thought to be buried at Petra, so it has been a place of religious significance to the dozens of generations of Bedouin who watched over it from ancient times until the nineteenth century. At that point, an intrepid Anglo-Swiss explorer, disguising himself as an Arab pilgrim, persuaded the locals to show him the city, which had been hidden from Western eyes for three hundred years, and Petra's splendid isolation was shattered.

Our day wandering around Petra was magical, climaxed by a forty-five-minute climb to Ed-Deir (The Monastery), one of the most stunning and massive buildings in the whole complex. From Ed-Deir, we could look down to the west, across the rust-red folds of Wadi Araba and the Israeli Negev to the Egyptian Sinai. Straining to the northwest, we could just make out the heat haze of the Dead Sea, and the Bedouin who sold us cold drinks insisted that on a clear winter's day one could see the sun glinting off the golden Dome of the Rock in Jerusalem. I had my doubts about this, but it did underscore how tight and intimate are the geographical relationships in the Middle East, where you can often see at least three countries at a time no matter what direction you look. Petra sits strategically on the old trade route that linked the vast deserts of Arabia with the Dead Sea, Gaza and the Mediterranean, in a time of no borders, no flags, no competing nationalisms, just tribes that jostled against each other over water rights and notions of God.

Visiting the great mountainous desert of the Sinai Peninsula should, in theory, have been easier than visiting Jordan, because Israel and Egypt are officially at peace. The Sinai had been captured by the Israelis during the Six Day War and held by them for fifteen years, until after the signing of the Camp David accords. During that time, Israel made an early start on developing the Sinai for tourism, based on the spectacular coral reefs that run the entire length of the Gulf of Aqaba into the Red Sea. They built a sleek four-lane highway down the coast from the Israeli border to Sharm el-Sheik, in an area that had had nothing but goat trails and tank paths before. That highway and an improbable high-rise Hilton hotel at Taba were thankfully all the Israelis managed to accomplish before the area reverted to the Egyptians, who let everything subside back to its natural state. (The natural state of a four-lane highway involves plenty of potholes and no lighting.)

We had heard from some Israeli friends about a wonderful Bedouin-style camp called Basata on the beach at Ras Bourqa, forty minutes south of the border in the Sinai. To book accommodation there, we had to phone the mother of the owner in Cairo, since there were, at that time, no telephones along the Sinai coast. Then we began looking into the possibility of taking our car into the Sinai and discovered that the peace between Israel and Egypt is frigid indeed.

Our problem was that Patrick was not coming with us on this trip, and the car papers were in his name. The Egyptian rule is that the only Israeli cars allowed over the border are "personal" cars, that is, cars driven by the person whose name is on the ownership. Presumably, this is designed to stop hordes of tourists renting cars in Israel and tootling around the Sinai; it forces them to rent cars in Egypt. For whatever reason, the regulation caught us in the crosshairs. When we went to the top Israeli bureaucrat at the customs department in Jerusalem, he shrugged in the familiar way. "Look," he said, "we Israelis have no problem with you driving your husband's car, so we have no form to give you that would satisfy the Egyptians.

If you want your name added to your husband's on the ownership papers, it'll cost you thousands of shekels in new taxes. Go to the Egyptians. Maybe they'll bend the rules."

So we drove to Tel Aviv for an appointment at the Egyptian Embassy with a functionary who had promised us over the telephone that he could help. As he listened to our story in person over tiny cups of sweet coffee, however, he looked crestfallen and said we were asking the impossible. "It is all spelled out in the Camp David accords exactly what kinds of vehicles can cross the Israeli–Egyptian border, and only personal owners of cars can drive them. Why not go to the Israelis and ask them to put your name on the ownership papers?" We were back to the beginning of the circle. The Egyptian diplomat turned to Patrick and issued the *coup de grâce:* "I am very sorry, sir, there is absolutely nothing we can do. Even if it was *your son* who wanted to drive the car across the border, he couldn't do it." We knew when we were licked.

In the end, my Canadian friend Suanne and I and my two boys drove four hours south from Jerusalem through the Negev Desert, parked our car just inside Israel and crossed the border on foot, hoping to find a taxi on the other side to take us to Basata. Evening was drawing on as we started the long, mysterious process of moving sixty metres through the border compound. The Israelis waved us through offhandedly, and we sank instantly into the quagmire of Egyptian officialdom. As we waited interminably outside one hut for an official to take our five Egyptian pounds and give us some stamps to take to the next hut, we puzzled over a gnomic sign that appeared to have been erected for the edification of travellers going in the other direction. It read:

Foreigners are departing to Israel and they have tourist resedent to visit all of Egypt and they like to going back Egypt througt the period of their resedent they will be getting re-entry visa from Taba immigration office before their leaving to Israel.

Eventually, in the inky blackness of a Sinai November night, we reached Basata and were welcomed into an enchanting world of Egyptian hospitality. The owner, Sherif, was an aristocratic Cairene, but he fancied himself a Bedouin and was decked out in the full flowing robes of a desert chieftain. His beach compound, built entirely by hand by Egyptian craftsmen and weavers, consisted of a central living and kitchen area open to the beach on all sides with rush mats laid directly on the sand as a floor, and about fifteen bamboo huts strung out along the cove. His visitors, Cairo-dwelling expatriates, trekkers and a few discerning Israelis, were sprawled on cushions at low tables, eating fresh fish from the Gulf of Aqaba, while Arab qanoun music wafted quietly out of Sherif's primitive sound system.

We sank into blissful sloth for the next three days and nights, rousing ourselves only to explore the exquisite Red Sea coral formations and dazzling tropical fish whose habitat began just fifteen metres out in the water in front of our beach hut. It wasn't until our final evening that we learned about the darker side of this tiny piece of paradise. That night, Suanne and I joined a pair of Israeli psychologists for dinner. Yoram and Yochanan told us they had met when doing their military service in the Sinai many years before. They had both fallen in love with the peninsula's spectacular austerity and emptiness, and since then, two or three times a year, they would snatch long weekends away from their jobs and families in Tel Aviv and come down to explore new areas of untouched grandeur in the Sinai. They adored resting and relaxing at Basata, but they commented that not many Israelis came here any more since the tragedy. What tragedy were they referring to, we asked.

In 1985, after Israel had given the Sinai back to Egypt and before Sherif had built his compound, a large group of Israeli families came down to camp on the beach here at Ras Bourqa. One day the children were running up and sliding down the sand dunes at the north end of the cove, when a soldier at the nearby Egyptian military guard post ran amok and started shooting. He killed his own commanding officer and hit many Israeli tourists. The situation then got worse because the Egyptians, in a panic, refused to allow any of the other Israelis, including some doctors, to come to the aid of the wounded until higher Egyptian officials could be summoned. That took agonizing amounts of time, and more victims bled to death. In the end, seven Israelis died, including four children, and the assassin, Suliman Khater, was hailed by many fundamentalist Egyptians as "the hero of Sinai". Ras Bourqa became another link in the chain of hatred and fear between Arabs and Israelis, a name to add to Deir Yassin, the Munich Olympics, Sabra and Shatila, the *Achille Lauro*, Kfar Kassem, Ma'alot, most recently Hebron. No wonder some of my neighbours in Jerusalem had looked at me askance when I told them we were going to Ras Bourqa for a holiday.

Some of the names on the preceding list may be unknown to those outside the Arab–Israeli conflict; four of them are Israeli (or Israeli-backed) attacks on Palestinians and four are Arab attacks on Jews. The equilibrium of pain and atrocity between the two sides is exquisitely balanced; I found it impossible after two years living in the middle of it all to award the crown of righteous victim to either side. There was a perfect and haunting symmetry between the destroyed Jewish communities of Europe, commemorated at the Holocaust memorial of Yad Vashem in Jerusalem, and the Arab towns and villages of Palestine that vanished without a trace under the Zionist onslaught.

To be sure, the Israelis have the upper hand and they use it like thugs: they have all the weapons, they manipulate all the laws, they treat Arabs like dirt. But they are on this land because of centuries of relentless and bloodthirsty persecution against them, culminating in the Nazi Holocaust; the country of Israel was voted into existence by a 33-to-13 vote with 10 abstentions at the United Nations, which gives it more legitimacy than most of the countries in the world. They live in a hostile environment where every one of their neighbours — including Egypt, with whom they have concluded a peace treaty — hates them and wants them eradicated from the Middle East forever.

The Palestinians are certainly victims, not only of the Israelis but of the rest of the Arab world, which has made endless windy promises of support against the Zionist entity and never delivered. They have lost their land, their honour and their freedom, and it is not clear that they can ever completely recover from such a full-blown calamity. But they are also virulently anti-Semitic, like the whole Arab world, and their public leaders over the years have almost never expressed regret, sorrow or shame over the litany of terrorist acts against innocent Jews that have been perpetrated by the militant extremists of Hamas or the PLO. These "warriors" are given comfort and support by their community; they are treated as heroes and martyrs. It is small wonder that Israelis say they cannot trust the Arabs, and that now that they have won control over them they are reluctant to let it go.

Trust is the most used and abused word one hears in the Middle East. "You can't ask us to trust the Israelis, they stole our land!" say the Palestinians. "How can you trust an Arab when you know he is capable of stabbing you in the back?" answer the Israelis. These questions are posed over and over again in every political conversation, and I soon came to feel that they were the wrong questions, completely beside the point. What will bring these two sides together is their own self-interest, nothing else. Both sides know it and in their calmer moments both sides already act on it.

In 1993 a scam was uncovered in which close to a billion dollars' worth of fresh fruits and vegetables were being smuggled annually from the Gaza Strip into Israel with the full cooperation of Palestinian farmers and Israeli truck drivers, who should have been deadly enemies. The Israeli trucks would drive into the Strip under Palestinian protection at night, load up and then sell their goods cheaply and illegally back in Israel. Everyone profited along the way and business was booming until they got caught. "I sure wish we could get this kind of cooperation at the peace table," opined the Israeli minister of agriculture. Ah yes, but at the peace table the name of the game is nationalistic posturing for the international media.

In the wake of the Hebron massacre, the Israeli military authorities erected a wall of concrete blocks between Arab and Jewish enclaves adjacent to the mosque where Baruch Goldstein murdered thirty Moslems at prayer. It is unclear whether the wall will ever come down. It is deplorable that a place of worship, or a city, or a country should be divided down the middle because its inhabitants cannot be trusted not to slaughter each other. But it is also the only practical solution in a place where the conflicting claims to the same piece of land are so compelling and so equally justified. Trust may come twenty or fifty years down the road, when both sides feel safe and secure inside their own borders. Good fences make good neighbours.

This is what I want to believe, but of course the situation is a great deal more complicated than Robert Frost's rather cynical homily can convey. If you build a fence between Israel and the West Bank today, at least 120,000 Jews end up on the Palestinian side: the settlers, many of whom are the most extreme and implacable enemies the Arabs will ever face on the ground. And if you try to adjust the fence to include the most populous settlements on the Israeli side and simply cast the others adrift, you then come up against the hard nut of Jerusalem, which is ringed by massive Jewish settlement on all sides. The Arabs will swallow a lot of humiliation for peace and separation, but they will not swallow the complete loss of Jerusalem.

"History teaches us," says Israeli statesman Abba Eban, "that men and nations behave wisely once they have exhausted all other alternatives." I desperately want to believe this as well, and yet the precipitous rise in extremism — on both the Moslem and Jewish sides — could prevent everyone from behaving wisely enough to bring about a peaceful end to this conflict. What do political and religious funda- mentalists know of exhaustion? The worse things get, the more fuel they have to stoke their terrible fires.

What I know in my bones is that Jerusalem today is a divided city, every bit as divided as Cold War Berlin, and that all Israeli protestations to the contrary cannot change that fact. Unless the Israelis are prepared to push the entire Arab population of Jerusalem out into the West Bank and militarily deny them access to the city — which they will not do — it will remain a perforated reality.

The other day I came across a poem called "Jerusalem," by Yehuda Amichai, Israel's most gifted poet, and it captured precisely the separa- tion and the sadness of the place that was my home for two years.

On a roof in the Old City
laundry hanging in the late afternoon sunlight:
the white sheet of a woman who is my enemy
the towel of a man who is my enemy
to wipe off the sweat of his brow.

In the sky of the Old City
a kite.
At the other end of the string,
a child
I can't see
because of the wall.

We have put up many flags,
they have put up many flags.
To make us think that they're happy,
To make them think that we're happy.

Amichai wrote this poem decades ago, long before the Six Day War, when Jerusalem was still physically divided by concrete walls and barbed wire between the Israelis and the Jordanians. The interesting thing is that it describes perfectly the psychological state of the city today, twenty-seven years after its so-called reunification.

One of our escapes from the Middle East took us to France for a four-week holiday. The damp Celtic mists on the coasts of Brittany were exactly the antidote we were seeking to our intense desert home. We gazed hungrily at the towering foothills of the Pyrenees just beyond Toulouse and could not get our fill of green. We ate wonderful food, drank splendid wines, drove through tamed and gentle landscapes that spoke eloquently of peace, prosperity and centuries of Western civilization.

And yet, an interesting thing happened. In every part of France, we came across vestiges and reminders of the Crusades, that convulsive moment in European history when Pope Urban II sent his Christian soldiers forth to recapture Jerusalem, which had been supposedly writhing under the bondage of the Moslem infidel since 864. The French answered the pope's call more enthusiastically than other Europeans at first, and every quiet town and village we entered seemed to have mustered its own pilgrim-warriors nine hundred years ago to add to the human river that flowed towards the Holy Land in the First Crusade, through the Rhineland, Hungary and Constantinople.

Like everyone educated in a Western culture, I always believed the Crusaders were the good guys. I still treasure a history of the kings and queens of England I was given when I was eight years old, which shows Richard the Lion-Heart resplendent on his medieval horse with a huge red cross on his chest and the flag of St. George carried proudly on his staff. Even though I was never a believing

Christian, it was easy to identify with the Crusaders as cultured, civilized heroes who had defended my way of life centuries earlier
against the alien and barbaric hordes of Islam. Those curved scimitars
and thin moustaches told you pretty quickly who were the villains.
As for the Jews, they weren't part of the story at all.

Living in Jerusalem, though, where the Crusader influence is one
of the most powerful cultural statements, I had begun to learn something about these religious warriors from the receiving end, so to
speak. My hero King Richard, for example, is best remembered by
the Palestinians for his cold-blooded slaughter of 2,700 Arab hostages
outside the town of Acre when his negotiations with the great
Moslem leader Saladin broke down. Israelis recall that huge Jewish
communities in Europe, such as those at Mainz and Prague, were dec-
imated by zealous Crusaders before they even left Europe, on the logical principle that if they were marching to Jerusalem to save Christ's
honour from the Moslems who had stolen His holy places, why not
avenge Him even more by liquidating the very people who crucified
Him? The blackest day for both Arabs and Jews was July 15, 1099,
when Godfrey of Bouillon's troops breached the wall of Jerusalem
near Herod's Gate, and thousands of Crusaders poured into the hapless city below. In Jonathan Riley-Smith's authoritative but entirely
Eurocentric history, *The Crusades,* what happened next is described in
just six words: "Jerusalem was given over to sack." For details, I had to
turn to an Israeli writer, Amos Elon, who in his book *Jerusalem: City
of Mirrors* quotes contemporary sources, which claim that fifty thousand Arabs and Jews were massacred in that attack by warriors "in
blood up to their knees and bridle reins." One of the chroniclers,
William of Tyre, wrote, "Even more dreadful than to observe the vast
number of slaughtered vanquished was to gaze upon the victors themselves, dripping in blood from head to foot, an ominous sight which
brought terror to all who met them." Half a year later, the alleys of
Jerusalem still reeked with the stench of unremoved corpses.

History evolves in strange ways, though. Instead of seeing themselves as the descendants of common victims of a brutal European
enemy, Israelis and Palestinians today both identify the Israelis as modern-day Crusaders. The Israelis have built feverishly since the Six Day
War to establish what they call "facts on the ground," particularly in
the West Bank, on the assumption that no one can make bricks and
mortar just disappear. Their settlements, mostly on the crests of lonely
hills, are eerily reminiscent of the great isolated castles throughout
Israel, Jordan, Syria and Lebanon from which the Crusaders ruled the
Holy Land for two hundred years. Will the Jews get more than two
hundred years? The Arabs take comfort from the fact that the
Crusaders were eventually swept away by the Islamic armies and pre-
dict that this, too, will come to pass with the Israelis. But Israel has
one thing in its favour that the Crusaders never had: a massive influx
of population from all over the world. The builders of great buildings
come and go — the Middle East is strewn with the empty relics of
twenty civilizations past — but the real facts on the ground are people. The Jews have learned that lesson well, from the Arabs.

One cool August evening in the southwest of France, Patrick and
I drove to the town of St. Bertrand de Comminges to hear an evening
of organ music and liturgical singing in the great medieval cathedral
that Bertrand himself, as bishop, had started building in the early days
of the First Crusade. Others had taken over the job later, so the cathedral is a splendid monument to the best in both Romanesque and
Gothic ecclesiastical architecture. The arches of its twelfth-century
cloisters overlook a ravine of spectacular proportions and luxuriant
foliage. We joined five hundred people along the sides of the nave and
listened, enraptured, to the powerful rolling waves of sound emerging
from the sixteenth-century organ and the cool, eloquent line of
Gregorian chant that came from an invisible choir and filled the vast
space around us with resonance and piety. Then a tenor stepped forward and began to sing one of the great eleventh-century liturgical

hymns, precisely the music that must have fired the imagination of hundreds of knights and princes to set off with their vassals on their spiritual journey of three thousand kilometres. "Ierusalem, Ierusalem," he sang in Latin, "Deus benedicat Ierusalem." His voice coiled in golden circles around the deeply carved decorations of the dark oak choir stalls, and echoed back sensuously from the high, slender stained-glass windows that glowed with the last rays of the August sun.

It was one of those moments that expressed the apotheosis of the European spirit, and it should have been glorious: the setting, the sound, the artistry, the awesome majesty of Christian belief and worship. But for me, what it summoned instead was the nightmare image of the streets of the very earthly Jerusalem running ankle-deep in Arab and Jewish blood, bid to flow by a thousand Christian European swords. It has been the sad misfortune of both Arabs and Jews to find themselves repeatedly at the wrong end of Western civilization's designs and dreams. This ill luck should perhaps draw them closer together, and yet it seems not to. To acknowledge their common victimhood may be more than human pride can bear.

I closed my eyes as the music swirled around my head and prayed, as the Bible enjoins us, for the peace of Jerusalem. Until I remembered the tart, realistic words of Israeli writer Meron Benvenisti: "You can have peace, or you can have Jerusalem. You can't have both."

I prayed for peace.

Suggested Further Reading

On Jerusalem:

Elon, Amos, *Jerusalem: City of Mirrors*, Fontana, 1991.

Hazleton, Lesley, *Jerusalem, Jerusalem*, Penguin Books, 1987.

Kaminker, Sarah, *Footloose in Jerusalem*, Footloose Publishers (Israel), 7th Edition, 1988.

Peters, F. E., *Jerusalem: The Holy City in the Eyes of Chroniclers, Visitors, Pilgrims and Prophets from the Days of Abraham to the Beginnings of Modern Times*, Princeton University Press, 1985.

Rabinovitch, Abraham, *Jerusalem on Earth: People, Passions and Politics in the Holy City*, The Free Press, 1988.

Rosovsky, Nitza, *Jerusalemwalks*, Henry Holt, 1982.

Storrs, Sir Ronald, *Memoirs*, Putnam's, 1937. (Storrs was British military governor of Jerusalem.)

Twain, Mark, *The Innocents Abroad*, ed. D. M. McKeithan, University of Oklahoma Press, 1958.

On Israel:

Brook, Stephen, *Winner Takes All: A Season in Israel*, Picador, 1990.

Don-Yehiya, Eliezer, and Charles Liebman, *Civil Religion in Israel*, University of California Press, 1983.

Eisenstadt, S. N., *The Transformation of Israeli Society,* Wiedenfeld and Nicolson, 1985.

Elon, Amos, *The Israelis: Founders and Sons,* Adam Publishers, 1971.

Golan, Matti, *With Friends Like You: What Israelis Really Think About American Jews,* The Free Press, 1992.

Melman, Yossi, *The New Israelis: An Intimate View of a Changing People,* Birch Lane Press, 1992.

Omer, Devora, *The Teheran Operation: The Rescue of Jewish Children from the Nazis,* B'nai Brith Books, 1991.

Paris, Erna, *The Garden and the Gun,* Lester & Orpen Dennys, 1988.

Segev, Tom, *The Seventh Million: The Israelis and the Holocaust,* Hill and Wang, 1993.

On the *Haredim:*

Heilman, Samuel, *Defenders of the Faith: Inside Ultra-Orthodox Jewry,* Schocken Books, 1992.

Landau, David, *Piety and Power: The World of Jewish Fundamentalism,* Secker and Warburg, 1993.

On the Middle East conflict:

Benvenisti, Meron, *Conflicts and Contradictions,* Villard Books, 1986.

Friedman, Thomas, *From Beirut to Jerusalem,* Doubleday, 1990.

Grossman, David, *The Yellow Wind,* Farrar, Straus and Giroux, 1988.

Oz, Amos, *In the Land of Israel,* Random House, 1984.

Oz, Amos, *The Slopes of Lebanon,* Vintage Books, 1989.

Shipler, David K., *Arab and Jew: Wounded Spirits in a Promised Land,* Penguin Books, 1986.

ON ARABS AND PALESTINIANS:

Graff, James A., *Palestinian Children and Israeli State Violence,* The Near East Cultural and Educational Foundation of Canada, 1991.

Grossman, David, *Sleeping on a Wire: Conversations with Palestinians in Israel,* Farrar, Straus and Giroux, 1993.

Harkabi, Y., *Arab Attitudes to Israel,* Valentine, Mitchell, 1972.

Pryce-Jones, David, *The Closed Circle: An Interpretation of the Arabs,* Paladin, 1989.

Rubinstein, Danny, *The People of Nowhere: The Palestinian Vision of Home,* Times Books, 1991.

Said, Edward, *Orientalism,* Random House, 1979.

Weir, Shelagh, *Palestinian Costume,* British Museum Publications, 1989.

ON WOMEN:

Cooper, Lisa, *The Status of Israeli Women: Resistance and Pressure for Change,* Hebrew University, 1991.

Lipman, Beata, *Israel, The Embattled Land: Jewish and Palestinian Women Talk About Their Lives,* Pandora, 1988.

Safir, Marilyn, and Barbara Swirski, *Calling the Equality Bluff: Women in Israel,* Teachers College Press, 1993.

Shaaban, Bouthaina, *Both Right and Left-Handed: Arab Women Talk About Their Lives* (no publishing information).

ON THE CRUSADES:

Riley-Smith, Jonathan, *The Crusades: A Short History,* Yale University Press, 1987.